Annie Ernaux

Modern French Writers

General Editor
EDMUND SMYTH
University of Liverpool

Consultant Editors

MICHAEL SHERINGHAM
Royal Holloway, University of London

DAVID WALKER
University of Sheffield

This series aims to provide a forum for new research on modern and contemporary French and Francophone writing. The volumes to be published in *Modern French Writers* will offer new readings of already widely-known writers in addition to those whose work is beginning to command attention. The contributions to the series reflect a wide variety of critical practices and theoretical approaches, in harmony with the developments which have taken place over the past few decades. Modern French writing will be considered in all its manifestations: novel, poetry, drama, autobiography, cinema, popular culture, theory. In keeping with the erosion of contours which characterises the modern period, 'canonical' and 'non-canonical' writers will be examined, both within France and the French-speaking world more generally. The volumes in the series will participate in the wider debate on key aspects of contemporary culture.

ANNIE ERNAUX

The Return to Origins

Siobhán McIlvanney
King's College, London

LIVERPOOL UNIVERSITY PRESS

First published 2001 by
Liverpool University Press
4 Cambridge Street
Liverpool
L69 7ZU

British Library Cataloguing-in-Publication Data
A British Library CIP record is available
ISBN   0–85323–537–6 cased
          0–85323–547–3 paperback

Typeset by Freelance Publishing Services, Brinscall, Lancs
www.freelancepublishingservices.co.uk
Printed and bound by CPI Group (UK) Ltd, Croydon, CR0 4YY

Contents

Acknowledgements

I would like to thank Elizabeth Fallaize, Diana Holmes and Diana Knight for their time and effort in reading and commenting on various parts of the manuscript. I would also like to thank my brother, Liam, for his helpful advice on earlier drafts. I am grateful to my students at King's for their enthusiastic questions and for enjoyable discussions on women's writing and Annie Ernaux in particular. The two people most deserving of my thanks for this project are my mother, Moira, whose love and encouragement were, and continue to be, a source of strength, and my partner Alan Overd, whose kind, supportive presence has long been invaluable to me.

S. M.

List of Abbreviations

Works by Annie Ernaux

CDR *Ce qu'ils disent ou rien* (Paris: Gallimard, 1977)
JDD *Journal du dehors* (Paris: Gallimard, 1993)
JSN *'Je ne suis pas sortie de ma nuit'* (Paris: Gallimard, 1997)
LAV *Les Armoires vides* (Paris: Gallimard, 1974)
LE   *L'Evénement* (Paris: Gallimard, 2000)
LFG *La Femme gelée* (Paris: Gallimard, 1981)
LH   *La Honte* (Paris: Gallimard, 1997)
LP   *La Place* (Paris: Gallimard, 1983)
LVE *La Vie extérieure, 1993–1999* (Paris: Gallimard, 2000)
PS   *Passion simple* (Paris: Gallimard, 1991)
UF   *Une femme* (Paris: Gallimard, 1988)

Others

LDS Simone de Beauvoir, *Le Deuxième Sexe*, 2 vols (Paris: Gallimard, 1949; reprinted 1976).

Author's note

Unless otherwise indicated, the use of italics in quotations reflects original emphasis.

Some material included in Chapter 3 previously appeared in my article 'Writing Relations: The Auto/biographical Subject in Annie Ernaux's *La Place* and *Une femme*', *Journal of the Institute of Romance Studies*, vol. 7 (1999), pp. 205–15.

To the memory of my mother

Introduction:
Con/textualising the Corpus

Annie Ernaux is one of the most commercially successful writers in France today. Her works appear repeatedly on bestseller lists, have been translated into more than fifteen languages, and she is a familiar figure on literary arts programmes in France, such as *Bouillon de cul-ture* and its predecessor, *Apostrophes*. Ernaux is also relatively well-known in Anglophone circles, due to the popularity of her texts on British school and university syllabi and to her regular visits to Britain in order to discuss her writing with students and academics. While Ernaux's writing clearly strikes a chord with general readers, who, like herself, are 'transfuge[s] de classe',[1] her success with an Anglophone readership may also be attributable to similarities between her confes-sional, autobiographical accounts of female experience written in the first person and the realist mode of feminist writing epitomised by American writers such as Marilyn French during the 1970s, a form of feminist *Bildungsroman* which continues to characterise much Anglo-American women's writing. In the manner of Christiane Rochefort and Marie Cardinal, Ernaux provides a predominantly 'existential' or materialist analysis of women's social situation, as opposed to the more 'essentialist' or differentialist branch of contemporary French wom-en's writing frequently referred to under the umbrella term of *écriture féminine*, a writing which typically focuses on linguistic or psychoana-lytic concerns, on the textual rather than the contextual.

Despite Ernaux's consistent popularity with both Francophone and Anglophone readers, her deceptively straightforward portrayal of or-dinary, everyday 'reality' has resulted in her writing being considered less theoretically challenging, and consequently less fashionable – par-ticularly in French academic circles – than that produced by the 'holy

1

trinity' of French women writers, Hélène Cixous, Luce Irigaray and Julia Kristeva, and other proponents of differentialist writing. However laudatory the reviews her writing receives from French magazines and newspapers, the academic criticism to engage with her work remains predominantly Anglo-American or French-Canadian in origin – Ernaux may be a best-selling author and an intellectual well-versed in current theoretical and literary trends, but no article on her writing by a French academic has ever been published in a French literary journal. As a woman writer of working-class origins, Ernaux has expressed her frustration at what she perceives to be the elitism of the French literary establishment and at the reception accorded to works whose displays of cerebral pyrotechnics she considers as largely irrelevant to the experiences of the ordinary French reader.[2] In other words, the very reasons for her popularity with a more general readership – the accessibility of her writing, its apparent simplicity and candour, its representation of everyday experiences – are exactly those which would seem to have discouraged a more academic appreciation of her work, particularly in France. It is one of the aims of this study to redress the imbalance between lay and academic appreciation of Ernaux's writing.[3]

Ernaux perceives her texts as giving expression to subjects passed over by conventional literary representation, subjects which, given the auto/biographical origins of her writing, centre on both working-class and gynocentric concerns. This dual focus and the politicised content of certain metanarrative remarks point to the importance Ernaux accords minority representation: she endeavours to diminish the social exclusion experienced by the 'petites gens' – whether women or members of the working class – through their inscription in literature. Throughout her corpus, Ernaux's narrators foreground the absence of, or shortcomings in, existent literary accounts of working-class or women's experience, thereby both drawing attention to and resolving such lacunae through their own more 'authentic' portrayal of marginalised subjects, in that her female narrators originate in the class they are portraying. References to earlier (male, middle-class) writers typically set them up as *repoussoirs*, rather than literary models to be emulated.[4] Ernaux's work broaches a range of 'taboo' subjects, from abortion to female sexual passion to the death of a parent from Alzheimer's disease, providing a detailed, and at times disturbing, representation of them. Ernaux views as paramount the disruptive function of literature and consequent destabilisation of readerly preconceptions: 'pour moi, l'écriture a eu toujours un petit peu cette fonction de dire ce que l'on sent mais sans oser le dire, de libérer des choses qui sont très refoulées dans les gens et qui ne se disent pas'.[5] Her popularity owes much to this candid depiction of the common, yet underrepresented components of her female narrators' *Bildung*, components which may be framed within the developmental parameters of education – both pedagogical and sexual – marriage, motherhood and the ageing process, and which generally take place against the background of the narrator's migration from working to middle class in the Norman town of Yvetot. Ernaux's writing constantly returns to the sense of betrayal following her narrators' change of class, to the traumatic ramifications of social mobility. Throughout her writing, it is her narrators' attendance at private school which marks the beginning of their assimilation of bourgeois values and consequent alienation from their working-class origins. As the title of one of her more recent works, *La Honte*, intimates, Ernaux perceives writing as an exculpatory medium through which her past may be restituted. If her early narrators express a desire to distance themselves from their origins, Ernaux's writing demonstrates her own desire to re-immerse herself in them, to validate her working-class childhood through literature. As Ernaux remarks, quoting fellow Norman, Gustave Flaubert: '"En art, Yvetot vaut bien Constantinople."'[6]

TOWARDS A FEMALE AUTO/BIOGRAPHY

Ernaux's writing points up a number of important areas in contemporary critical thought. These areas include the categorisation of genre and its particularly fluid manifestations in the realm of autobiography; the subject position articulated by minority groups and the role played by language in identity formation; the deconstruction of strategies of oppression; and the continuing significance of feminist ideologies. If Ernaux's writing from *La Place* onwards is difficult to categorise, one constant is its auto/biographical subject matter. Ernaux's first three works are autobiographical novels, yet after the publication of *La Femme gelée*, Ernaux requested that Gallimard remove specific reference to fictional classification. From *La Place* onwards, Ernaux's writing incorporates a variety of different genres, including ethnography, sociology, fiction, the diary form and, most obviously, auto/biography.[7] Ernaux perceives the fluid generic form of her works as inherently related to the innovative aspect of their content. Her perception of the representational field of her writing as audacious translates itself into a lack of adherence to traditional categories of literature: 'J'ai ce désir, je crois, de transgresser les formes établies. Quand je cherche à dire quelque chose de vraiment très fort, il faut que la forme éclate aussi d'une certaine manière; on ne peut pas faire autrement.'[8]

This desire for generic transgression, or cross-fertilisation of genres, is commonly associated with women writers. It is variously interpreted as constituting a response to what is perceived as the androcentric rigidity of conventional generic categories; as indicative of women's relational, rather than separatist, perception of the self/other duality; and, in the case of autobiography, as attributable to women's traditional lack of self-esteem and reluctance to consider themselves as suitably eminent subjects for autobiography, leading them to conflate it with other genres.[9] It has also been suggested that autobiography's emphasis on the construction of identity through the act of writing corresponds to many women's perception of having their own identity socially constructed, in that their 'public self' may incorporate superimposed, fictional elements the better to correspond to patriarchal norms. The consequent 'split self' which results from this disparity between women's private and public personae – a split self visible in Ernaux's writing – may complicate the referential act requisite to autobiography and the location of the pre-existent 'real' self to be represented by it, producing a greater incidence of generic transgression. Conversely, the articulation of a previously marginalised 'private self' may fuel the drive for representativeness seen as characteristic of women's self-inscription: the transgressive act of disclosing unrepresented aspects of female experience is accompanied by the desire to have them normalised.[10]

Studies of women's autobiography repeatedly point to this drive for representativeness and relationality as key features. These features are contrasted with a more 'masculine' self-regard which foregrounds the extraordinary traits distinguishing the male autobiographical subject from other members of his community.[11] Susan Stanford Friedman maintains that women, rather than perceiving themselves as autonomous individuals, tend to consider themselves part of a general community of women. She subverts Georges Gusdorf's definition of a culture *without* the required preconditions for autobiography in order to describe those conditions generally visible in women's autobiography, and in Ernaux's auto/biographical writing:

> Autobiography is possible when 'the individual does not feel *herself* to exist outside of others, and still less against others, but very much *with* others in an interdependent existence that asserts its rhythms everywhere in the community ... [where] lives are so thoroughly entangled that each of them has its center everywhere and its circumference nowhere. The important unit is thus never the isolated being.' The very sense of *identification, interdependence,* and *community* that Gusdorf dismisses from autobiographical selves are key elements in the development of a woman's identity.[12]

As illustrated in the parental portraits of *La Place* and *Une femme*, Ernaux's auto/biographical writing repeatedly highlights the representative elements of both her narrators' existence and those with whom they come into contact. For those outside the dominant group, the desire to have their experience corroborated through an identification with others is particularly strong and, in works such as *Les Armoires vides* and *Passion simple*, is given self-reflexive articulation in the narrators' explicit wish to discover the degree to which other women have shared their experiences.

Ernaux's adaption of the genre of autobiography reflects her politicised perception of literature's function: by an accurate representation of her own autobiographical trajectory, Ernaux seeks to extend the relevance of her 'personal' account in order to embrace the experience of numerous others, to locate her first-person narratives not in an idiosyncratic, unique subjectivity, but in a 'je transpersonnel'.[13] She endeavours to distil subjectivity to the essential, to whittle it down until she arrives at its base line, and the autobiographical 'I' serves, not to limit, but to increase the representativeness of her first-person accounts: 'Ce qui me gêne dans le terme "autobiographique" c'est qu'on a toujours l'impression au sens strict qu'on ne va parler que de soi et de sa vie.'[14] Ernaux's use of the first-person pronoun, while anchoring the text in the subjective, endeavours to implicate the reader in a way a third-person work does not.[15] As the narrator of *Journal du dehors* remarks:

> En écrivant cette chose à la première personne, je m'expose à toutes sortes de remarques, que ne provoqueraient pas 'elle s'est demandé si l'homme à qui elle était en train de parler n'était pas celui-là'. La troisième personne, il/elle, c'est toujours l'autre, qui peut bien agir comme il veut. 'Je', c'est moi, lecteur, et il est impossible – ou inadmissible – que je lise l'horoscope et me conduise comme une midinette. 'Je' fait honte au lecteur. (JDD, pp. 18–19)

It is by encouraging the reader to take up the narratorial position, to fill, in a sense, the 'je' with his/her own identity, that Ernaux seeks to inscribe a textual 'je transpersonnel'. The desired representativeness is not, however, that of a sterile New Critical experience, but of an historically-specific auto/biographical account which, through its detailed portrayal of the social mores and customs of a stratum of French society, acquires ethnographical resonance. The centrality of representativeness to Ernaux's literary conception points to her quasi-determinist belief in the role played by environment in identity formation: public and private are inherently intertwined in her writing, in that the self is always implicated in the portrayal of the Other, whether that Other take the form of the narrator's parents, her lover or the everyday men and women she observes in public spaces.

In the following study, Ernaux's narrators are treated as variations along a continuum, which, while pointing to their common grounding in the auto/biographical 'I' and marked similarities in terms of background experience, facilitates comparisons between their respective narrative roles. The narrator in *Les Armoires vides* is called Denise, in *Ce qu'ils disent ou rien*, the blurring of identities between author and narrator is reflected in the protagonist's name, Anne, and, in *La Femme gelée*, she has become nameless, foregrounding her increased representativeness. The renunciation of the category *roman* to designate *La Place* and *Une femme* is further substantiated by this progression from fictional to more ambiguous first-person narratives. If the abandonment of the novel format after the early trilogy serves to promote an auto/biographical reading of subsequent works, so too does the correspondence in ages between narrator and author, a correspondence absent in the early texts, particularly in *Ce qu'ils disent ou rien*, in which the narrator is only 15 years old. The numerous intertextual references to particular events or characteristics, references which complicate the task of recalling in which work(s) a particular account takes place, reinforce their auto/biographical veracity. These references encompass a range of subjects, whether general observations about the narrator's upbringing or more precise details, such as her father's inability to understand the pleasure to be gained from reading (CDR, p. 33; LFG, pp. 24–25; LP, p. 80) or her grandmother's foreshortened academic career (LAV, p. 128; LFG, p. 12; UF, p. 25).[16]

If the auto/biographical foundation of Ernaux's writing is undeniable, its generic categorisation as 'pure' autobiography ignores both the ethnological emphasis of works subsequent to *La Femme gelée* and the narrator's desire to destabilise such categorisation in the first place: Ernaux's writing repeatedly advocates and, by its example, legitimates, the cross-fertilisation of genres. Not only is the ostensive subject of these works the life of someone other than the narrator, but the term 'autobiography' nowhere appears in the numerous references to generic definitions in the corpus.[17] Ernaux's works are auto/biographical, but do not constitute autobiographies, positing instead a metonymic relationship between narrator and author: the narrator connotes, rather than denotes, the author. Ernaux's writing may establish a relationship between the inter-textual narrator and the extra-textual author, yet to define it as autobiography is to confine it to unnecessary generic constraints. Such constraints have long been endured by women's literature, which has frequently been viewed as little more than 'personal expression', in which the female authorial and narratorial 'I' are automatically conflated, and which, in the case of Ernaux's writing, may have discouraged closer engagement with the metanarrative comments of later works. This conflation may partly account for the criticism that her work lacks 'literariness', in that the common categorisation of women's auto/biographical writing as 'life writing' implies an unmediated transcription of everyday experience requiring little creative artistry. The very ordinariness of its subject matter and sparse expression have led to the accusation that Ernaux's work is underwritten, that it scarcely merits the term 'literature' at all.[18]

THE CORPUS

Ernaux's corpus to date comprises eleven books and a number of short texts. Her first three works, *Les Armoires vides*, *Ce qu'ils disent ou rien* and *La Femme gelée* make up a triptych of texts examining the female socialisation process from childhood through to adulthood. Ernaux's principal aim in this trilogy is to deconstruct ideology's powerful role in the formation, or, rather, deformation, of subjectivity, in order to divest it of its more 'innocent' guises. The narrative of all three texts takes the form of a retrospective interior monologue by a first-person female narrator and deploys a range of similar techniques to chart the transformation of a contented, sexually curious child into an unhappy and rancorous young woman. That transformation is shown to begin with the narrator's attendance at the *école libre* and to be bolstered subsequently by a variety of ideological reinforcers or cultural representations of womanhood. The interrogative function of these narratives is reflected in the similar epistemological positions inhabited by narrator and reader, as both endeavour to identify significant moments in the developmental trajectory of the narrator. Only a meticulous, and retrospective, dissection of childhood and adolescence can uncover the principal sources of ideological pressure, the cultural mechanisms instrumental in bringing about the different predicaments of the older narrators. That predicament is abortion in *Les Armoires vides* (an allegory for the narrator's feelings of alienation from her milieu and desire to purge herself of links with it); in *Ce qu'ils disent ou rien* solitude and deception stemming from the disparities between romanticised discourse on heterosexual relations and the narrator's own sexual experiences; and, in *La Femme gelée*, postmarital stagnation following the assimilation of female stereotypes.

In all three works, it is the gradualness of the narrator's estrangement from her social origins which complicates the task of uncovering the processes responsible for it: 'Quand ai-je eu une trouille folle de leur ressembler, à mes parents ... Pas en un jour, pas une grande déchirure' (LAV, p. 50). That estrangement produces identical corollaries in the trilogy: the narrator, who enjoys a secure and happy childhood in which her mother represents an idealised female role model, is shown to inhabit successfully the environments of home and school until approximately the age of 12, when her consciousness of class differences renders her existence in these parallel universes increasingly problematic. As her private education continues to valorise middle-class values, the narrator comes to despise her working-class origins. Throughout the trilogy, it is language and linguistic dexterity which constitute the most effective indicator of social status, and the narrator's exposure to its written form in canonical literature heightens her awareness of the degree to which her family falls short of the ideals represented by it.[19] Similarly, the narrator's introduction to gender stereotypes at school gives rise to a growing resentment at her mother's lack of conformity to these types and at her general disregard of the feminine attributes deemed essential by the narrator's educational environment.

All three texts comprise an intricately woven web of alternating narrative perspectives. While the principal narrative is retrospective, the narrator's thoughts at different stages of her maturation process, as well as her current feelings, combine with a polyphonic medley of voices from past and present which continually intercept the narrative flow. The complexity of such heteroglossia is increased by the absence of textual indicators to signal different interlocutors. The impression is of remarks inserted pell-mell as they enter the narrator's consciousness, forming a mélange of chronological perspectives. The language of the early trilogy and its general style of composition are starkly different from those of subsequent works. These early works convey a sense of unbridled energy, a desire on the part of the narrators to give immediate expression to their thoughts and feelings – as highlighted by the prevalence of the present tense throughout – which creates an impression of 'unfinishedness' characteristic of oral discourse: having had free expression censored during childhood, they appear to give release to years of pent-up bitterness and frustration. The syntax of these works is irregular, with sentences truncated and words or phrases elided or omitted.[20] If the numerous typographical gaps of *La Place* and *Une femme* highlight their more reflective and analytical nature, the infrequent paragraphs or page breaks throughout the trilogy reinforce its sense of urgency. As the trilogy progresses, the language of the narrators becomes gradually less vibrant and violent. *La Femme gelée* is very much a transitional text, in that, while resembling its sister texts in style and subject matter, it pre-empts the metanarrative comments and greater authorial control of later works, as well as their more conciliatory approach to the past. This desire for restitution of the past in *La Femme gelée*, while aided by the narrator's greater distance from her origins, also stems from her prolonged experience of being a bourgeois wife and mother. Unlike Denise and Anne, who admire the bourgeoisie from afar, this narrator's first-hand experience of its restrictive stereotypes leads to a reappraisal of the benefits of the working-class model of womanhood which dominated her childhood.

The *mise en abîme* of the act of literary composition which recurs throughout the early trilogy mirrors these changes in emphasis in Ernaux's writing project. The working-class narrator of *Les Armoires vides* writes fiction as a result of her valorisation of middle-class values. Similarly, in *Ce qu'ils disent ou rien* Anne's manner of composition 'à la troisième personne' (CDR, p. 65) signals a desire to distance herself from her own working-class experiences and to disown her past through a fictionalisation of it: 'j'ai cherché un beau prénom, Arielle, Ariane, Ania, que la première lettre au moins me ressemble, mais avec un beau nom pareil, c'était plus moi' (CDR, p. 106). This quotation may be read as an allusion to the autobiographical content of this most fictional of Ernaux's works, since the protagonist of *Ce qu'ils disent ou rien* is called Anne. (The narrator of *Passion simple* also comments on the 'forme romanesque où les apparences sont sauves' [PS, p. 70].) As the trilogy progresses, the narrators become more intent on restitution rather than rejection, demonstrating a willingness to confront the past more directly through a reduction of the fictional framework, as reflected in the move to a nameless narrator in *La Femme gelée*. An examination of the narrator's role in the trilogy reveals a progressive development from the 'timid' use of the fictional protagonist Denise to a more assertive approximation of author and narrator.[21]

If the early trilogy may be classed as autofiction, from *La Place* onwards Ernaux's writing abandons the novelistic framework and engages explicitly with factual material. This abandonment stems from her retrospective perception of the earlier works, the form and content of which she views as inherently contradictory. In its dissection of the internalisation process, the early trilogy condemns the bourgeois disparagement of working-class experience, yet Ernaux comes to consider its fictional form as corroborating such disparagement by the implicit suggestion that the texts' working-class subject matter requires fictional embellishment in order to gain literary acceptance by her bourgeois readers. (However, as Chapter 3 argues, the narrator's indifference to her bourgeois readers' sensibilities in *La Place* and *Une femme* is less resolute than it appears.) Ernaux's style of writing in *La Place* and *Une femme* consequently becomes more objective and controlled as language is stripped of every unnecessary adjective or qualifier, a linguistic pruning reinforced by the absence of transitional explanations throughout the works. If the initial stage of reconciliation with the past involves an emotional articulation of its principal components, the subsequent stage would appear to necessitate a distancing from them in order to gauge their significance: where fiction was previously a facilitator in the narrators' representation of their past, it becomes an obstacle to their coming-to-terms with it.

In works following *La Femme gelée*, Ernaux adopts a more conventional, 'classic' style of composition, as if to reflect the mature narrator's development from rebellious, working-class girl to established member of the middle class. From the mélange of registers which characterises the earlier works, Ernaux's writing after *La Femme gelée* tends to confine working-class vocabulary to a sociological role when seeking to illustrate the lexicon of the narrator's parents and those from the same social class.[22] In *La Place* and *Une femme*, the narrative focus embraces a wider stratum of society than the interior monologues of the early works, a broadening of perspective reflected in the narrators' foregrounding of the works' ethnographical relevance. However, if the subject matter of these texts is the narrator's father and mother respectively, and, by extension, the working class to which they belong, the impetus behind their composition is the daughter's desire to make amends for previous shortcomings in her relationship with her parents, shortcomings initiated by her migration to the bourgeoisie. In works subsequent to *La Femme gelée*, Ernaux's narrator possesses both an insider's perspective on working-class culture which increases her epistemological authority vis-à-vis the reader and the outsider detachment of a class migrant, a combination which results in a self-reflexive analysis of familiar subject matter. If *La Place* and *Une femme* extend the narrative focus to represent the social class of the narrator's parents, that focus becomes still further removed from the familial in Ernaux's next two works: *Passion simple* portrays the narrator's recent relationship with a married man from a previously Eastern-bloc country, while *Journal du dehors* comprises vignettes of strangers the narrator comes across in her everyday life in a Parisian new town. The experiential extremes to which her sexual liaison exposes her in *Passion simple* can be seen to be reflected in the marginalised individuals who populate *Journal du dehors*. As with *La Place* and *Une femme*, however, narratorial interest in the Other in these two works is fundamentally anchored in an interest in the self, in that the Other is valorised above all for its ability to promote greater self-awareness in the narrator.

While the fictional is usurped by the auto/biographical in works subsequent to *La Femme gelée*, Ernaux's writing continues to comprise a fictional element in its literary transformation of 'reality', an element most explicitly acknowledged in *Passion simple* and to which the publication of Ernaux's next two works, *'Je ne suis pas sortie de ma nuit'* and *La Honte*, indirectly testifies. From *Passion simple* onwards, the narrator draws attention to literature's limitations as a referential medium, highlighting the inherently inferior ersatz 'reality' it produces. If works like *La Place* and *Une femme* indicate the narrator's belief in the well-rounded definitiveness of the parental portraits they provide, later works, which are no less anchored in 'real-life' events, foreground the constraints of the literary medium, its approximation of, rather than substitution for, 'reality'. If the narrators' constant reworking of auto/biographical subject matter points to the pivotal role of 'reality' in Ernaux's literary conception, this repeated return to origins can also be interpreted as an acknowledgement that the transcription of 'reality' inevitably distorts or omits aspects of it, necessitating a further attempt to capture its essence. Ernaux's corpus can be viewed as reflecting the theoretical shift from the homogeneous autobiographical certainties of the past to the contemporary emphasis on fragmentation and on the transformative, rather than reflective, relationship between 'reality' and literary representation.

This revised narrative perspective is apparent in '*Je ne suis pas sortie de ma nuit*' and *La Honte*. In these works, Ernaux's narrators view the publication of previously concealed information about their parents and childhood as contributing to a more *vraisemblable* portrayal of them than the 'definitive' earlier versions. Where previously the narrator in *Une femme* had no desire to discover new information about her parents posthumously, later narrators consider a coherent, integrated portrayal of them inauthentic in its simplistic suppression of their many contradictions. Consequently, in the diary of '*Je ne suis pas sortie de ma nuit*' the reader is provided with details of Ernaux's mother's demise from Alzheimer's disease, details which should be read in conjunction with the more extensive biographical account of her mother's life provided by *Une femme*. In *La Honte*, Ernaux's narrator goes further in destabilising previous representations with the suggestion that the impetus to her writing project is her father's earlier attempted murder of her mother; new angles and interpretations immediately force themselves on readings of previous works. *La Honte* takes up the theme of social inferiority central to the early trilogy, and, to a lesser extent, the biographical descriptions of the parents in *La Place* and *Une femme*, and combines this 'subjective' content with the topographical treatment of the Other most evident in *Journal du dehors*. The personal is portrayed in a highly objective manner in *La Honte*, unlike the subjective '*Je ne suis pas sortie de ma nuit*', in which the work's original status as private diary frees the narrator from the drive for representativeness characteristic of the parental portraits in *La Place* and *Une femme*.

Ernaux's two most recent publications can be seen to duplicate the disparate narrative approaches of *La Honte* and '*Je ne suis pas sortie de ma nuit*' – works also published concurrently – in their comprising both an objective, detached account of 'reality' – *La Vie extérieure* – and a more personal account of a past experience, *L'Evénement*. In *La Vie extérieure*'s predecessor, *Journal du dehors*, Ernaux's narrator highlights her valorisation of both forms of literary *engagement* with the 'real':

> Je m'aperçois qu'il y a deux démarches possibles face aux faits réels. [...] Les fragments, comme ceux que j'écris ici, me laissent insatisfaite, j'ai besoin d'être engagée dans un travail long et construit (non soumis au hasard des

jours et des rencontres). Cependant, j'ai aussi besoin de transcrire les scènes du R.E.R., les gestes et les paroles des gens *pour eux-mêmes*, sans qu'ils servent à quoi que ce soit. (JDD, p. 85)

The narrator's ongoing political objective to provide representation of ordinary working-class existence finds realisation in the existence of a 'public' text in conjunction with her more 'private' compositions. Like *Journal du dehors*, *La Vie extérieure* constitutes a diary of the narrator's suburban environment in a Parisian *Ville Nouvelle*, and provides chronological continuation of *Journal du dehors*, beginning the year after the earlier diary concludes. The imbrication of the personal and public continues to inform *La Vie extérieure*, in that the narrator's subjective needs or memories influence the selection process governing diary entries. The work's focus may be on the same circumscribed community of Cergy-Pontoise, yet its portrayal is imbued with a stronger representative resonance than *Journal du dehors*. *L'Evénement* provides a detailed depiction of the circumstances surrounding the narrator's illegal abortion in 1964, the numerous obstacles to be surmounted and the very real physical dangers it incurred.

Whatever the differing treatment of Ernaux's subject matter or modified perception of the relationship between literature and 'reality' throughout the corpus, a constant return to origins forms the leitmotif of Ernaux's writing. If, for Ernaux's narrators, the past continues to inform the present, so the ever-changing elements of the present lead to a constant re-presentation of the past. Her texts comprise a circularity which is not merely intratextual in the explanatory structure of the works, in the mature narrator's desire to seek out personal and social truths through a revision of the past, but is also apparent in this overview of her literary trajectory: as the Conclusion remarks, with her two most recent non-diary works, *La Honte* and *L'Evénement*, Ernaux comes back to her point of departure in *Les Armoires vides*, to the key events which confirmed the daughter's estrangement from her working-class origins.

CRITICAL PERSPECTIVES

In addition to a number of articles on Ernaux's writing in both French and English, two critical studies of her corpus have been published in French and she is also included in a work examining the mother/daughter relationship in the writing of three contemporary French women writers. The only existent study in English of her writing provides a general introduction to its thematic recurrences and examines both its popular and critical reception. Ernaux has also been included in two English anthologies on French women's writing.[23] While much Ernaux criticism has proved pertinent and insightful, it has also been charac- terised by a tendency to reiterate the professed aims of Ernaux's narra- tors, rather than to challenge or nuance them. This critical reluctance may stem from the somewhat coercive nature of certain metanarrative remarks, as well as from the first-person blurring of narrator and au- thor, which can be seen to inhibit critical dissension by 'personalising' comments made about the role of the narrator. Such reticence may be further aggravated by a form of political correctness, in that Ernaux's writing portrays the difficulties encountered by a working-class woman in gaining access to literature, and potential critics do not wish to be affiliated to a bourgeois cultural domain seen to perpetuate such difficulties.

While adhering to a broadly feminist hermeneutics, the following study does not rigidly apply one particular theoretical approach to textual analysis. Indeed, the adoption of a purely theoretical approach to her writing generally is to misread the entire ideological thrust of Ernaux's literary project. Rather, as the first comprehensive study of Ernaux's corpus to provide close readings of each of her texts indi- vidually, this book is underpinned by a variety of theoretical perspec- tives which are suggested by the texts themselves rather than imposed upon them – most particularly, perspectives supplied by the work of Pierre Bourdieu and, above all, Simone de Beauvoir, probably Ernaux's most important theoretical and literary predecessor. The work of Bourdieu can be viewed as providing a class-based analysis of social structures which parallels Beauvoir's examination of gender acquisi- tion detailed in her principal theoretical work, *Le Deuxième Sexe*. Both these writers deny the existence of inherent class- or gender-based characteristics in the individual, positing instead the overriding forma- tive influence of environment on subjectivity: it is man-made nurture which moulds human beings, not given nature. Beauvoir and Bourdieu seek to deconstruct the naturalisation of culturally-imposed differences, whether in the form of 'feminine behaviour' or 'good taste': if Beauvoir's focus is on the sexual classification systems grounded in patriarchy, Bourdieu's is on the 'class' classification systems which determine an individual's access to economic and cultural capital. Ernaux's percep- tion of the individual as fundamentally rooted in and influenced by the familial, the social and the historical can be seen to provide literary representation of Bourdieu's sociological and Beauvoir's philosophical and theoretical approaches. For Ernaux, one is indeed not born a woman or, more importantly, working- or middle-class, but is taught to become it. Her corpus documents the corrosive effects of class and gender distinction and, in the majority of works following the early trilogy, does so with a quasi-sociological detachment. The recent renewed critical interest in Beauvoir reaffirms her continuing relevance to contemporary feminist thought and testifies to the eclectic complexity of her writing beneath its accessible exterior.[24] Similarly, the following study seeks to demonstrate that, by looking beyond the surface information with which her narrators provide us, Ernaux's writing is more sophisticated than has often been acknowledged: it is by reading against, as well as with, Ernaux's narrators that the intellectual intricacies of her literary project are revealed. While the purpose of this book is to introduce readers unfamiliar with Ernaux's writing to her works, it also aims to engage readers familiar with her writing on less familiar terrain, to open up and problematise future avenues of analysis.

The following chapters provide close readings of the individual works which make up Ernaux's corpus, and can be read as self-contained analyses. Given the fundamentally intertextual nature of Ernaux's writing, a degree of repetition is inevitable. That each of Ernaux's texts has a potential sister text with which it either shares common ground or complements well has led to the grouping of two texts per chapter – or, in the case of Chapter 4, three – allowing both for easy consultation and, where appropriate, for comparisons to be drawn between them. Broadly speaking, the intertextual parallels which dictate the choice of grouping are as follows: the adolescent sense of alienation in *Les Armoires vides* and *Ce qu'ils disent ou rien*; the differing perspectives on mature womanhood offered by *La Femme gelée* and *Passion simple*; the similar treatment of the paternal and maternal legacies of *La Place* and *Une femme*; the diary form of '*Je ne suis pas sortie de ma nuit*', *Journal du dehors* and *La Vie extérieure*; and the circular return to origins represented by *La Honte* and *L'Evénement*. *La Honte* and *L'Evénement* simultaneously represent both the genesis and cyclicality of Ernaux's literary trajectory: if *La Honte* represents a return to origins *par excellence* in its supra-objective excavation of familiar childhood sites and in its portrayal of a key event in initiating the social divide between parents and daughter, *L'Evénement* depicts the ultimate

termination of childhood in the form of class and generational proximity between parents and daughter, a termination given clear symbolism in the narrator's abortion, and for which Ernaux's corpus offers a form of textual panacea.

CHAPTER 1

The Early Years:
Classifying Sexuality in
Les Armoires vides and
Ce qu'ils disent ou rien

As the title of this study suggests, the formative influences of child-hood shape the many themes and concerns which make up Ernaux's corpus – even, as Chapter 2 argues, in a work as firmly anchored in the present as *Passion simple*. Underlying and uniting these thematic recurrences is the role played by social class in the narrator's socialisation process, and the psychosexual consequences of the confrontation between her working-class childhood and her middle-class education. If, for Ernaux, class and sexuality are imbricated in the construction of individual subjectivity, it is nonetheless the former which provides the conditions for the development of the latter: 'Comme je l'ai raconté dans *Les Armoires vides* on appartient d'abord totalement au milieu dans lequel on naît et on est, dans les deux sens du mot.'[1] To interpret the narrator's developmental trajectory independently of the sociocultural environments in which it evolves is to produce a reductionist reading of the text, and, indeed, of Ernaux's corpus as a whole. Toril Moi's regret at the paucity of feminist studies on the inter-connection between class and gender – which remains valid – is surely redundant in analyses of Ernaux's writing, in which the portrayal of female sexuality cannot be read without reference to the formative parameters of social class.[2]

More than any other work by Ernaux, *Les Armoires vides* illustrates the corrosive consequences – both physical and psychological – of these influences on female sexuality. The social divide between the working class and the bourgeoisie, or, as Ernaux prefers, adopting Bourdieuian terms of reference, between 'la classe dominée' and 'la classe dominante', and the traumatic ramifications this entails for the self-image of the female protagonist, constitute the subject matter of the work. As the first of Ernaux's texts, *Les Armoires vides* details that divide with a violence which appears gradually to burn itself out in the remainder of the trilogy: while the narrator of *Ce qu'ils disent ou rien* manifests a less virulent form of parental loathing, her counterpart in *La Femme gelée* adopts a still more conciliatory position towards her origins, manifesting a tolerance which may stem from her greater maturity and reflective distance vis-à-vis the events she is relating, as well as the fact that she is now a parent herself and better able to comprehend her own parents' conduct. Later still, the narrators we encounter in *La Place* and *Une femme* are intent on reconciliation with, and restitution of, their past, rather than retribution. The angry young women of Ernaux's early trilogy give way to older, more composed narrators, who, having achieved a degree of emotional distance from their childhood, seek to expiate their previous vilification of it through the act of writing.

LES ARMOIRES VIDES

The formal properties of *Les Armoires vides* foreshadow those adopted in the subsequent works of the trilogy, in that the narrative chronology comprises an intermingling of the narrator's retrospective narrative, which traces her trajectory from earliest childhood to the present, with voices from her childhood – whether her own or other people's – which, in turn, merge with her present thoughts on aspects of her past and on her current situation. The polyphonic nature of the narrator's thoughts engages the reader in an active process of interpretation, as a multiplication of viewpoints is layered one upon the other, producing a dense conversational matrix. This con/fusion of narrative voices can be viewed as echoing the con/fusion of formative influences to which the narrator has been subject and which the narrative of *Les Armoires vides* strives to disentangle. The tightly woven web of predominantly first-person narrative voices is all the harder to unravel given the anger and resentment which account for its existence in the first place. The emotional impetus of the work is reflected in the fragmented syntax and vulgar lexicon, and in the narrator's tangential diatribes throughout.

The work opens *in medias res* as the reader accesses the turbulent stream of thoughts of the 20-year-old narrator, Denise Lesur. Gradually, the immediate source of the narrator's emotional turmoil is disclosed: she is in her student bedroom waiting for an abortion to take its course, having visited a backstreet abortionist on the previous day when two months' pregnant.[3] It is, however, the less readily discernible sources of turmoil which the narrative sets out to uncover: 'Ne pas pouvoir aimer ses parents, ne pas savoir pourquoi, c'est intenable' (LAV, p. 117). As with the sister works in the triptych, the narrative's interrogative function is reflected in the older narrator's determination to understand her current situation by a dissection of the events leading up to it. Indeed, all of Ernaux's narrators place their faith in the power of deductive reasoning, in the establishment of causal links between their recent or distant past and their present sociocultural situation. This quasi-determinist belief in the structuring influence of the past on the present results in the circularity characteristic of Ernaux's writing, and, as the Introduction and Chapter 5 argue, of her corpus. The absence of a clear catalyst for the alienation Denise experiences vis-à-vis her family and class forces her to undertake a painful excavation of childhood and adolescence. That excavation is given allegorical resonance in the act of abortion, in that the self-interrogation of *Les Armoires vides* may be viewed as the psychological equivalent of the physical catharsis abortion represents for the narrator.[4] Throughout Ernaux's writing, the body and female sexuality generally are viewed as important sources of self-knowledge, in that they are somehow less imbued with patriarchal ideology than the more conventionally 'intellectual' indicators of development acquired through reading and education.

The retrospective narrative follows a broadly linear development, beginning in early childhood with the description of a typical week in the narrator's home life, the very predictability of which is shown to contribute to the sense of security which permeates the young child's domestic environment.[5] Having progressed through Denise's education at school and university, this principal narrative thread returns to its point of departure with a description of her relationship with the man who made her pregnant. Punctuating the retrospective narrative are interjections relating to the narrator's present situation, whether in the form of previous maternal warnings about the dangers of pregnancy or imaginary comments made by her parents on learning of her abortion. Like a Greek chorus, these remarks reinforce the narrator's sense of inevitability regarding her current crisis. The overwhelming importance of the narrator's childhood in *Les Armoires vides* is also highlighted by these interjections: as the mature narrator endeavours to advance the narrative chronology, past influences constantly seethe under the narrative surface, and appear to affect her at what is almost a subliminal level, disrupting the narrative flow to take her back to earlier events or statements. It is as if, despite her efforts, the narrator cannot contain the effects of her past, but must allow them repeated expression if she is to have any hope of neutralising their potency. If the retrospective narrative is generally linear, the present one is circular, weaving in and out of the retrospective narrative, before merging with it to conclude where it began – with the narrator undergoing an abortion in her bedroom. The circularity of the present narrative underlines the narrator's inability to progress beyond the formative influences of her early years and to interpret events in her adult present without recourse to her past.

That inability is illustrated in Denise's constant disparagement of her parents and their value system ('moches, minables, péquenots' [LAV, p. 14]), a disparagement which merely accentuates their continuing influence on her. She may perceive her attendance at university as the realisation of her aim to eradicate all traces of her working-class origins – 'Je ne suis pas la fille Lesur ici' (LAV, p. 15) – yet the entire narrative thrust of *Les Armoires vides* points to the narrator's continuing subjection to the mores of her working-class childhood and adolescence, particularly in the realm of sexuality. Evidence of that subjection is highlighted in the opening page of the work, when, as she undergoes the contractions of her abortion, the narrator makes an association between her mother's sexual censorship and what is presumably an expression of her bourgeois boyfriend's sexual desire: 'Il ne faut pas toucher ton quat'sous, tu l'abîmerais ... laisse-moi embrasser les petits bonbons, là, entre les lèvres ...' (LAV, p. 11).[6] This dichotomised representation of censorship and its transgression pervades the narrative of *Les Armoires vides*, and the narrator's perception of her abortion as a form of divine justice, as penance for her immoral conduct – a conduct which she attributes to her working-class origins, thereby reinforcing the correlation of class and sexuality – represents its culmination.

Denise's dichotomous attitude to sexuality is intimated in the younger narrator's Manichaean perception of the world around her, a perception reinforced by her exposure to the precepts of Catholicism. While the narrator's qualification of the constituents of good and evil is shown to depend on her degree of assimilation of the bourgeois value system encountered at school, one constant which spans both her pre- and post-school existence is the representation of premarital sex as sinful. Indeed, the condemnation of sexual pleasure encountered at her single-sex, Catholic school is one of the few points in common between her home and educational environments: both advance an apocalyptic view of those who fall short of the requisite moral standards, yet the taboo nature of sexuality prohibits all further clarification of its 'immorality'. The narrator's ambivalent attitude to sexuality – her awareness that it is forbidden fruit and consequent desire to taste it for herself – is conveyed in her quasi-masochistic pleasure when she eventually transgresses sexual taboos, a pleasure which combines the enjoyment of sex with fear of parental reproof. In *Les Armoires vides*, this combination is illustrated in the common conflation of pleasure and pain experienced by the narrator, a conflation apparent in the opening paragraph of the work, in which the narrator describes the physical effects of her abortion as '[P]resque du plaisir' (LAV, p. 11). The narrator later associates losing her virginity with the backstreet abortionist's intervention, again combining pleasure and pain: 'Le plaisir, la petite voie pour lui, et couic, le déverrouillage, l'enfonçure, "ça rentrera bien, c'est toujours rentré!", avec la main piquetée de lentilles. La douleur, la douleur' (LAV, p. 180).[7] Given the vehemence of the Catholic Church's interdictions on the most anodyne piece of carnal knowledge and the coupling of censorship and transgression throughout *Les Armoires vides*, it is not surprising that the narrator's association of pain and pleasure frequently occurs in religious contexts: 'Mal aux genoux, tiraillements dans les cuisses, plaisir et douleur, toujours, à l'église' (LAV, p. 36).

The taboo status of female sexuality and the social sanctions accompanying its transgression are present from the narrator's earliest childhood in the form of overheard conversations in her mother's shop (one of which prefigures the recent situation of the older narrator, '"Elle n'a pas vu depuis deux mois"' [LAV, p. 29]). The sexual conduct of local women is under constant surveillance, as reputations are destroyed in the mini-courtroom of the *épicerie* with her mother as presiding moral magistrate, a role analogous to that of the priest at confession. The illicit nature of these conversations produces vicarious sexual desire in the narrator, which she partly satisfies by taking food from the shop, an act which, through its own minor transgression of parental laws, enhances her pleasure. Denise's early childhood is portrayed as a Rabelaisian festival of the senses, as she indulges her need for physical gratification through touch and taste: 'Chaud aux cuisses d'y penser, bouche ouverte, collante de sucre ...' (LAV, p. 30).[8] The transference of sexual gratification to the act of eating which follows such conversations results in a highly erotic experience, as illustrated in the narrator's correlation of comestible and sexual pleasure when she hides her sweets 'dans la culotte, le seul endroit où on n'ira pas farfouiller' (LAV, p. 32).

The recurrent sublimation of sexual desire through eating in *Les Armoires vides* points to the omnipresence of sexuality in the young narrator's thoughts, a presence indicated not merely by the eroticised manner in which the narrator describes eating or in the numerous references to cream – the least subtle of which refers to 'la laitance crémeuse' (LAV, p. 48) – but equally by the phallic imagery she employs to denote a variety of unrelated objects: 'tuyaux', 'petits serpents', 'un gros ver' (LAV, p. 35), 'Serpent de lait' (LAV, p. 57). A more obviously phallic image occurs when the narrator refers to the abortionist's probe as 'le serpent rouge' (LAV, p. 11), reinforcing the association of sexual penetration and abortion already mentioned. The narrator's intense interest in sexual matters is further highlighted by her imaginary transformations of ordinary events into utopian opportunities to satisfy her sexual curiosity – opportunities which always involve young men and tend to take place in an adult-free zone – and by her fascination with urinary functions (see, for example, pp. 42, 46, 48, 56). It is not merely the narrator who appears overly focused on her genitalia through scarcely veiled references to them, but, it would appear, this preoccupation afflicts most of the people who populate her universe, whether customers in her home environment – 'Hé, Ninise, baisse le capot, on voit le moteur!' (LAV, p. 57) – or teachers at school: 'la vieille Aubin [...] regardait sous les tables à cause des mains ...' (LAV, p. 58).

This overriding focus on sexuality which permeates the text from the narrator's earliest childhood to her young adulthood can be attributed to the abortion she is undergoing in the present, to the sexual origins of her current suffering. There is no sentimentalisation of abortion on the part of the narrator, but it is presented as a pragmatic, if temporarily unpleasant, solution to an unwanted pregnancy; in other words, it is not merely the subject matter of the work which may be disturbing for the reader, but, equally, the blunt manner of its reporting: 'Je sais seulement que ça meurt petit à petit, ça s'éteint, ça se noie dans les poches gorgées de sang, d'humeurs filantes ... Et que ça part. C'est tout' (LAV, p. 12). This manner accords with the representation of taboo subjects to provocative effect which is fundamental to Ernaux's

literary project. The absence of literary representations of abortion –
an absence which may explain both the narrator's frustrated frankness
in discussing the topic, as well as any consequent unease experienced
by the reader on reading the account – reinforces the narrator's sense
of isolation: 'Il n'y a rien pour moi là-dedans [her university syllabus]
sur ma situation, pas un passage pour décrire ce que je sens maintenant,
m'aider à passer mes sales moments' (ibid.).[9] While the narrator has
adhered to bourgeois models of conduct throughout adolescence and
early adulthood in an endeavour to eradicate all evidence of her working-class origins, the public condemnation of abortion – whatever the
private approbation – prohibits the existence of a relevant 'modèle'
(LAV, p. 55) for her to consult. The sole accounts of abortion are to be
found in arid medical journals written by men and intended to frighten,
rather than enlighten, female readers.[10] The narrative of *Les Armoires
vides* can be seen as countering this non- or mis-representation: by
expressing her thoughts and feelings throughout her abortion, the narrator both raises and partially resolves the problem of such literary
lacunae, providing her own much-needed account of abortion, and
giving voice to an area of female experience which has traditionally
been excluded from literature.

The suffering endured by the narrator goes beyond the physical
effects of abortion to encompass acute psychological repercussions.
The narrator perceives her abortion as a punishment for being born
working-class, a perception which accounts for her feelings of aggres-
sion towards her milieu: 'Gosse mal embouchée, vicieuse, et je leur
[her mother's customers] pisserais à la gueule tout accroupie ...' (LAV,
p. 46). (The term 'vicieuse', which the narrator first hears during a
conversation between her mother and a customer, recurs throughout
Les Armoires vides as a term of self-designation and conveys the self-
castigation of the narrator, her awareness of the social and, more importantly, maternal perception of premarital sexual pleasure for women
as immoral, an awareness which both increases her enjoyment of it
and reinforces her association of sexual immorality with her working-
class origins.) The damaging consequences of the sexual interdictions
the narrator encounters at both home and school, and of the bourgeois denigration of her working-class background, are apparent in
her interpretation of abortion as a form of divine retribution. The
confessional monologue of *Les Armoires vides* reveals the erroneousness of Denise's conviction that a sexual relationship with a member
of the bourgeoisie would suffice to cleanse her of the 'original' sin of

being born working-class, a conviction which leads her to transgress the parental interdiction on premarital sex. Her working-class past is shown to haunt her like a spectre she may temporarily conceal, but can never completely exorcise.

The consequence of this belief in a type of class curse, a belief which indicates the success of the naturalisation of culturally imposed differences, is a defeatism, a reluctance on the part of the narrator to accept responsibility for her actions.[11] As well as attributing various occurrences to her working-class origins, the narrator 'personalises' responsibility, blaming events on specific individuals such as her parents, her friend Odette, or even God: 'Encore un coup de Dieu, c'est lui qui veut tout ça ...' (LAV, p. 90). The narrator may experience moments of guilt when she admits to her own inadequacies and lack of filial respect, but such moments are short-lived, rapidly submerged beneath a wave of anger at the injustice of belonging to the working class. The narrator's passivity and acceptance of her lot – an attitude she may have inherited from her father – can be viewed as indicative of both her internalisation of ideological hierarchies and of her peripheral position on the cusp of both the working and middle classes, a position which prevents her from fully participating in either. As manifested in her narrators' constant return to their working-class childhood, the belief in the ineradicable influence of social origins on psychosexual development underlies Ernaux's entire literary project.

That her sexual experiences tend to take place at home strengthens the association of class and sexuality – or, rather, sexual depravity – in the narrator's mind. As her exposure to Catholic values continues at school, she begins to view her home life as evil, to perceive herself as eternally condemned to sin. The uneasiness this perception generates in the narrator is Sarrautian in its tropistic vagueness: 'Quelque chose de poisseux et d'impur m'entoure définitivement, lié à mes différences, à mon milieu. Toutes les prières de pénitence n'y feront rien. Il faut que je sois punie' (LAV, p. 67). This correlation between social class and sexual immorality is confirmed for the narrator during her first confession. The priest's condemnation of the narrator's masturbation fuels the sense of inferiority instilled by the constant denigration and exclusion of her working-class culture at school. Envisaged as a opportunity to expiate the minor sins of her past, her first confession represents instead the definitive end of Denise's childhood innocence: the narrator feels more entrenched in, and unable to escape from, her working-class conditioning. Indeed, given the narrator's association of religious condemnation and masturbation, of sexual censorship and its transgression, it is no coincidence that she has a spontaneous orgasm while studying her Latin homework, or that she is convinced her menarche has arrived during her first communion, reinforcing the symbolism of her transition from childhood to womanhood: the narrator's body rebels against the constraints to which religion subjects it.[12] Her religious education reveals its continuing influence on her in her reference to the advent of menstruation as 'la purification' and 'la grâce des règles', adding 'Je suis neuve, je suis propre, ma naissance' (LAV, p. 121). For Denise, her menarche demonstrates both that masturbation has not irredeemably tainted her, allowing her to begin afresh in her desire to conform to the rules of sexual morality, and that, irrespective of class, women's physiology comprises certain universal components.

Lessons of Value

In *Les Armoires vides*, the narrator's childhood universe centres on the kitchen, symbolically situated between the paternal domain of the café and the maternal domain of the *épicerie*.[13] The young narrator's early childhood is characterised by a sense of fulfilment, as exemplified in her designation of it as 'vrai', while that of her schoolfriends is termed 'faux'. In a similar vein, it is her home life which represents 'reality' for the young narrator, yet, as school begins to exert an influence on the child – an influence partly encouraged by the parental reverence towards it – the narrator realises the benefits to be accrued from working the system: 'Comme le café-épicerie était plus réel. L'école, c'était un faire comme si continuel, comme si c'était drôle, comme si c'était intéressant, comme si c'était bien' (LAV, p. 54). The narrator learns the art of duplicity in order to gain acceptance and enjoys the power academic success brings, until the ludic aspect of her academic participation acquires more sinister overtones, signalling her allegiance to a class hierarchy which judges her home environment as inferior. If the 'middle' position occupied by the narrator during her early years is one of security, safely ensconced between her parents, it comes to acquire more claustrophobic and limiting associations as the halcyon days of childhood recede into the past: 'Ligotée. Denise Lesur, la fille de l'épicière et du cafetier, coincée entre l'alignement de mangeaille d'un côté, de l'autre les chaises remplies de bonshommes qui s'affalent autour de la table, attendent d'avoir leur chouïa' (LAV, p. 101).[14] This 'middle' position is subsequently represented by her constant shuttling between home and school, and by her anomalous class status: she may not belong to the social class of her schoolfriends, yet is at the top of the working-class hierarchy, due to the commercial success of her parents. The harmonious coexistence of her working-class domestic environment and middle-class educational one begins to break down, as the disparities between them necessitate an ever greater degree of role-playing on the part of the narrator, foreshadowing the 'split' personality which figures in both *Ce qu'ils disent ou rien* and *La Femme gelée*. The narrator's consequent sense of isolation, apparent in her perception that she alone is guilty of masturbating – 'Moi seule je reste avec mon vieux péché inclassable' (LAV, p. 87) – continues to be felt by the mature narrator as she endures her abortion on her own, and contrasts sharply with the lack of privacy which characterises early childhood.[15]

As in both *Ce qu'ils disent ou rien* and *La Femme gelée*, the narrator's assimilation of the values proffered at school is illustrated by the reversal of her terms of reference, in that her home life comes to be described as 'faux', while it is the school environment which is considered 'vrai'. This assimilation is further conveyed in the narrator's account of her lovemaking with Marc – 'J'ai trouvé mon vrai lieu, ma vraie place' (LAV, p. 173) – and her reference to 'Marc et ma vraie vie' (LAV, p. 174). Similarly, while pretence plays a prime role in facilitating her acceptance at school, it later becomes a necessary survival tactic in her home environment: 'Pour m'en sortir, il fallait fermer les yeux, faire comme si je mangeais, lisais, dormais dans un vague hôtel' (LAV, p. 100).[16] Reinforcing this volte-face in the narrator's attribution of values is her reversal of the Manichaean judgements made earlier, in that she now views middle-class people as 'gens bien' (LAV, pp. 83, 88, 89, etc.), and refers to the middle class in general as 'milieux bien' (LAV, p. 100), while the world of her parents is relegated to the shameful, the peripheral – in short, to the 'unreal': 'j'aurais voulu qu'ils soient autrement, convenables, sortables dans le véritable monde' (LAV, p. 111). As she grows older, the realisation that her parents' taste in reading material and music is considered lamentable by 'la classe dominante' she esteems so highly intensifies the humiliation she feels towards her origins – along with 'honte', 'humiliation' is one of the most common nouns in *Les Armoires vides*: 'On ne parle jamais de ça, de la honte, des humiliations, on les oublie les phrases perfides en plein dans la gueule, surtout quand on est gosse. Etudiante ... On se foutait de moi, de mes parents. L'humiliation' (LAV, p. 60).[17] The likes and dislikes of her parents are vilified by the narrator's middle-class schoolfriends – 'Les rires des filles, "tu aimes Luis Mariano!"' (LAV, p. 124) – illustrating the classist and classifying nature of the concept of taste, of cultural consumption.[18]

At school, taste is presented as a natural predisposition, rather than culturally acquired.[19] It is the professed neutrality of her educational environment which makes the transmission of its middle-class values – and the consequent reification of the class hierarchy – difficult to resist. The divisive consequences of such 'neutrality' become apparent when Denise, like her counterparts in *Ce qu'ils disent ou rien* and *La Femme gelée*, begins to conflate socioeconomic class differences with an inherent physiological or intellectual superiority: 'Mais je ne faisais pas le rapport. Je croyais que sa [one of her middle-class schoolfriends] légèreté, ses moqueries alertes étaient de purs dons, rien à voir avec le magasin, le hall d'entrée aux plantes vertes' (LAV, p. 62). If the younger narrator, who at first accepts differences between the world of school and her home life indiscriminately, is taught to view taste as a 'natural' indicator of distinction, to employ Bourdieuian terminology, her older counterpart, while capable of deconstructing the ideological indoctrination of her schooling, continues to be influenced by it: 'Le goût. La sonde, le ventre, ça n'a pas tellement changé, toujours de mauvais goût. La Lesur remonte' (LAV, p. 61).[20] Only at the text's conclusion does the narrator begin to question the value system she so much wishes to appropriate, a questioning also articulated in the text's epigraph, foregrounding the circular structure of the work. Taken from Paul Eluard's *La Rose publique*, the epigraph's first line – 'J'ai conservé de faux trésors dans des armoires vides' – points to the narrator's misplaced appreciation of the cultural indicators of middle-class status: having succumbed to the superficial attractiveness of middle-class values, the narrator comes to realise that their acquisition guarantees nothing.

The narrator's sole means of transcending the perceived limitations of her working-class origins and demonstrating her superiority over classmates is to excel academically. Having failed to achieve redemption for her working-class origins through sexual abstinence, Denise determines to redeem herself through her marks at school: 'j'avais la grâce, des facultés' (LAV, p. 72). In a sense, the satisfaction she achieves through her academic prowess, through the validation of her intelligence in a middle-class environment, mirrors the satisfaction she feels when taking food illicitly from her mother's shop or experimenting sexually, all of which, in different ways, signal a severance from her social class through a rejection of its value system. Education represents a form of innoculation against the influence of her working-class environment, in that the imaginary vistas it conjures up allow Denise to enjoy vicarious experience of a world beyond the parameters of her milieu. Indeed, so desperate is she to eschew a working-class future that she considers prostitution – or a somewhat idealised version of it – preferable to marrying within the working class: 'Je partais, je m'évadais, je cherchais dans le *Larousse* les mots étranges, volupté, lupanar, rut, les définitions me plongeaient dans des rêveries chaudes, destin blanc et or, salles de bains orientales, je me coulais dans des cercles de bras et de jambes parfumés' (LAV, p. 107). This perception of sexuality as a key to transcending social origins – as illustrated by the fact that her exoticisation of prostitution involves only middle-class clients – accounts for the resolute middle-classness of all her future boyfriends and, ultimately, for the narrator's pregnancy. Going out with a member of the bourgeoisie constitutes revenge for the narrator – 'un gars "bien", c'est la purification' (LAV, p. 130) – and allows her to participate in the middle class by proxy. As with her earlier use of 'purification' in relation to menstruation, the term signals the redemptive power with which the narrator invests sexually-related events which distance her from her working-class background. Indeed, part of the narrator's pleasure at attending university stems from the fact that she no longer has to verify the class credentials of future partners: her utopian childhood dream of existing in an adult-free universe with an infinite array of potential sexual partners is finally realised.

Flattered to be considered an honorary member of the middle class through her relationships with men, the narrator looks back on her previous self with ironic detachment. Throughout Ernaux's writing, the use of irony is indicative of middle-class status:[21] 'je regarde ironiquement la grognasse que j'étais hier encore' (LAV, p. 154). That detachment transmutes into a quasi-masochistic pleasure in being seduced by men who denigrate her – if ridicule reflects class difference, then the greater the humiliation, the more impressive the narrator's 'catch'. This masochism is, however, more apparent than real, and is not portrayed as inherent in the narrator's perception of sexual relations, but as firmly rooted in her valorisation of the bourgeoisie.[22] Indeed, her submissive behaviour towards her partner is extremely purposeful: rather than epitomising the passively masochistic female, the narrator can be viewed as a ruthless and calculating duper, who sees men as little more than a means to social ascension. (The importance the narrator accords the social class of her boyfriends is highlighted by the fact that she keeps a record of their parents' professions.) In earlier relationships, when differences in social class are less conspicuous, the narrator assumes a more dominant role sexually, as highlighted by the repeated references to her first boyfriend as 'proie' (LAV, pp. 131, 132, 133). She is shown to objectify men, to view them as interchangeable instruments for her own physical gratification: 'Je ne pensais qu'à moi-même, j'étais une vraie boule de plaisir des orteils à la queue de cheval' (LAV, p. 143).

When the narrator loses her virginity, the vocabulary she employs has a religious air, further reflecting her sense of redemption at having been validated by a member of the bourgeoisie and corroborating the connection between penetration and abortion already mentioned: 'hurler de délivrance, et macérer doucement, crevée, du sang, de l'eau' (LAV, p. 171).[23] That redemption is clearly linked to heterosexual activity – which both gives pleasure to men and incorporates a reproductive function – as opposed to masturbation: 'Je me sentais toute neuve, faible, écaillée de mes vieux péchés. A deux, dans le petit sentier, ce n'était pas sale' (LAV, p. 141).[24] Denise re-experiences the festival of physical indulgence of early childhood thanks to the 'purifying' presence of middle-class men; heterosexual relationships represent regeneration for the narrator, allowing her to distance herself from her social origins not only in the form of defying parental interdictions, but also by providing indubitable proof of middle-class approbation. However, as the narrative of *Les Armoires vides* testifies, the ultimate consequence of such approbation – her pregnancy – serves to entrench the narrator more deeply than ever in the class from which she seeks to escape. Her mother's favourite phrase – the portentous 'si jamais, si jamais il t'arrive un malheur' (LAV, p. 147), which forms a leitmotiv of the narrative, rising up repeatedly through the heteroglossic diversity of voices – becomes a self-fulfilling prophecy.

Linguistic Representation

The principal signifier of difference between the narrator's home and educational environments, and one to be addressed in greater detail in *Ce qu'ils disent ou rien*, is language. In Ernaux's writing, language use is never innocent and cannot be analysed as a self-contained, neutral system in the manner of structuralist linguistics. Rather, it reverberates with social and cultural implications, designating both the contextual specificities of the speaker's position within the social hierarchy and their consciousness of the linguistic components appropriate to their various speech interactions. The protagonist's use of language in *Les Armoires vides* reflects her dual sociolinguistic identity, expressing the class dichotomy of the parallel universes she has been forced to inhabit throughout childhood and adolescence: the profane *argot* stems from her working-class origins, and her more poetic, literary French from her bourgeois education. These linguistic variations demonstrate that language use, like the phenomenon of taste, is not a natural ability, but a cultural acquisition, the lexicon and execution of which are dependent on the speaker's sociocultural situation. As Bourdieu comments:

> La compétence linguistique n'est pas une simple capacité technique mais une capacité statutaire qui s'accompagne le plus souvent de la capacité technique, ne serait-ce que parce qu'elle en commande l'acquisition par l'effet de l'assignation statutaire ('noblesse oblige'), à l'inverse de ce que croit la conscience commune, qui voit dans la capacité technique le fondement de la capacité statutaire.[25]

As the state-sanctioned voice of authority, the narrator's teacher in *Les Armoires vides* manifests a dexterity and confidence absent from her parents' speech. It is not merely what is said, but how it is said – what the narrator refers to as 'ces intonations qui classent' (LAV, p. 158) – which situate the speaker socially. The narrator is conscious of switching 'languages' as she switches environment, but considers the language spoken at school, despite its more 'legitimate' status, to have a transience and abstractness absent from the language of her home life. The vulgar expressiveness and density of the latter perfectly denote the atmosphere of the café, the roughness of its customers, her parents' brutal manner of speaking to one another, as well as the pent-up frustration the narrator feels at times towards her school environment. In a remark which, by its incorporation of the value judgements already discussed in this chapter, signals the narrator's continuing affiliation with her home environment when she first attends school, the narrator draws attention to the colourful corporeality of the working-class expressions of childhood: 'Le vrai langage, c'est chez moi que je l'entendais, le pinard, la bidoche, se faire baiser, la vieille carne, dis boujou ma petite besotte' (LAV, p. 54).

As the narrator's education continues and she assumes the *Weltanschauung* inscribed in pedagogical discourse, facility in language use, given its pivotal role as an indicator of social class, grows increasingly important for her: 'N'avoir rien à dire, le nez dans son assiette, c'est une langue étrangère qu'ils parlent. My mother is dirty, mad, they are pigs!' (LAV, p. 114). The narrator first refers to the language spoken at school as 'une langue étrangère' (LAV, p. 53), hence this designation of her parents' language indicates the inversion of values undergone by the narrator, and the linguistic domination exerted by the school environment. Her parents may belong to the upper echelons of the working-class hierarchy, yet their lack of verbal proficiency (as determined by middle-class criteria) distinguishes them from those higher up the social ladder. As with other culturally acquired attributes, the success of ideological conditioning is illustrated in its naturalisation of taught verbal skills: 'L'impression que c'était inné, ça aussi, si on l'avait manqué à la naissance, c'était fichu' (LAV, p. 134). Given the importance the narrator accords linguistic competence, it is not surprising that it also plays a key role in her relations with men.[26]

The differences between the languages of home and school are reinforced when the narrator begins reading and continues to increase her lexicon, acquiring a vocabulary alien to her home environment. The narrator is effectively exposed to four variations of French: the working-class language spoken at home; a more 'purified' and stilted middle-class version spoken at school; a popular written French; and a lexically richer 'classic' literary French. Given its lack of familiarity to her and inappositeness when describing her home environment, the language the narrator encounters in literature, like its oral equivalent – the language spoken at school – initially has an air of unreality for her: 'Abat-voix, abaisse-langue, allégorique, ça, c'était toujours un jeu, et je récitais les pages roses, la langue d'un pays imaginaire … C'était tout artificiel, un système de mots de passe pour entrer dans un autre milieu' (LAV, p. 78). In contrast to the ephemeral unreality of literary language, the concreteness of working-class language continues to make itself felt in the present in imaginary comments from the narrator's mother apropos of her abortion: 'embroquée comme une traînée que dirait ma mère, les jambes écartées par le spéculum de la vioque, c'est comme ça que je dois dire les choses, pas avec les mots de Bornin, de Gide ou de Victor Hugo' (ibid.). As with the subjects portrayed in the patriarchal literary canon and its middle-class male perspective on 'representative' experience, the language it employs is profoundly alienating for the narrator and incapable of conveying the concrete physicality of the specifically female event she is enduring.[27]

Literature plays an increasingly important role in the narrator's life – at university, she refers to the library as 'l'église à livres' (LAV, p. 165),[28] echoing the parental reverence towards education. That reverence, whether in its general form of paying for private education or, more specifically, satisfying the narrator's appetite for new books, serves to entrench class divisions between parents and daughter: 'Entre *Bonnes Soirées*, que ma mère poisse de son café au lait, et *Le Château* de Kafka, je m'aperçois encore qu'il y a un monde. Continuellement des distances, avec mon milieu ...' (LAV, p. 156). In a manner analogous to her idealised perception of prostitution, literature allows the narrator to enjoy vicarious freedom from the constraints of her milieu while awaiting its actual realisation, to participate in the ruling class by proxy. The narrator's access to a plethora of literary works – and the surplus of middle-class indices they contain – facilitates her construction of an imaginary persona: 'L'épicerie-café, mes parents n'étaient certainement pas vrais, j'allais un soir m'endormir et me réveiller au bord d'une route, j'entrerais dans un château, un gong sonnerait, et je dirais "bonjour, Papa!" à un élégant monsieur servi par un maître d'hôtel stylé' (LAV, p. 80).[29] By introducing the narrator to numerous potential character permutations and future selves, literature contributes to the 'split' personality which the narrator gradually assumes, a personality she perceives as comprising her temporary actual self and her 'real' virtual self to be actualised some time in the future. The imaginary middle-class persona which reading helps create is paradoxically referred to as 'la vraie Denise Lesur, la nouvelle Denise Lesur' (LAV, p. 79), a persona at once both pre-existent and new. This fabrication of a middle-class persona does not remain at a virtual stage in the narrator's imagination, but also becomes the focus of written stories and essays: books inspire the narrator's own attempts to approximate her ideal future through writing.

So disparate are the linguistic – whether written or oral – and experiential strands of the narrator's current existence that language fails to provide any meaningful bridge between her parallel universes: while there exist no works of literature portraying abortion or any working-class experience recognisable to the narrator, her perception of that abortion as stemming from her working-class origins means that the oral language she learnt at school is incapable of expressing how she feels. The narrator also claims to have forgotten the vocabulary of her parents, buried as it is under years of learning, a claim which is inconsistent with the emphasis throughout Ernaux's writing on the ineradicable influence of childhood – indeed, with reference to her parents' language, she remarks: 'je les ai dans la tête ces boniments' (LAV, p. 103).[30] The oral nature of the early trilogy makes the narrator's dichotomised categorisation of spoken and written language all the more untenable: the narrator may claim to have different 'languages' for speaking and writing, yet the interior monologue of her narrative clearly blurs the boundaries separating them. Indeed, much of the work's potency lies in the oral frankness of its language, an orality comprising short, staccato comments ('Presque du plaisir' [LAV, p. 11], 'Et que ça part' [LAV, p. 12]), incomplete sentences, ('Si toute la récré se passait aux chiottes ...' [LAV, p. 56]) and elliptic ones.[31] Given the narrator's association of written discourse with the bourgeoisie and oral discourse with her working-class origins – an association which reflects the Manichaean values already discussed, in that *écriture* is valorised over *parole* – her failure to acknowledge her own use of working-class French can be interpreted as evidence of her internalisation of the linguistic and cultural hierarchies taught at school. Her school's assessment of her spoken language as 'Expression orale maladroite' (LAV, p. 77) may further account for the narrator's explicit distancing from her early language use. In light of this dichotomised portrayal of spoken and written languages in *Les Armoires vides*, Ernaux's desire to study literature at university and to pursue writing as a career may be seen to represent the definitive attempt to escape the oral language of child-hood and to align herself with the bourgeoisie.

It is perhaps Denise's abortion – the catalyst to her quasi stream-of-consciousness narrative – which provides the clearest illustration of the linguistic influences to which she is subject. Her description of abortion can be seen to reflect the language of the text in microcosm, in that it is characterised by an unusually lyrical combination of work-ing- and middle-class elements. Her perception of sexuality as a pass-port to the bourgeoisie, yet instinctive association of its more negative effects – of which her abortion is the nadir – with her working-class origins results in a hybrid linguistic representation of her suffering. Just as her relationships at university are imbued with a romanticism stemming from the middle-class environments in which they take place, her account of abortion further reveals her literary culture in her em-ployment of poetic images, in the cumulative use of synonyms and in descriptions of a surreal Baudelairian nature: 'Le soleil traverserait la peau, décomposerait les chairs et les cartilages, la bouillie filerait en douceur à travers le tuyau ...' (LAV, p. 12). However, as if to illustrate the narrator's belief that her working-class origins can never be eradicated, the working-class language of childhood erupts into the narrative in moments of anger and frustration, pointing to the intense swell of emotion which subtends Denise's fragile linguistic façade. *Les Armoires vides* portrays Denise's expression of her sexuality as an ongoing negotiation between the 'oral' working-class option of silence or a distortive vulgarity, and the 'written' middle-class alternative of an alienating, since phallocentric, literary discourse.

CE QU'ILS DISENT OU RIEN

The narrative of Ernaux's second work covers a much shorter period of time than *Les Armoires vides*, relating events which take place one summer, during the vacation separating the end of the narrator's education at a *collège* in June and her attendance at a *lycée* the following September. The narrative does delve into the more distant past, briefly recounting, for example, the narrator's experience of primary school, but in no sense do we have the extensive timescales of *Les Armoires vides* or *La Femme gelée*. The symbolism of the narrative's temporal framework, a framework which can be viewed as spanning the transitional period from childhood to adulthood, is reinforced by the events it portrays. *Ce qu'ils disent ou rien* centres on the representation of Anne's first sexual experiences, including the loss of her virginity, and the increased parent/daughter estrangement this precipitates, an estrangement which finds expression, or, more accurately, fails to find expression, in language. The narrator's sense of alienation from her representation in parental discourse, and, in particular, from its prescriptive role in the construction of identity, is intimated in the work's title. Anne's impression of being both central yet peripheral to parental discourse characterises the narrative as a whole: her parents' principal concern may be her academic success and future well-being, yet they deny her the subjecthood to engage in dialogue about them. That denial is epitomised in one of her father's remarks, a remark which was to have provided the work's original title: 'tu n'as rien à dire que tu ne parles pas' (CDR, p. 143). While generational and class differences reinforce the linguistic divide separating Anne and her parents, *Ce qu'ils disent ou rien* portrays the consequences rather than the causes of that divide. The work's short-term perspective prohibits the more comprehensive analysis of familial divisions provided by *Les Armoires vides* and *La Femme gelée*. Unlike these works, within the retrospective narrative of *Ce qu'ils disent ou rien* the thrust is very much forward-looking – the youth of the narrator and her adolescent impatience to gain sexual experience lead her to focus firmly on the present and future, as exemplified in her tendency to state her age as 'bientôt seize ans' (CDR, p. 19).

From the work's opening, Anne experiences detachment from the discourse of her parents, and – whether she be subject of the *énoncé* or of the *énonciation* – bemoans the inadequacies of language to provide meaningful articulation of her feelings. While the narrator's lack of communication with her parents is compounded by her gradual migration to the bourgeoisie and consequent resentment of her working-class origins, Anne's transition is described with neither the vituperative intensity of *Les Armoires vides* nor the expository clarity of *La Femme gelée*, but is, rather, deduced from the narrator's accounts of her parents' conversations and general habits, and from her use of 'détails concrets'.[32] The narrator's appropriation of bourgeois values is less notable in *Ce qu'ils disent ou rien* than in *Les Armoires vides* due to both the minor role played by education in the work and the greater financial security of Anne's parents. Indeed, when compared to the framing works of the trilogy, the reader is obliged to take up a more 'proactive' role when interpreting the content of *Ce qu'ils disent ou rien*. While the narrator in *La Femme gelée* is a wife and mother when she relates her retrospective account and the narrator in *Les Armoires vides* has left home to attend university, their counterpart in *Ce qu'ils disent ou rien* has only recently experienced the events she describes: she has neither the reflective nor the geographical distance to understand, and make explicit, their significance. The narrator's linguistic isolation is aggravated not merely by her mis- or non-representation in parental discourse but equally by her inability to articulate her sexual experiences. While language's androcentric bias is shown to profoundly distort such experiences, the parental attitude to sexuality forbids even the attempt to verbalise them: 'Si j'avais pu tout leur dire, je n'aurais pas eu ces idées bizarres' (CDR, p. 92). The recurrent use of the adjective 'bizarre' (CDR, pp. 9, 20, 22) points to the narrator's indeterminate self-image during this adolescent period of flux, and foreshadows an important theme of the work, that is, the patriarchal correlation of female sexual freedom and social deviance. The impossibility of giving verbal expression, and, consequently, validation, to a fundamental part of her identity – her sexuality – has resulted in an internalised sense of abnormality.

The narrator's marginalisation in language is made worse by the absence of an interlocutor with whom to converse. While loneliness features prominently in the lives of the narrators throughout the trilogy (whether stemming from generational and class divisions between parents and offspring, or from gender divisions between men and women), the narrator's loneliness in *Ce qu'ils disent ou rien* is particularly acute. Anne's isolation may be intensified by the location of the family home: in contrast to the representation of the busy *café-épicerie* elsewhere in Ernaux's corpus, the portrayal of the narrator's house in *Ce qu'ils disent ou rien* foregrounds its geographical seclusion. With no customers to occupy them, her parents' constant surveillance of the narrator exacerbates the atmosphere of tension and claustrophobia in the work's opening section. The narrator's loneliness is further reinforced by her transitional position both between two social classes – an intermediacy analogous to the 'middle' position occupied by her counterpart in *Les Armoires vides* – and between childhood and adulthood: she may have the physical maturity to enjoy sexual relationships, but does not possess the psychological maturity to cope with their consequences. Even at the work's conclusion, the narrator remains suspended between two phases of her development, having temporarily stopped menstruating. This cessation may be viewed as signifying Anne's rebellion against the maternal policing of her body, as well as her desire to arrest her physical development and entry into womanhood, a desire fuelled no doubt by the negative repercussions of recent sexual experiences.

Too young to possess a well-defined class consciousness, the narrator is unable to decipher the wider political motives underlying her parents' involvement – or, to her mind, interference – in her day-to-day life. This involvement clearly has its source in fear: after years of sacrifice in order to ensure a successful future for their daughter, her parents wish to minimise the likelihood of extraneous factors entering, and unbalancing, their carefully calculated equation. Petrified that their social aspirations will come to nought and unfamiliar with more sophisticated forms of rhetoric, they subject Anne to constant and vociferous verbal policing. The screaming and shouting – which, along with the reverential tones reserved for members of the professional classes, characterises parental communication throughout Ernaux's corpus – is merely an indication of their inferior social position, a position which they do not wish to see duplicated in their daughter's future. This desire that Anne eschew the parental model of achievement accounts for the inflexibility of the conditions they impose on her: 'il faut que je sois ce qu'ils disent, pas ce qu'ils sont' (CDR, pp. 10–11). Unsure as to what the small print of such a future will contain, her parents seek to guarantee unquestioning assimilation of its main features through their constant reiteration. The narrative of *Ce qu'ils disent ou rien* highlights the shortcomings of such an approach: at an age characterised by a need for dialogic exchange, the narrator is frustrated by her parents' confinement within rigid conversational parameters.

Unable to give adequate oral expression to her feelings, the narrator voices a desire to write in order to provide the self-representation she so desperately needs. As in *Les Armoires vides*, it is the inadequacies of existent literary accounts in reflecting the narrator's experience which are put forward to justify Anne's attempts at writing in *Ce qu'ils disent ou rien*. The tentative nature of these attempts is conveyed by the narrator's use of the third person, foregrounding both her feelings of alienation and lack of confidence in her writerly ability. That lack of confidence and the influence of previous literary models are evident in the narrator's recourse to clichéd romantic scenarios in her compositions, since, as she remarks of her family, 'nous ne sommes pas des personnages de roman, c'est assez visible et il ne m'arrive rien' (CDR, p. 64). Just as she succumbs to the heady seductiveness of the *déjà-dit* in the form of reading romances in *Femmes d'aujourd'hui*, Anne gives up trying to mould language to suit her personal writerly needs: 'ça ressemblait à un début d'*Intimité*, une rencontre dans un train, le wagon de première, mais la fille s'était trompée de wagon, le hasard, il fallait, pour la faire aimer par un P.-D.G.' (CDR, p. 65). Where the narrator's related attempts fail to reflect her own existence – 'Très loin de la pluie ici, des carrés de jardins, de l'histoire enfermée quelque part dans ces murs' (ibid.) – *Ce qu'ils disent ou rien* succeeds: as with *Les Armoires vides*, *Ce qu'ils disent ou rien* addresses the lacuna its narrator perceives in literature generally by providing a candid account of heterosexual relations – with the emphasis predominantly on the sexual – unlike the sterilised versions of romantic love on which she has been raised.

Ce qu'ils disent ou rien differs from the rest of Ernaux's corpus not only in its representation of an extreme form of alienation but also in its general content. *Ce qu'ils disent ou rien* is the most fictional of Ernaux's works, in that it is the least anchored in auto/biographical details. Here, the narrator's parents have lived in the *cité* before moving to their current home; both parents work outside the home – the father is foreman in a refinery, the mother now works in a café, having previously worked in a factory; and the characters of the narrator's parents deviate from their otherwise consistent portrayal in Ernaux's writing – in *Ce qu'ils disent ou rien*, for example, the mother is houseproud and the usually abstemious father is shown to drink moderately.[33] While sharing many of the temporal and focal complexities of *Les Armoires vides*, overall *Ce qu'ils disent ou rien* is more conventional in its deployment of narrative techniques. In contrast to the predominance of the 'oral' present in the interior monologue of its predecessor, *Ce qu'ils disent ou rien* includes more traditional literary elements, whether in its use of past tenses or in the deliberate creation of suspense throughout its opening section. (This self-conscious use of suspense provides further evidence of the narrator's familiarity with novelistic conventions, in contrast to *Les Armoires vides*, where the gradual dissemination of information is appropriate to the naturalistic use of the interior monologue.) Throughout the early part of the work, the narrator makes recurrent, if fleeting, reference to the unhappy outcome of the events she is describing and to the distortive effect her position of epistemological superiority has on her representation of these events: 'de savoir la suite maintenant ça me fausse tout' (CDR, p. 81). This explicit acknowledgement of the constructed nature of *Ce qu'ils disent ou rien* can be seen to foreshadow the role played by metanarrative comments in subsequent works. It may be that the extreme form of loneliness experienced by Anne in *Ce qu'ils disent ou rien* requires a stronger panacea than the 'oral' version of events presented in *Les Armoires vides*.

The narrator's reluctance to reveal the source of her current misery and confusion throughout the text's opening section subjects the reader to a frustration analogous to that endured by Anne's younger self during the first part of her summer vacation: a sense of expectation embraces both the narrator who longs for the advent of a sexual rite of passage, and the reader, who is aware that such an event is shortly to be recounted and who seeks clues as to its precise nature. The gradualness of the narrative build-up to the pivotal encounters with Mathieu is shown to stem from both the limitations of language in providing accurate expression of the narrator's feelings – 'Je me vois dégringoler et je ne sais même pas comment appeler ce que je sens' (CDR, p. 11) – and from her disinclination to relive events: she would prefer either to rewind her 'life narrative' to the beginning of the summer – a time which she retrospectively perceives as a period of innocence before the Fall –

or to fast-forward it to when she is an adult, and her current suffering will be consigned to the past, again highlighting the intermediacy which characterises her present position. The climactic tension which permeates the first section of the work is given further impetus by Anne's constant references to the date and by the claustrophobic atmosphere at home. This atmosphere, combined with the stifling heat, serves to fuel the narrator's pent-up sexual energy, as reflected in her provocative manner of dressing.[34] Both the intensity of the narrator's sexual longing and the significance of this particular vacation for her sexual development are signalled by her act of masturbation at the beginning of the summer, an act she has resisted for the previous six months due to her perception of masturbation as sexually aberrant: 'La première fois l'année dernière, je n'ai pas osé regarder ma mère, ni personne, ils devaient savoir, et ce n'est pas permis aux filles normales' (CDR, p. 23). Anne, like Denise before her, has internalised the belief that the expression of female sexuality is psychologically detrimental unless it occurs within the confines of the heterosexual, preferably married, couple, and is therefore safely consigned to patriarchal control.[35] Anne fears that she may be considered 'braque' or 'folle' (CDR, p. 36) if she discloses her sexual desires. Throughout *Ce qu'ils disent ou rien*, the narrator differentiates between sex or sexual fantasies and their representation in language, between the private and public realm: it is above all when such fantasies are voiced that they become morally reprehensible. As in *Passion simple*, it is the potential misappropriation of her sexual experiences by others which most concerns the narrator: 'La chaleur me donnait des idées gluantes dont j'aurais eu honte de parler aux autres, mais que je n'avais pas honte d'avoir' (CDR, p. 16).

The narrator's anxiety at failing to correspond to the ideal of the sexually naïve Catholic schoolgirl stems from the fact that if she is not 'ce qu'ils disent' ('ils' being her parents, and 'ce que' the circumscribed future they have envisaged for her), she is 'rien'. (The title of the work can also be interpreted as referring to a specifically male imposition of acceptable female behavioural paradigms – an imposition clearly illustrated by Mathieu and Yan's double standards regarding monogamy – and to the inability of androcentric discourse to accommodate female sexual experience.) This void is emphasised on several occasions when, confronted with her parents' verbal representation of her, Anne feels only emptiness: 'Toujours, pendant leurs disputes à mon sujet, je suis gênée, comme s'ils ne parlaient pas de moi mais d'une autre Anne, la bonne petite fille à ses parents, ils se chicanent dans le vide au fond'

(CDR, p. 34). The linguistic vacuum which Anne views as characterising her inscription in parental discourse points to its monologic, as well as monolithic, quality. In order to minimise parental policing while preserving her own vision of subjecthood, the narrator is obliged to adopt two personae. If, as the Introduction suggests, the portrayal of this 'split' personality forms a recurrent feature of women's writing, its prevalence in Ernaux's texts may be further necessitated by the crosscultural locus her narrators inhabit and the consequent parental apprehension vis-à-vis their future. Anne's domestic persona – whose appearance consists of glasses, sensible clothes, no make-up or perfume and a childlike gait – is designed to draw attention to her intelligence and moral uprightness, in short, to conform to her parents' ideal. Her public persona once beyond the censorious maternal gaze is that of a sexually attractive, coquettish woman. These two personae typify the dilemma faced by Ernaux's narrators throughout the trilogy, and one to be examined in greater detail in Chapter 2, that is, how they may reconcile the personal fulfilment of intellectual potential with a continuing physical attractiveness to the male Other. Indeed, the extent of Anne's disillusionment in sexual relations following the end of her relationship with Mathieu is clearly illustrated in her full-time assimilation of the domestic persona.

Mother/Daughter Individuation

If the representation of adolescence in *Ce qu'ils disent ou rien* reflects the estrangement characteristic of parent/child relations throughout Ernaux's writing, unlike Denise in *Les Armoires vides* the narrator does not trace her trajectory from contented child to embittered adolescent, but focuses on her present disaffection. She may recall a period when she was closer to her parents, yet the reasons for her change in attitude are not examined in detail. Foreshadowing the use of affective images in *Une femme*, the narrator's memories of childhood are predominantly visual, rather than verbal, made up of images 'loin des mots' (CDR, p. 147). These images focus on a fun-loving, free-spirited woman antithetical to the censorious mother of the present and point to the emotional intensity of the earlier mother/daughter symbiosis. The end of this 'pre-verbal' symbiosis concurs with the narrator's consciousness of the significance of language's content. In Lacanian terms, the advent of the Symbolic leads to the devaluation of the Semiotic: 'quand on est gosse on n'écoute pas les paroles, à peine si on les entend, juste un fond' (CDR, p. 77). While the mere sound of her mother's

voice provides security for the young child and a sense of pre-individu-
alised fusion, as the narrator matures the content of her mother's speech
becomes all-important; the increasing disjunction between that content and the narrator's own experiences and perceptions – a disjunction intensified by the narrator's continuing absorption of middle-class
values – serves to reinforce the daughter's separation from the mother:
'Tout est désordre en moi, ça colle pas avec ce qu'ils disent' (CDR, p.
146). Throughout *Ce qu'ils disent ou rien*, parental discourse is represented as clichéd and insular. Anne dismissively refers to her parents'
speech as 'du bruit de fond' (CDR, p. 18) or 'leur baratin' (CDR, p.
19), and their act of conversing is described as 'épiloguer' (CDR, p.
52) or 'blablater' (CDR, p. 53).[36] With no interest in political issues
and unable to provide explanations to her queries, her parents limit
their conversation to commenting on local gossip and *faits divers*, or
to discussing practical matters: 'Qu'est-ce qu'elle m'avait dit
d'intéressant depuis longtemps. Début juillet, j'ai découvert qu'au fond
je n'avais pas besoin d'elle, sauf pour bouffer et dormir, m'acheter des
affaires. Elle ne m'apprenait rien, c'est ça' (CDR, p. 29). (This emphasis on 'utilitarianism' is also exemplified in her parents' view of education above all as a means to social betterment rather than intellectual
development.)

In an article entitled 'Annie Ernaux, filial ambivalence and *Ce qu'ils
disent ou rien*', Lucille Cairns relates the narrator's need for
individuation from the mother to the developmental paradigm posited
by, among others, Luce Irigaray, in which the young girl's original
desire for the mother must be repressed through a form of metaphorical matricide in order that successful socialisation take place.[37] The
psychoanalyst Nancy Chodorow also considers this erosion in intimacy a common development in the mother/daughter relationship:

> Before she can fully develop extrafamilial commitments, therefore, a girl must
> confront her entanglement in familial relationships themselves. It is not sur-
> prising, then, that […] the pubertal/adolescent transition is more difficult
> and conflictual for girls than for boys, and that issues during this period
> concern a girl's relationship to her mother.[38]

An event of key importance in reinforcing the narrator's individuation
from the mother is the death of the maternal grandmother. This death
can be interpreted as signalling the end of Anne's childhood, an end
given allegorical significance in her act of masturbation on the evening
of her grandmother's funeral: 'Ç'a été ma façon à moi de l'enterrer'
(CDR, p. 79). Analogous to the role played by mealtimes throughout

Ce qu'ils disent ou rien, the family meal following the funeral crystallises the narrator's feelings of hostility towards her family by feeding her distilled doses of their conversation. The narrator's incomprehension at her mother's grief testifies to her own feelings of estrangement towards her mother.[39] Anne's rejection of the mother/daughter symbiosis culminates in the wish for her own mother's death – the definitive physical severance – a wish which is presented as the logical conclusion to the narrator's psychological estrangement from her: 'Là j'aurais aimé autant qu'elle soit partie, morte, puisque de toute façon je suis partie d'elle dans ma tête' (CDR, p. 126). Judith Kegan Gardiner comments on the diffusiveness of the 'bad mother' figure in much recent women's writing: 'The most disturbing villain in recent women's fiction is not the selfish or oppressive male but instead the bad mother. This mother-villain is so frightening because she is what the daughter fears to become and what her infantile identifications predispose her to become.' Similar instances of 'matrophobia' in women's writing indicate the daughter's resistance to positional identification with the mother, a resistance clearly articulated in *Ce qu'ils disent ou rien*: 'Il m'a semblé que ma mère ressemblait à ma grand-mère, sa jambe était enflée, elle mourra dans trente ans, et moi je serai au retour d'âge, une chaîne atroce' (CDR, p. 125). In contrast to the Œdipus myth in which the son murders his father in order to replace him, the daughter's metaphorical murder of her mother in contemporary women's writing may represent, then, a determination to avoid taking her place through the eradication of existent maternal models.

That desire for eradication is further expressed in Anne's choice of heterosexual partner. Like Denise before her, Anne's motivation for losing her virginity to Mathieu is less a positive affirmation of her feelings towards him than a vengeful gesture towards her milieu and a means of liberating herself from the maternal. Indeed, immediately after her first sexual experience, she exclaims 'si ma mère me voyait' (CDR, p. 90), describing this exclamation as a 'cri de victoire' (ibid.). Like Denise, Anne strives to free herself from the sexually oppressive atmosphere at home and school, to transgress classist and sexist codes of conduct, through the physical. Anne's wish to have sexual relations with Mathieu in order to escape the constraints of her working-class background extends to linguistic constraints – she feels both intellectually and sexually imprisoned, 'quadrillée de leurs mots' (CDR, p. 145), when exposed to the language of her family: 'Plus tard quand j'aurai vécu longtemps, ou quand j'aurai couché avec un garçon, je pensais alors, je saurai m'exprimer' (CDR, p. 64). Since early childhood, her mother has either designated her daughter's genitalia by a childish euphemism which merely alienates the narrator from her own bodily experience – 'Ma mère lui donne un drôle de nom, son crougnougnous, objet innommable, pouah, je n'avais pas ça en moi' (CDR, p. 106) – or else refused to acknowledge – and thereby to legitimate – their existence. The psychoanalytic perception of woman as lack finds its linguistic equivalent in the literal absence of signifiers of female genitalia in *Ce qu'ils disent ou rien*: 'si on se lave le' (CDR, p. 125). At one point in the text, the narrator refers to her genitalia as belonging to her mother, 'Sa propriété' (CDR, p. 129). If this mode of designation foregrounds the mother's desire to contain her daughter's sexuality through appropriation and consequently accounts for the vehemence of the daughter's need for individuation, it can also be read as evidence of the physiological identification between mother and daughter, an identification which above all subtends the early childhood and late adulthood of Ernaux's narrators and which finds its most intense expression in *'Je ne suis pas sortie de ma nuit'*.

Gender Divides

Anne's most constant female companion in early childhood, and the only one for whom she feels emotional and physical intimacy, is Alberte. References to Alberte recur throughout the narrative – indeed, on occasion the narrative voice seems to be addressing her directly. The associations with Proust's Albertine are wholly appropriate, given the lesbian subtext to Anne's relationship with her. Indeed, the narrator attributes the repression of any homosexual tendencies between Alberte and herself to the social conditioning which posits heterosexuality as the key to a 'normal' healthy female sexuality, rather than to any 'natural' disinclination on her part: 'Du provisoire, toujours, rien que du provisoire, sinon, peut-être que je n'aurais pas eu peur de toucher Alberte, que j'aurais aimé' (CDR, p. 87).[41] In the narrator's childhood, Alberte represents social trangression and – or, indeed, through – sexual initiation. Her role as sexual initiator to the narrator is one fulfilled by female friends throughout Ernaux's corpus, given the maternal interdiction on all reference to female sexuality, including menstruation. The failure of the narrator's mother to provide her with the most rudimentary of sex educations is reflected in Anne's apparent ignorance of the basic, and profoundly sexist, rules of sexual conduct, an ignorance which has damaging repercussions for her platonic relationships as well.

Apart from her relationship with Alberte, female friendship has no intrinsic value for the narrator, but merely represents a means of meeting potential sexual partners. Her friendship with Gabrielle provides her with the pretext to escape the claustrophobic confines of the home and is instrumental in introducing her to Mathieu and other supervisors at the holiday camp where he works, yet the narrator has no qualms about having a sexual relationship with Gabrielle's boyfriend – Gabrielle is as expendable to Anne as Anne is to men. Anne's ignorance of the norms governing male and female sexual conduct may, however, be less complete than she admits, in that her claim to misunderstand the rules of courtship – as in *La Femme gelée*, there are repeated references to 'le code' – and her putative belief that 'sharing' Gabrielle's boyfriend is a sign of sisterhood are undermined by the very vocabulary she uses to describe her action: 'Peut-être que je n'ai pas le sens de la propriété, en imagination au moins, j'aurais bien volé l'autre main pour moi, fifty-fifty' (CDR, p. 71). She employs a synonymous verb later in the text, in a remark which clearly indicates her sense of triumphalism over Gabrielle: 'De l'avoir piqué à Gabrielle me paraissait déjà beau' (CDR, p. 90). The narrator condemns the gendered norms governing men and women's sexual mores, and men's deceitful exploitation of them in order to achieve their sexual objectives (*Ce qu'ils disent ou rien* repeatedly highlights men's hypocrisy in encouraging women's sexual liberty for personal pleasure, while publicly condemning them for promiscuity), yet behaves in a similarly misogynous manner towards Gabrielle.

If linguistic exchanges between the narrator and her parents are impeded by issues relating to class and generation – like Denise's, Anne's parents are constantly referred to as 'les vieux' – outwith the domestic realm the inadequacies of language are felt most strongly by the narrator when confronted with men's representation of female sexuality. In such cases, language is so tainted with misogynous prejudice as to alienate the narrator completely. Extreme vigilance is required in order to counter men's sophistic manipulation of the female interlocutor: 'Là j'écoutais presque sans penser que c'étaient des garçons et qu'il y a toujours des intentions derrière les paroles dans ce cas' (CDR, p. 83). That manipulation is also apparent in the anodyne-sounding binary oppositions in Anne's father's and Mathieu's sexist clichés: 'l'homme propose la femme dispose [...] la femme se donne et l'homme se prête' (CDR, p. 101).[42] The narrator is appalled by the seemingly ubiquitous vulgarity in men's discussion of sexual relations, relations which she has only previously known narrated in the euphemistic language of song lyrics and romantic literature. The emotional sterility of the language men use to describe sexual relations is unambiguously conveyed in Anne's assessment of her third sexual relationship with a man for whom she feels only disgust: 'Je sentais ça, le sexe il faut dire, le mot général, oui ça convenait bien cette fois' (CDR, p. 141). While the narrator's difficulty in providing an account of her erotic experiences is compounded by the challenge of giving expression to the less tangible aspects of female sexuality, the patriarchal bias in everyday language use, the reiterative deadening of the *déjà-dit*, cannot but misrepresent such experiences. Anne views men as adopting a highly reductive approach to language, in that behind most of their conversations lies insecure machismo; conversational competitiveness typifies male discourse in *Ce qu'ils disent ou rien*, reducing both sexes to their physical characteristics. For Anne, the predictability and detachment of 'men's' language is at odds with her own intimate and ever-developing awareness of female sexuality, indicating the lack of correspondence between Anne and Mathieu's 'background' system of experiences and assumptions:[43]

> [L]es mots ne m'ont pas semblé bons, il y avait un côté vécé municipal et puis après, ne dis pas que t'as jamais trifouillé avec une fille, vous êtes toutes un peu gouines. C'est la première fois que j'entendais ce nom, il se comprenait bien mais tout ce vocabulaire me déplaisait et j'ai été triste. Je trouve que c'est mieux de ne pas nommer, ou alors inventer. Peut-être que les garçons n'ont pas beaucoup d'imagination qu'ils se répètent les mêmes mots d'une génération à l'autre. (CDR, p. 95)

If masculine discourse alienates Anne through its crude objectification of her body image, in its extreme form such discourse not only objectifies, but obliterates the female subject:

> [D]is donc j'espère que tu lui as déjà fait sauter la capsule, moi de mon temps je craignais personne pour la farce. Ils étaient tout bouffis de rire, l'un restait muet et l'autre s'excitait encore plus, c'est que je te l'enfilerais encore bien ta bonne amie. Mathieu trouvait ça très sympa, naturel. (CDR, pp. 102–03)

The female interlocutor of previous androcentric discourse has been effaced. In this respect, masculine discourse emulates parental discourse by denying Anne the possibility of self-representation – once again, she is the third-person object of the *énoncé*, rather than the first-person subject of the *énonciation*.

Since the sexual lexicon available inaccurately reflects her personal experience from a patriarchal viewpoint, Anne prefers to create her own vocabulary, reclaiming what was previously eliminated. As a woman, her form of linguistic subversion takes place within the private forum of her diary, allowing Anne to achieve a degree of correlation between her sexual experiences and their inscription in language: 'J'écrirais, oui, un journal intime, je décrirais sa chambre, peut-être, son sexe, avec d'autres mots' (CDR, p. 113).[44] This distinction between the private and public articulation of her sexuality parallels Anne's earlier distinction between harbouring sexual fantasies and exposing them to misappropriation through verbal representation to the Other. Anne's innovative, more feminist perspective on language is further apparent in her attempt to destabilise the coherence and authority of the grammatical subject – and, consequently, that of gender identity – by her reversal of gender denominations. Male genitalia are feminised through both the use of the feminine article and the feminine diminutive: 'Alberte et moi on avait plein de mots secrets, pour les hommes une titite, une baisette, pour nous le carabi ou "celui-là", on inversait les sexes dans nos dénominations' (CDR, pp. 95–96). This ludic reversal of gender reveals the narrator's awareness of the significant role played by form in language's designatory function, and of the interrelation between the extralinguistic hierarchy of gender attribution and metalinguistic discourses.[45]

If Denise's vacillating sense of self in *Les Armoires vides* is aggravated by her increasingly crosscultural locus and uncertainty as to the precise components of her future, she does not question the ability of language to give representation to that self. The overall tone of *Ce qu'ils disent ou rien* is, however, more pessimistic. Throughout the work, Anne's isolation foregrounds the class, generational and gender bias which infuses linguistic exchanges. While Ernaux's second work, like her first, ends on a note of uncertainty, such uncertainty embraces the very instrument through which the narrator seeks to articulate her sense of alienation. Both narrators straddle a crosscultural position and consequently embrace a multilingualism, yet Denise's negative sexual experiences spur her to articulate them any which way: her intense need to express herself predominates, rather than the accuracy of the language she employs to do so. Denise may feel frustrated at having to negotiate the divergent linguistic paradigms of working- and middle-class lexicons in order to express her sexuality, yet appears to opt for a mixture of the two, while Anne, in a sense, chooses neither. Anne's sexual experiences produce a more subdued sense of resignation and less frenetic textual energy. The valorisation of the Symbolic in the form of the public domain has not brought with it the successful socialisation desired by the narrator. Her 'extrafamilial commitments', to quote Chodorow, reveal themselves to be no less problematic than her interfamilial ones. In *Ce qu'ils disent ou rien,* individuation blurs into solitude as the narrator feels linguistically isolated from the community surrounding her. The public meanings posited by the languages around Anne force her to retreat into her private 'muted' realm in an endeavour to achieve greater correspondence between her world-view and its inscription in language.

CHAPTER 2

The Adult Woman:
Female Behaviour Paradigms in
La Femme gelée and
Passion simple

This chapter provides a feminist reading of Annie Ernaux's portrayal of the female condition in *La Femme gelée* and *Passion simple*. While the contrasting degrees of emotional *engagement* reflected in the respective titles of these works would suggest that they have little in common, *La Femme gelée* and *Passion simple* are unusual among Ernaux's works in their representation of a female narrator as a sexually active wife or mother. The narrator's migration from working to middle class and her ongoing process of adjustment, which form the main subject matter of Ernaux's writing, are replaced in these texts by an emphasis on gender and female sexuality. The narrator's early childhood and schooling may be portrayed in *La Femme gelée*, yet it is the adolescent and adult narrator's endeavours to negotiate the tensions between personal and public gender models which are foregrounded. *La Femme gelée* focuses less on the narrator as desiring subject and more on her marital and maternal roles, on her petrification into an accomplished Stepford wife – or, in this case, Annecy wife – while *Passion simple* portrays the narrator's sexual passion during a short-term affair with a man from the then Eastern bloc. In a sense, *Passion simple* can be read as the adult narrator's rejection of conventional expectations that female sexuality be channelled into a monogamous future within marriage; as a more sexually confident, older woman with economic independence, the narrator can at last allow her sexual desires free rein.

La Femme gelée is the only work in Ernaux's corpus which provides a detailed discussion of marriage and motherhood. In it, the older narrator charts her younger self's gradual indoctrination into socially-approved gender roles, and identifies the more surreptitious effects of sexism. While, as the previous chapter demonstrates, the daughterly perspective figures heavily in Ernaux's first two publications – and will recur in subsequent works – *La Femme gelée* is unusual in that it also depicts the mother–child relationship from the perspective of the mother. According to Marianne Hirsch, insofar as it extends the boundaries of conventional representations of women to give voice to what has traditionally been silenced, the inscription of the maternal perspective in literature may be viewed as radical: 'Feminist writing and scholarship, continuing in large part to adopt *daughterly* perspectives, can be said to collude with patriarchy in placing mothers into the position of object – thereby keeping mothering outside of representation and maternal discourse a theoretical impossibility.'[1] If the inclusion of the maternal viewpoint is taken to corroborate a feminist reading of *La Femme gelée*, the general critical consensus of the work considers it feminist in its politicised exposition of the female internalisation process, in its highlighting of the social and cultural factors which lead the female narrator to assimilate an oppressive model of gender relations, culminating in postmarital mental atrophy. In characteristic Ernaux fashion, the retrospective narrative focuses on key stages in the developmental process of the protagonist in order to illustrate the trajectory from 'liberated' past to 'oppressed' present, a trajectory which culminates in the production of the eponymous 'femme gelée'. While there is no doubt that *La Femme gelée* provides a strongly gendered analysis of the narrator's past, this chapter will argue that an interpretation of the text as feminist would seem to be based as much, if not more, on its politically aware use of rhetoric than on the events it portrays, on what it tells rather than on what it shows.

If *La Femme gelée* is considered feminist in its politicised representation of the daily drudgery which makes up the adult narrator's *condition féminine*, *Passion simple* is a more ambivalent narrative to appropriate for feminist interpretation in that much of the narrator's conduct appears to revoke the feminist tenets of *La Femme gelée*.[2] While the retrospective viewpoint may have contributed to the narrator's embellishment of her younger self's feminist consciousness in *La Femme gelée*, her counterpart in *Passion simple* does not even attempt to put a feminist gloss on events: where the narrative of *La Femme gelée* documents the narrator's entrapment within the confines of marriage and motherhood, in *Passion simple* she is shown to embrace willingly a dependence on her lover. Nonetheless, feminist readings of the work focus on the narrator's sexually voracious attitude to her lover and on the frank portrayal of sexual desire from the perspective of a middle-aged female: the narrator may be obsessed by her lover, yet her extreme self-interest is seen to undermine the usual paradigm of inequality in such relationships. Her lover A. is viewed as playing the conventional role of the female muse, inspiring the narrator's autoportrait in *Passion simple*. In *La Femme gelée* the narrator's personal desires are subordinate to the fulfilment of her social duties; in *Passion simple* everything else – including, at times, the welfare of her children – is subordinate to the fulfilment of her personal desires. In order to assess the degree to which feminist readings of *La Femme gelée* and *Passion simple* are vindicated, this chapter incorporates a variety of feminist texts in its analysis, drawing principally on what may be considered the Ur-text of contemporary French feminist writing – Simone de Beauvoir's *Le Deuxième Sexe*.

LA FEMME GELÉE

As part of its feminist credentials, *La Femme gelée* makes three explicit references to Simone de Beauvoir's seminal feminist text, *Le Deuxième Sexe*. Ernaux has acknowledged the important role played by Beauvoir's writing, and *Le Deuxième Sexe* in particular, in shaping her awareness of the norms governing gendered behaviour. Throughout Ernaux's corpus, Beauvoir remains a frequent point of reference for her narrator, but it is in Ernaux's third publication that Beauvoir's influence is most visible.[3] The subject matter of *La Femme gelée* – the female maturation process from childhood to adulthood – provides a close parallel to Beauvoir's account of the socialisation undergone by the young girl in *Le Deuxième Sexe*, particularly volume two, which deals with the experiential results of the ideological conditioning described in greater detail in the first volume. In both *La Femme gelée* and *Le Deuxième Sexe II*, the young girl is confronted with a range of objectifying cultural concepts and social institutions, which reinforce a rigidified notion of femininity, an *en soi*, at odds with her self-perception as an individual consciousness, a *pour soi*. Indeed, the namelessness of Ernaux's narrator, while foregrounding her representativeness, may be taken to indicate the usurpation of her personality by her social role. Both works relate the traumas and struggles which consciousness goes through in order to conform to societal expectations of what such femininity should entail, and, by dissecting the female socialisation process, endeavour to demystify its work-ings. The retrospective viewpoint in *La Femme gelée* articulates the same political thesis as Beauvoir's narrative voice in *Le Deuxième Sexe*. Ernaux's narrator has lived through and processed the events she is re-counting, with the reflective distance this requires, a distance which, as we shall see, may equally serve to distort as to elucidate her interpreta-tion of events. The retrospective position of the narrator in *La Femme gelée* allows her to superimpose a feminist interpretation on her earlier behaviour – an interpretation clearly not available to her during her formative years – and to deconstruct her childhood influences. She dis-locates the temporal coherence of the narrating 'I', enabling her to step outside the constructed discourses of gender and critique them, as well as take up a position within them; the self-representation of the narrator can challenge the patriarchal representation of the female self. As this chapter highlights, the recurrent parallels between *La Femme gelée* and *Le Deuxième Sexe II* suggest that Ernaux's debt to Beauvoir extends beyond the occasional textual reference to her.

La Femme gelée represents the third and final contribution to Ernaux's early triptych of texts, and both duplicates and extends the chronology of the earlier works, portraying the narrator not merely as a child and adolescent, but as a young adult in her role of wife and mother. The work's narrative structure resembles that of its predeces-sors, in that a first-person female narrator in the present looks back and reassesses events from her past, yet it differs by its inclusion of occasional instances of metacommentary in which the mature narra-tor acknowledges her role as writer. Throughout the trilogy, there is a gradual increase in remarks highlighting the structuring role of the retrospective narrator, remarks which find their correlation in the more contained writing style of *La Femme gelée* when compared to *Les Armoires vides* and *Ce qu'ils disent ou rien*. These metanarrative re-marks become both more prominent and more reflective in subsequent works, as the fictional façade is lowered and generic categories blurred. The nameless narrator of *La Femme gelée* offers the most conciliatory representation of her working-class origins in the trilogy. Like Anne in *Ce qu'ils disent ou rien*, she acknowledges her mother's inability to provide in-depth explanations to her queries, yet chooses instead to foreground their almost instinctive empathy with one another; equally, literature's role in *La Femme gelée* is similar to that of *Les Armoires vides*, providing the narrator with the components of an idealised persona which she fashions into an imaginary self, yet – unlike Denise's imaginary self – one which happily coexists with her real self rather than desiring its effacement. The narrator's more benevolent analysis of the components of her *Bildung* in *La Femme gelée* stems from the absence of self-fulfilment following her assimilation of the ideal feminine role model posited at school and her integration into the middle class through education, marriage and professional success. While the lexicon of *La Femme gelée* incorporates the slang and spoken French of the early works, the narrator's greater maturity and bourgeois status are further reflected in her use of a markedly less vulgar language.

'Enfance'/'La Jeune Fille'

By beginning the work in her pre-school childhood, a childhood populated with independent, opinionated women, who, while caring little for physical appearance, are nonetheless formidable physical presences, Ernaux's narrator aims to demonstrate the verity of Beauvoir's thesis in *Le Deuxième Sexe*, expressed in the second volume's opening sentence: 'On ne naît pas femme: on le devient.' In *La Femme gelée*, Ernaux's narrator links the comparatively liberal nature of her preschool upbringing and its jettisoning of more restrictive gender roles with its working-class origins.[4] She enumerates three 'modèles' of female conduct, which broadly correspond to the three social strata of the middle class, the petite bourgeoisie and the working class.[5] If the enumeration of these different 'modèles' of womanhood points to the variations between them, it nonetheless reveals the limited behaviour paradigms available to women, and the social expectation to conform to them.[6] By highlighting the typicality of these class-based characteristics in its opening section, the work immediately intimates its main thesis: to speak of choice in relation to women's future possibilities is to be guilty of *mauvaise foi*, in that such choice is restricted to the assimilation of the class role model deemed most appropriate to a woman's particular stage of development, a model which inevitably culminates in marriage and motherhood. The alternative – the refusal to choose from within the approved range of options – results in isolation and ostracism.

In *La Femme gelée* and throughout Ernaux's corpus, the reader has the impression of a rigidly dichotomised pre- and post-school existence and value system, in which, broadly speaking, the retrospective narrator appears to consider her early childhood years as constituting an innocent, ideology-free state, and her attendance at school as responsible for shattering the idyll and corrupting her childlike innocence.[7] The work reverses the usual feminist developmental paradigm from sexual oppression to politicised enlightenment in that, chronologically, the narrator's most liberated period is childhood. The fact that the working-class conditioning of Ernaux's narrators precedes their bourgeois schooling endows it with a more 'natural' status in contrast to their cultural education. Similarly, that education always constitutes an education into bourgeois ideology, with the consequent denigration of working-class values this entails. From the narrators' retrospective position, the Edenic world of childhood represents freedom, a period of epistemological grace, before their schooling reveals to them the 'error' of their ways. While this representation of childhood as a golden age before societal expectations succeed in curtailing future possibilities is a common motif in women's writing, the politically dichotomised representation of the female condition in *La Femme gelée* is reinforced by the narrator's conviction that the bourgeoisie exerts more severe limitations on the female individual's potential for development than the working class.

By focusing initially on the independent working-class women of her childhood, the narrator not only points to the man-made origins of femininity, but indirectly emphasises the surreptitious efficiency of ideology, thereby validating the consciousness-raising exercise which implicitly subtends the narrative of *La Femme gelée*. If, despite her earliest role models, the narrator subsequently assimilates the bourgeois model of femininity, women from more traditional middle-class backgrounds are even less likely to eschew the conventional path of marriage and motherhood. Numerous interjections pertaining to the narrator's later life as wife and mother – and the work's title itself – serve to remind the reader that strength of character and feminist role models are of little consequence when social conditioning begins to exert its grip: however liberal her early working-class environment, the narrator must inevitably step outside its familiar parameters and come into contact with more oppressive models of gender relations, models which are shown to erode her aspirations and desires. The concurrent existence of past and present narratives and the hermeneutic authority this confers on the reader serve to focus their attention less on specific events than on the general reasons underlying them: that the reader is forewarned of future developments early in the work allows them to concentrate on the socialisation process which brings them about. The young narrator's reiterated conviction that she will escape the shackles of marriage and motherhood, a conviction which makes her subsequent volte-face all the more disturbing, further points to the importance of understanding the social mechanisms which temporarily efface her political and emotional affinities with the women of her childhood.

The woman who best encapsulates the positive qualities of working-class womanhood represented by female relatives is the narrator's mother. The mother's job as shopkeeper, as the family representative most in contact with the outside world, fuels her dynamism and thirst for knowledge, attitudes which galvanise the young narrator's own desire to engage with and explore her surroundings: 'Par elle je savais que le monde était fait pour qu'on s'y jette et qu'on en jouisse, que rien ne pouvait nous en empêcher' (LFG, p. 30).[8] That working-class women in *La Femme gelée* generally have to work for a living is shown to undermine the social topography separating the female domestic sphere from the male public sphere. In the case of the narrator's mother, this contact with the public domain – a contact Beauvoir considers essential for individual growth and fulfilment – results in a corresponding lack of interest in stereotypical female roles within the private domain. In contrast, the middle-class women in *La Femme gelée*, referred to as 'des femmes peureuses' or 'des femmes d'ombres' (LFG, p. 20), are portrayed as isolated in their large, silent houses. Indeed, when the narrator assumes the role of middle-class housewife after her own marriage – a marriage ironically presented as a concession to social integration – solitude becomes the defining feature of her existence. The narrator acknowledges that the sense of freedom which characterises her early childhood and her resultant self-confidence stem not merely from the working-class female role models to which she is exposed but also from her status as an only child:[9] all parental hopes and ambitions rest on her, and education is viewed, not as a temporary distraction until the advent of a suitable husband, but as providing the key to a secure future through intellectual development.

In the young narrator's home life, normality takes the form of a non-conventional, non-gender-specific division of labour, with her father playing the traditional maternal role, looking after the child and taking her to school, while her mother undertakes more cerebral tasks. With such a prototype of heterosexual relations, it is hardly surprising that the mature narrator's overwhelming impression of her pre-school childhood is one in which gender is irrelevant. Her early home life is characterised by freedom, physical activity and adventure, qualities which partly explain the narrator's lack of interest in the quintessentially female toy, the doll. The sheer inertia of dolls frustrates the narrator, and she begins to take them apart in an endeavour to render them more interesting.[10] Paradoxically, this reaction provides further ratification of Beauvoir's theses in the 'Formation' section of her work, in which she argues that young girls frequently identify with the passive toy and use it as a means of duplicating their own mother–child relationship: the narrator's failure to identify with the passivity embodied in the doll may be attributed to her unconventional upbringing, in that her father is primary carer and her mother largely free from conventionally feminine traits, as well as to her 'transcendent' attitude at this stage of her development[11] – she is neither treated nor behaves like a 'poupée vivante'.

The parental belief in the expansive power of education is confuted by the system's inability to accommodate any values which do not conform to its monolithic model of gendered normality, an inability no doubt aggravated by the fact that the narrator attends a private, single-sex Catholic school. At school, the narrator is taught the 'anomalousness' of her childhood gender models and of her unfettered aspirations resulting from them: 'j'en ai bavé surtout d'avoir été élevée d'une façon tellement anormale, sans respect des différences' (LFG, p. 32). There she learns that femininity is an integral component of womanhood, a learning process which foregrounds the concept's cultural, rather than 'natural' or physiological, origins. Just as the narrators of *Les Armoires vides* and *Ce qu'ils disent ou rien*, by the fluctuating relativity of their perceptions of the notions of truth and falsehood, reveal their continuing absorption of bourgeois values, so the narrator of *La Femme gelée* reveals the ideological basis of 'natural' or 'normal' behaviour. As Beauvoir demonstrates throughout *Le Deuxième Sexe*, the success of bourgeois ideology depends on this naturalisation of the internalisation process, on the slippage between 'cause' and 'effect': women's acquiescence to their inferior social status and limited social opportunities must be presented as antecedent to such restricted opportunities, indeed, as their justification in the first place.

While school teaches the narrator the code of feminine conduct to which she is expected to conform, as she grows older a variety of ideological reinforcers in the form of different media continue the inculcation. Beauvoir comments on patriarchy's need to deploy all available means – what Michèle Le Doeuff refers to as a 'polymorphous network of limitations'[12] – in order to minimise deviations from gendered behaviour norms. It is this continual assimilation of bourgeois ideology following the narrator's initial exposure to it in *La Femme gelée* which finds close correlation in Beauvoir's description of the female formative process in *Le Deuxième Sexe II*. The gradual merging of narrative content between the two texts as Ernaux's narrator conforms to bourgeois norms further ratifies the criticism that Beauvoir's work portrays a predominantly middle-class female socialisation process, which it endeavours to pass off as universal. As the narrator becomes increasingly exposed to the 'portrait-robot' (LFG, p. 60) of motherhood at school, whether through the explicit eulogising of it or indoctrination into its components through more 'innocent' means – 'Maman fait le ménage soigneusement, elle époussette, deux t verbes en eter, avec un plumeau' (LFG, p. 21) – she gradually realises the extent to which her own mother deviates from gender norms. (Her mother has a very Beauvoirean view on the futility of housework and, in particular, dusting.) If the maternal influence is at first capable of neutralising the pedagogical position, the 'innocence' of the indoctrination process encountered at school means that the narrator cannot immunise herself against it completely: 'De leur [the nuns'] discours, j'en prends donc et j'en laisse. On en laisse toujours moins qu'on s'imagine' (LFG, p. 58).[13] At this early stage of her subjection to normative behaviour paradigms – she is approximately 10 years old – the young narrator continues to perceive her femaleness in an unequivocally positive light, admiring her female schoolteachers, who, like her mother, provide her with role models of intelligent, professional women. This conforms to Beauvoir's representation of *la condition féminine* in *Le Deuxième Sexe II*, when the young girl's limited perspective on life means that she is not yet aware of the negligibility of women's power – in that it is generally circumscribed to the domestic domain – when compared to men's.[14]

Following Beauvoir's developmental trajectory in *Le Deuxième Sexe II* in which the young girl initially admires and emulates the mother, it is unsurprising, given the independence and strength of character of the maternal role model in *La Femme gelée*, that the narrator takes longer to cast off its influence: if the narrator's assimilation of stereotypically feminine traits is more protracted than that of her female counterpart(s) in *Le Deuxième Sexe II*, it is surely due to the alternative model represented by her home life, a model which differs from the typical family unit of frustrated, and at times sadistic, mother and quasi-divine paterfamilias portrayed by Beauvoir.[15] The maternal role model in *La Femme gelée* is more ambitious and outgoing than the paternal model, who, conversely, could be seen to epitomise the traditionally feminine characteristics of tenderness and gentleness. The mother's drive is reflected in her conviction that academic success is prerequisite to her daughter's personal and professional fulfilment, while, at school, it is motherhood itself which is proferred as the ideal female profession in which women can exercise their 'natural' capacity for self-sacrifice. In a manner analogous to that portrayed in *Les Armoires vides* and *Ce qu'ils disent ou rien*, the realisation that her mother's qualities of independence and self-fulfilment are not 'normal' feminine qualities, that her parents are the exception rather than the rule, induces a gradual inversion of the narrator's original value system: 'Obscurément, en ces occasions, je sentais avec malaise que ma mère n'était pas une vraie mère, c'est-à-dire comme les autres' (LFG, p. 59). Both the dominance and nonconformity of the maternal model may account for the vehemence of the daughter's subsequent rebellion against it.

'L'Initiation sexuelle'

The liberal element in the narrator's upbringing which encourages her to achieve her professional ambitions does not extend to the realm of sexuality. As with *Les Armoires vides* and *Ce qu'ils disent ou rien*, female sexuality in *La Femme gelée* is portrayed as the area of women's experience most vulnerable to linguistic misrepresentation, or, indeed, to a complete absence of representation: her mother's fears that her daughter become pregnant, rather than leading her to verbalise such fears in an endeavour to exorcise them, cause her to censor all mention of female sexuality.[16] Beauvoir acknowledges the prevalence of such censorship when she comments on the taboos surrounding female sexuality and on the fact that, while the male genitalia are designated through a variety of valorising synonyms, both the lack of visibility of, and linguistic signifiers for, the female genitalia conspire to efface their existence. Ernaux's narrator bemoans this paucity of terms of reference: 'Pas beaucoup de noms, on ne soupçonnait pas qu'il puisse même y en avoir des sérieux dans le dictionnaire pour ces choses. C'est le "ça", pour tout' (LFG, p. 42). Indeed, this absence of naming extends to other areas of female sexuality in *La Femme gelée*, whether sexual relations ('Ensemble, on parlait de "ça"' [LFG, p. 70]) or the arrival of menstruation: 'Et quel triomphe de lui annoncer [to Brigitte] que je suis comme "ça" moi aussi' (LFG, p. 71). Like her counterparts in the trilogy, the narrator also criticises the sexism in language used to describe sexual relations and the double standards in sexual conduct it legitimates: 'La bourde, l'inversion des rôles, tout de suite taxée de fille facile, dans la pochc. Il n'existe pas de garçon facile' (LFG, p. 90). Beauvoir draws attention to a similar slippage between behavioural paradigms and their linguistic designation, in which the term 'femme libre' comes to denote 'femme facile' (LDS II, p. 610). Again, when the narrator describes resisting her partner's sexual advances, her assessment of their encounters echoes Beauvoir's remarks on the vocabulary used to describe the sexual act in *Le Deuxième Sexe II*. In *La Femme gelée*, we read: 'Chaque plaisir s'est appelé défaite pour moi, victoire pour lui' (LFG, p. 96).[17] This combative approach to sexual relations is illustrated in the narrator's association of the corporeal with the territorial, as she gradually concedes bodily terrain to her male partners.

As her intellectual ability repeatedly incurs social disapproval, the narrator is forced to take on board the dichotomy between attractiveness and intelligence – a dichotomy mentioned repeatedly by Beauvoir in *Le Deuxième Sexe II* – to which women are commonly subject.[18] In an endeavour to neutralise the threat female intelligence represents and to court approval, the narrator seeks to emulate the feminine attributes of her middle-class schoolfriends. A narcissism based on intellectual ability is replaced by one based on physical appearance. From an early childhood characterised by indifference to the impression she is making, the adolescent narrator's self-worth becomes dependent on her adoption of a prefabricated façade of femininity and on the Other's opinion of that 'genre' (the recurrent use of the term 'genre' in *La Femme gelée* gives greater emphasis to the physical attributes of femininity than 'modèle'). The narrator in *La Femme gelée* provides clear illustration of the tension described by Beauvoir, in which the young girl is torn between her desire for subjecthood and the social requirement that she repress it if she wishes to be sexually desirable. As Beauvoir observes in *Le Deuxième Sexe II*, p. 65: 'La fillette sent que son corps lui échappe, il n'est plus la claire expression de son individualité; il lui devient étranger; et, au même moment, elle est saisie par autrui comme une chose.'[19] With the adolescent narrator's increasing awareness of her interpellation as desired Other and the consequent usurpation of the intellectual by the physical, the maternal model is superseded by the paradigm of middle-class femininity. The destructive ramifications of this objectification are apparent in the mature narrator's negative perception of her younger self's physical appearance. (Throughout *La Femme gelée*, the repeated use of 'encore' highlights the continuing influence of past conditioning on present self-perception.) The pivotal role played by physical attractiveness in dictating women's social value is further reflected in the narrator's consciousness of the ageing process – it is no coincidence that, on the two occasions when she describes looking in the mirror, she states her age – and in her fear of being alone as a result of it, a fear articulated in the final words of the text: 'Au bord des rides qu'on ne peut plus cacher, des affaissements. Déjà moi ce visage' (LFG, p. 182).

'La Femme mariée'/'La Mère'

While the normative effects of social conditioning are shown to be responsible for the narrator's assimilation of 'feminine' behaviour during adolescence (and, it is intimated, the containment of possible homosexual tendencies, 'peur de tomber dans l'anormal' [LFG, p. 103]), these effects do not reach their usual culmination in a desire to get married or to have children. Given the formative role her education plays in the narrator's childhood and its positing of marriage and motherhood as women's ideal, it is somewhat surprising that it appears to have had little success in influencing the narrator in these areas. This absence of desire in the narrator may partly derive from her childhood impressions of working-class marriage: whatever the liberal model represented by her parents, the benefits of married life and, in particular, of motherhood for the working-class women with whom she grew up were few. Equally, the narrator's exposure at university to a literature which valorises the individual's rejection of social norms is shown to reinforce her negative opinion of married life. The institution of marriage is presented as possessing an alien theatricality for the narrator, as reflected in the disparity between her current private persona and her future public one of consumer housewife: 'j'avais l'impression d'être dans les monstrueuses coulisses, bourrées d'accessoires, d'une pièce qui me faisait horreur même si elle n'était à jouer que plus tard' (LFG, p. 102).[20] Subsequent events would suggest, however, that the narrator's feminist dismissal of marriage originates more in her desire to espouse a particular intellectual position than in a profound political conviction.

If university education provides the rhetorical tools with which the narrator may denounce the institutions of marriage and motherhood, her acute consciousness of her appearance, and the importance of femininity for her generally, undermine her feminist stance, preparing the reader for her later reappraisal of the benefits of married life. The narrator's political disingenuousness may further be seen in her endeavour to give her acceptance of marriage a more radical slant by focusing on the picaresque nature of her courtship with her husband-to-be and the light-hearted, informal manner in which the marriage ceremony is accomplished. (That her wedding ring does not fit may be taken as a symbol of her future maladjustment.) If her premarital relationship with her husband is portrayed as one of relative equality and autonomy, once that relationship has been sanctified by marriage it begins to deteriorate, substantiating Beauvoir's belief that the institution of marriage corrupts the freely assumed nature of a *concubinage* by transforming it into a social duty. Indeed, the trajectory of Ernaux's narrator conforms closely to that of the traditional 'femme mariée' described by Beauvoir in her work: marriage is presented as prerequisite to social acceptance, yet, once married, she feels that her individuality has been usurped by her role, a role which stultifies her with its daily drudgery, while her husband leads a fulfilling existence in the public domain. In an unacknowledged reference to Beauvoir's analogy between the futility and repetitiousness of housework and Sisyphus continually pushing his rock up a mountain, the narrator comments: 'Sisyphe et son rocher qu'il remonte sans cesse, ça au moins quelle gueule, un homme sur une montagne qui se découpe dans le ciel, une femme dans sa cuisine jetant trois cent soixante-cinq fois par an du beurre dans la poêle, ni beau ni absurde, la vie Julie' (LFG, p. 155).[21] The result of this marital oppressiveness is quintessentially Beauvoirean – 'l'aliénation' (LFG, p. 167).

Isolated at home, the narrator's earlier observation on the absence of a gender-based solidarity among women is experienced first-hand: 'Décidement pas tellement frangines les filles, différence sociale d'abord' (LFG, pp. 100–01).[22] Her husband does little to reduce her sense of isolation, his premarital belief in equality never extending beyond the verbal. As the narrator feels increasingly underconfident intellectually and her professional ambitions dwindle, his career goes from strength to strength – her energy is expended guaranteeing his success, rather than her own. While the narrator does not renounce all professional goals, her focus on their realisation is necessarily sporadic. The fragmented nature of women's existence, their inability to devote themselves to the task in hand, predictably leads to underachievement: the narrator fails the Capes examination on her first attempt,[23] perceiving any activity not related to her role as wife and mother – whether teaching or writing – as of subsidiary importance. Following Sandra

M. Gilbert and Susan Gubar's diagnosis in *The Madwoman in the Attic*, Ernaux's narrator displays a condition common among women writers, a condition which is less a variant of Bloom's 'anxiety of influence' than a far graver 'anxiety of authorship', questioning her ability to write at all.[24]

It is perhaps the section of *La Femme gelée* relating the narrator's experiences of motherhood which most closely corresponds to its counterpart in *Le Deuxième Sexe II*, Beauvoir's chapter 'La Mère'. Just as Beauvoir begins her section with a discussion of abortion, so Ernaux's narrator is tempted to see an abortionist on discovering she is pregnant.[25] Indeed, even when her first child is a toddler, she voices her regret at having been prevented from visiting the abortionist by the ideological representation of motherhood as the most enriching of women's experiences. Beauvoir acknowledges this relentless pressure on women to experience motherhood, and points to the consequent role played by revenge in the mother–child relationship, in which the mother's occasionally sadistic attitude has its origins in her frustration and discontent at the constrained opportunities which tend to accompany motherhood. Ernaux's narrator also presents her half-hearted decision to have the child as a form of vengeance for her diminished existence, as a means of forcing her husband to accept more responsibility within the couple. However, it is when she describes the physiological state of pregnancy that Ernaux's narrator most closely reflects Beauvoir's remarks in *Le Deuxième Sexe II*. Throughout *Le Deuxième Sexe*, Beauvoir represents the conventional female maturation process as a gradual transformation from a state of transcendence to immanence, as women become increasingly objectified. Pregnancy typifies this struggle between transcendence and immanence, between woman's concern for her own future, and her role as progenitor of the species: 'elle est la proie de l'espèce qui lui impose ses mystérieuses lois et généralement cette aliénation l'effraie: son effroi se traduit par des vomissements', *Le Deuxième Sexe II*, p. 353. Ernaux's narrator is familiar with the psychosomatic interpretation of pregnancy symptoms as signalling the effort required to accommodate another, not merely physiologically, but psychologically.

Pregnancy and the various maternal functions it involves do not constitute activities for Beauvoir. Similarly, Ernaux's narrator feels passively inhabited during pregnancy, further entrenched in the inessential: 'Entre le monde et moi s'étend une mare grasse, des relents de pourriture douce. Arrachée à moi-même, flasque' (LFG, p. 138).

Such passivity makes her dismissive of the kudos accompanying pregnancy, of the belief that pregnancy epitomises the apogee of femaleness, and she echoes Beauvoir's opinion on the absurdity of women enjoying being the centre of attention during pregnancy, given the immanence which characterises their repository role: 'cet orgueil-là ne vaut pas mieux que celui de la bandaison' (LFG, p. 139). The narrator's entire attitude towards motherhood points to the non-existence of a maternal instinct, a sentiment Beauvoir articulates unequivocally in *Le Deuxième Sexe II*, p. 369, when she remarks that 'il n'existe pas d'"instinct" maternel: le mot ne s'applique en aucun cas à l'espèce humaine.' As the references to her future child as a 'poupée vivante' (LFG, p. 139) indicate,[26] the narrator experiences a similar detachment from, or sense of unreality in, her role as mother as she did with that of wife, partly because the skills required for motherhood, like those required for marriage, are learned, rather than 'instinctive' for the narrator, and partly because such detachment is a means of self-preservation: she does not wish her maternal role to completely usurp her few remaining professional aspirations.[27]

Ideological Reinforcers

From earliest childhood, the narrator's mother introduces her to the pleasures of reading: witnessing the importance literature represents for her mother, the narrator in turn becomes a bibliophile.[28] *La Femme gelée* repeatedly points to the significant role literature plays in the narrator's life, a role also highlighted by Beauvoir in *Le Deuxième Sexe II* in her many references to the influence literature exerts over women's imagination (see, for example, LDS II, pp. 51, 105, 459, 532). Indeed, Beauvoir maintains that one of the few positive outcomes of women's oppression under patriarchy is the advanced development of their psychological and emotional capacities, due in part to their exclusion from the public sphere of action: women compensate for this exclusion by vicariously experiencing activities forbidden to them, whether observing from the periphery or dreaming up imaginary existences, thereby developing their 'internal sensibilities'. However, while references to the formative role of literature in *Le Deuxième Sexe II* implicitly criticise certain literary genres for romanticising heterosexual relationships and furnishing women with unrealistic expectations of them, Ernaux's narrator in *La Femme gelée* is more positive in her assessment of the escapist function of literature.[29] For her, literature represents freedom from her mundane existence, and, when she is married, respite from her husband's demands – a quiet refusal to accept mediocrity as her lot. It may be their awareness of this contestatory function of literature in its depiction of alternative existences which accounts for men's unease at women reading in *La Femme gelée*. While reading works of literature acts as a springboard for the narrator's imagination and that of her mother, allowing them to experience fleetingly another existence, their awareness of the divide separating the factual from the fictional ensures that romantic literature's role as archetype of 'reality' is not taken for 'reality' itself: 'Non, ma mère ne confondait pas sa boutique et les rivages de Californie, le feuilleton glissé sous le linge à repasser au coup de sonnette ne l'empêchait pas de calculer ses pourcentages' (LFG, p. 26). Equally, the disparities between fictional representations of romance and their 'real-life' equivalents are too glaring for the narrator to ignore, as the inverted commas and her very unromantic detachment in the following quotation demonstrate: 'Je reste perplexe, je n'ai pas défailli sous "son baiser brûlant", j'étais en train de regarder les lapins grignoter la biscotte que je leur avais apportée' (LFG, p. 47).[30]

As she grows older, these disparities lead the narrator to progress from reading stereotypical representations of romance to works with more intellectual substance and, to her mind, less gender-specific content, such as *La Nausée* or *L'Etranger*. The narrator's interest in these works demonstrates her continuing need to envisage a more fulfilling future for herself, albeit one which differs radically from that portrayed in the romantic literature she reads as an adolescent. When studying literature at university, the narrator does not always differentiate between narratives relating male and female experience, but may identify with the protagonist regardless of gender: 'quand je lisais Eluard, "moi je vais vers la vie, j'ai l'apparence d'homme" c'est à moi que je pensais' (LFG, p. 109). Much feminist reader-response theory perceives this identification with the male hero as evidence of the surreptitious coercion of the female reader, yet its liberating function for the narrator of *La Femme gelée* intimates its empowering potential.[31]

As the introduction to this chapter remarks, the narrator mentions *Le Deuxième Sexe* and its importance to her on different occasions throughout *La Femme gelée*. Ironically, like the romantic fiction she reads as a young girl, it represents as its ultimate goal an ideal, rather than attainable, relationship, in that the reciprocity it advocates as a prerequisite to forming a healthy heterosexual relationship turns out to be elusive for the narrator. The narrator's degree of engagement with Beauvoir's text alters depending on her personal circumstances. On first reading the work, she wholeheartedly embraces its subversive analysis of the female socialisation process, only to reject temporarily Beauvoir's negative representation of marriage when she is still in the 'honeymoon period' of her own: 'Qui parle d'esclavage ici, j'avais l'impression que la vie d'avant continuait, en plus serré seulement l'un avec l'autre. Complètement à côté de la plaque, *Le Deuxième Sexe*!' (LFG, p. 129). Later, however, as the role of efficient wife and mother threatens to become all-consuming, the narrator clings to certain arguments or remarks made in Beauvoir's work in an attempt to avoid complete engulfment by her role: 'Surtout pas le balai, encore moins le chiffon à poussière, tout ce qu'il me reste peut-être du *Deuxième Sexe*, le récit d'une lutte inepte et perdue d'avance contre la poussière' (LFG, p. 150). A further 'feminist' writer referred to in *La Femme gelée* is Virginia Woolf, whose culinary skills are cited by the narrator in an endeavour to convince herself that the traditionally feminine and the intellectual can successfully coexist.

It is the literature the narrator encounters at school which she considers most harmful: the numerous accounts of saints' lives are shown to be detrimental to her self-image in that they normalise female self-sacrifice, presenting it as an integral component of womanhood. This mythicisation of femininity, however tenuous its links to *le vécu*, is shown to exert a powerful influence on it. Indeed, according to Beauvoir, it is precisely the tenuousness of such links that renders the content of mythical reinforcers unassailable – the mythicisation of femininity exists as an homogenising ideal to be emulated by multifarious real women (LDS I, p. 395). Other examples of literature provided by the school environment include *Toi qui deviens femme déjà*, her Catholic school's attempt at sex education, an attempt which, by describing men as 'victimes d'un "mouvement brutal, impérieux, dont ils ne sont pas maîtres"' (LFG, p. 80) and thereby exonerating them of all sexual responsibility, ultimately condones rape.

As the narrator grows older, again it is not romantic literature which is presented as exerting a pernicious influence on her, but, paradoxically, works which deny all escapist potential. It is this oppressive, constraining role of literature which is most apparent in the narrator's child-rearing manual, *J'élève mon enfant*. So stereotypical is its content that she feels obliged to quote an excerpt from the work, along with page number, in order to authenticate its factual accuracy:

"[P]apa, c'est le chef, le héros, c'est lui qui commande c'est normal, c'est le plus grand, c'est le plus fort, c'est lui qui conduit la voiture qui va si vite. Maman, c'est la fée, celle qui berce, console, sourit, celle qui donne à manger et à boire. Elle est toujours là quand on l'appelle", page quatre cent vingt-cinq. (LFG, p. 157)

Adherence to such gender stereotypes and to the impeccable moral conduct they advocate is rewarded in literature by the portrayal of happy, idyllic futures for middle-class women. The narrator in *La Femme gelée* implicitly condemns the paucity of portrayals of working-class women when she comments on the disparity between the older female members of her family and their literary equivalent: 'Des femmes noires et coties, leurs jupes sentent le beurre oublié dans le garde-manger, rien à voir avec les mamies sucrées du livre de lectures, surmontées d'un chignon neigeux et qui moumoutent leurs petits-enfants en leur racontant des histoires de fées, des aïeules ça s'appelle' (LFG p. 10). As Chapter 1 remarks, it is partly the desire to reduce such disparities by providing literary representations of working-class experience which fuels Ernaux's writing project.

It is not merely certain types of literature which present the traditional components of middle-class women's existence as the norm against which all deviations must be measured. A further source of ideological reinforcement in *La Femme gelée* is women's magazines, which encourage female readers to devote their lives to the upkeep of the domestic realm and, consequently, to the retention of their husband. It is magazines such as *Femme pratique*, *Bonnes soirées* and *Echo de la mode* which first introduce the narrator to the notion of *maîtresse de maison*, a notion which remains abstract until she visits the homes of middle-class schoolfriends and, above all, until she comes across its perfect incarnation in her mother-in-law. Her parents-in-law's conformism to stereotypical gender roles and lack of individuality are reflected in their designation in the text as 'madame mère' and 'monsieur père' (LFG, p. 136). The mature narrator recognises the difficulty in resisting the ubiquitous message that women's happiness is dependent on obtaining and, more importantly, retaining a husband. An exemplary pupil in the art of good housekeeping, she is acutely aware of the distortion inherent in the mediatic valorisation of conventional feminine attributes: 'Dix ans plus tard, c'est moi dans une cuisine rutilante et muette, les fraises et la farine, je suis entrée dans l'image et je crève' (LFG, p. 61).

If the narrator acknowledges the influence of women's magazines on her internalisation of female behaviour paradigms, that influence is, once again, not as straightforward as Beauvoir maintains in *Le Deuxième Sexe*. While *La Femme gelée* shares Beauvoir's view of the normalising role played by women's magazines which, according to Beauvoir, 'enseignent avec cynisme aux jeunes filles l'art d'"attraper" un mari comme le papier tue-mouches attrape les mouches' (LDS II, p. 232), the 'real-life' stories of magazines such as *Confidences*, aimed at a predominantly working-class readership, also act as correctives to any romantic fantasies the young narrator may harbour by their vivid presentation of 'femmes mariées malheureuses, filles séduites et abandonnées, la grosse chaîne d'un désastre féminin, fatal' (LFG, p. 26). The narrator's more nuanced reading of ideological influences in *La Femme gelée* is also reflected in the different associations magazines hold for her: if *Nous Deux* provides the optimistic young narrator with the appropriate lexicon to discuss future romances, a copy of *Elle* or *Marie-France* bought by her husband acts as a depressing indicator of her successful espousal of the ideal of middle-class femininity.

Advertising also plays an important role in encouraging conformism to gender norms, and its surreptitious influence is conveyed in *La Femme gelée* through the insertion of advertising slogans in the main body of the narrative. The narrator traces her trajectory from young, liberated girl to oppressed wife and mother by gauging her degree of conformism to advertisement images: 'Mais je sentais que je ne serais jamais plus une fille du bord de mer, que je glisserais dans une autre image, celle de la jeune femme fourbisseuse et toujours souriante des publicités pour produits ménagers. D'une image à l'autre, c'est l'histoire d'un apprentissage où j'ai été refaite' (LFG, p. 134). Beauvoir makes a similar comment on the self-serving and manipulative power of ideology in encouraging women to have children in *Le Deuxième Sexe II*, p. 386: 'Que l'enfant soit la fin suprême de la femme, c'est là une affirmation qui a tout juste la valeur d'un slogan publicitaire.' After she is married and begins to assume the role of ideal homemaker, the narrator becomes increasingly aware of the coercive power of advertising which masks consumerism and everyday drudgery behind a façade of creativity, a façade highlighted in *Le Deuxième Sexe*. The narrator also intersperses song lyrics throughout her own discourse, further suggesting both the pernicious power of the media in reinforcing behaviour norms and the intense cross-fertilisation of discourses to which she is subject: 'Je ferais n'importe quoi, si tu me le demandais, Piaf a raison' (LFG, p. 80).

Narrative Techniques

As noted earlier in this chapter, it is in *La Femme gelée* that the narrator first adopts the technique of metacommentary to highlight the veracity of the account she is providing, a technique which also signals the transitional status of this closing text of the trilogy, in that it recurs in many of the later publications and may be viewed as foreshadowing their more explicit auto/biographical content. In these metacommentaries, Ernaux's narrator acknowledges the temptation to rewrite history, to provide a revised, more politically correct account of her past, and the necessity of resisting such embellishment if she and others are to learn anything from that past.[32] However, as this chapter has suggested, the narrator's temptation to superimpose a feminist interpretative grid on past experiences is not always successfully resisted, raising questions about the suitability of such a reading on the part of the older narrator. The mature narrator's acknowledgement that her early behaviour was often more conventional than she realised further points to the potential falsification of certain feminist interpretations of childhood experiences.[33]

The reader of *La Femme gelée* may feel that many of the older narrator's assessments of the feminist sentiments of her younger self are overly definitive, and are therefore inevitably contradicted by subsequent developments. The narrator appears to wish to round off phases of her childhood and adolescence by emphasising her lack of awareness of inequality between the sexes, only to have her character do just that a few pages later. For example, on page 82, we read: 'L'idée d'inégalité entre les garçons et moi, de différence autre que physique, je ne la connaissais pas vraiment pour ne l'avoir jamais vécue.' Yet, during her first experience of seduction, she describes her reaction and that of Brigitte as 'Murmures d'esclaves, encens élevé vers le dieu' and 'La soumission dans toute sa perfection à quatorze ans' (LFG, p. 86). While a degree of disparity between the narrator's earlier *vécu* and her subsequent assessment of it is inevitable, in many cases the disparity is such as to cast doubt on the accuracy of certain remarks made by the older narrator about her younger self. Given her pessimistic perception of her current situation, and her validation of feminist beliefs, it is perhaps not surprising that she seeks to play down both her character's desire to conform to gender norms and the existence of such a desire at an early stage in her life.

As the narrative voice grows in self-consciousness in *La Femme gelée*, it becomes more defensive in many of its remarks. In their dogmatic tone, certain narratorial assertions would appear to require no further ratification.[34]On several occasions, the narrator dialogues with an imaginary interlocutor, characterised as an upstanding member of society, who criticises her lack of enthusiasm for conventional behaviour paradigms. As she becomes more outspoken in her rejection of the stereotype of the ideal wife and mother, these imaginary interjections increase, allowing the narrator to play the role of both prosecution and defence by constructing her response to such criticisms and thereby justifying her conduct to the reader – and, it could be argued, to herself. With a less rigid fictional façade to hide behind, the vulnerability of Ernaux's narrator is also apparent in her desire to seek readerly approval, when, despite having dismissed the socially-sanctioned components of motherhood, she cannot resist foregrounding her own exemplary assimilation of them: 'Je n'ai pas besoin de me souvenir de tout pour prouver que j'étais "aussi" une vraie mère, comme autrefois une vraie femme' (LFG, p. 160).

The narrator's retrospective desire to present herself from a more radical feminist position is above all apparent in her discussion of motherhood. The narrator admits to enjoying motherhood and the thought of devoting herself to it completely, but makes a political decision to remain partially detached from her role. This disparity between actual sentiment and political beliefs may account for certain inconsistencies in the narrator's words and actions. As a student at university, the narrator's dislike of children is unequivocal: 'dégoût absolu pour les poulots, larvaires et visqueux' (LFG, pp. 101–02). Yet, while still at university, she conquers her doubts about marrying her boyfriend by risking the one thing she has always claimed to abhor more than marriage itself – motherhood: 'Ma super lâcheté, l'inavouable, dans les derniers cercles de l'amour, je désire que mon ventre se fasse piège et choisisse à ma place' (LFG, p. 123). It is difficult to conceive of the narrator making a decision about her participation in an institution she professes to detest by deliberately courting even less desired consequences. This action, or non-action, contradicts the entire thrust of Beauvoir's arguments in *Le Deuxième Sexe*, which is that, without the exercise of conscious choice and the assumption of responsibility which goes with it, women will be confined to a state of immanence. Ernaux's narrator has that choice – a choice Beauvoir spent a lifetime battling to give her – and, in the ultimate act of *mauvaise foi*, fails to take it up.[35]

As the narrator becomes more conformist to the model she has spent so long railing against, many of her remarks appear merely to pay lip service to a rather nebulous feminist agenda: 'Je n'en veux pas de cette vie rythmée par les achats, la cuisine. Pourquoi n'est-il pas venu avec moi au supermarché' (LFG, p. 124). Further evidence of what may be construed as a form of retrospective political correctness can be found towards the work's conclusion: 'Depuis le début du mariage, j'ai l'impression de courir après une égalité qui m'échappe tout le temps' (LFG, pp. 166–67). The representation of marital relations in *La Femme gelée* does little to substantiate this claim: rarely does the narrator verbalise her frustration and misery to her husband. In fact, not only does she fail to communicate her feelings to him, but sends out contradictory signals by becoming pregnant a second time, an act which remains incomprehensible given the narrative up until this point: having finally achieved her one remaining ambition to become a teacher, an achievement which allows her to escape temporarily the domestic confines she supposedly hates, the narrator does not even consult her husband about his wishes regarding a second child, but confronts him with a *fait accompli*. The reader is tempted to draw the conclusion, made by the narrator on another occasion, that 'tous les langages peuvent se rejoindre quand on veut' (LFG, p. 125).

Ernaux's narrator in *La Femme gelée* underlines bourgeois ideology's surreptitious manner of operating, endorsing the Althusserian perception of the individual as passively subjected to events, while believing s/he is actively participating in them. Throughout *La Femme gelée*, the narrator attributes her increasing assimilation of female stereotypes to the indoctrination begun at school, which is then continually buttressed by a variety of cultural representations of women, whether in the form of advertising or literature – in short, by the order of society. The work's principal thesis is that, in its current form, the normalising function of ideological conditioning gradually eradicates all potential for an alternative social order based on alternative choices for women. The narrator's husband, as a representative of that normative patriarchal order, is also held responsible for the perpetuation of it: 'De lui ou de cet ordre, je ne sais pas lequel des deux m'a le plus rejetée dans la différence' (LFG, p. 151). Indeed, the dedication of *La Femme gelée* to Ernaux's husband at the time ironically reinforces this attribution of responsibility. Blame for the narrator's conformism is also assigned to postmarital consumerism and its ongoing effects: possessing both beautiful objects and the means to look after them in the form of state-of-the-art cleaning products, women are obliged to devote the time to doing so. The narrator's reluctance to assume responsibility for certain actions is exemplified by her frequent use of the term 'engrenage' when relating her developmental process in *La Femme gelée*: in a very unBeauvoirean manner, the narrator, rather than strive to assert her will over facticity, over obstacles which stand in its way, appears to succumb before them.

Ultimately, then, the reader is left with an impression of *mauvaise foi*, of a denial of transcendence, on the part of the narrator, with a frustration at her continuing refusal to assume greater responsibility for her actions, a refusal which renders ineffectual the tacit objective behind writing the work, which is, presumably, to initiate a type of political global warming, which will help defrost those women petrified into 'femmes gelées' by patriarchal conditioning. If, despite a well-grounded 'feminist' upbringing, the individual is presented as powerless to resist social pressure to conform, it would appear politically futile to signal the various pitfalls in advance. At least if the individual fully acknowledges her complicity in her own oppression, a complicity foregrounded throughout *Le Deuxième Sexe II*, the possibility of achieving transcendence remains. Indeed, underpinning Beauvoir's project is an optimistic vision of women's future existence, a vision based on the pivotal role played by conscious choice. In Ernaux's work, however, such optimism is less apparent. While her narrator occasionally acknowledges her weakness and cowardice in failing to challenge the patriarchal order through her actions, even this failure can be attributed to the social pressure to conform. The politicisation of Ernaux's narrator never progresses beyond the virtual: the further removed her existence becomes from the feminist sentiments she articulates, the more vociferous that articulation becomes. The courage required to espouse feminist beliefs from within the haven of conventionality which is marriage and motherhood is rather less than that needed to reject the shelter they provide in the first place.

When discussing the political optimism of both accounts and its relevance to a feminist reading of *La Femme gelée*, it is useful to bear in mind Toril Moi's definition of feminism: 'Feminism, one might say, requires us not simply to describe the status quo, but to define it as unjust and oppressive as well. It also requires a vision of an alternative: a utopian perspective which inspires and informs the struggle against current oppression.'[36] While *La Femme gelée* fulfils the first part of Moi's requirement, incorporating many Beauvoirean elements into its fictional representation of the maturation process, it fails to fulfil the second. It could, of course, be argued that the act of writing the work represents an optimistic gesture on the part of Ernaux herself, and that her character at the work's conclusion is not irredeemably lost to patriarchal convention, 'Juste au bord, juste' (LFG, p. 182). Nonetheless, the passivity of her narrator, her reluctance to shoulder responsibility for her immanent condition, would appear to limit the likelihood that she enjoy authentic agency. As the narrative highlights, the narrator's awareness of her own objectification does not lead to a reduction in her *mauvaise foi*. At the text's conclusion, we read, 'Toute mon histoire de femme est celle d'un escalier qu'on descend en renâclant' (LFG, p. 178), an assessment with which the reader is inclined to agree. The narrative content of the work seeks to demonstrate that the narrator was, if not continually pushed, than at least nudged, into a downward spiral of oppression from her schooldays onwards. The repeated and sustained criticism of the diverse forms of social pressure to conform portrays patriarchy as a type of monolithic force against which the individual can do little except lament.

As this analysis has aimed to illustrate, by its fictional representation of the female socialisation process described in *Le Deuxième Sexe*, *La Femme gelée* ratifies Beauvoir's principal theses. However, Beauvoir presents women's sexual oppression not purely as a matter of acculturation, but, vitally, also as a matter of choice. To *become* a woman means to possess the capacity to assimilate, but equally to reject, certain cultural norms, and Beauvoir's existentialism invests the individual will with the capacity to transcend existent developmental paradigms, allowing women to participate in the construction of their own identity. It is all the more ironic, then, that, in a work which owes so much to Beauvoir's text, the narrator fails to take the essential first step towards liberation advocated by Beauvoir: to exercise choice through the acceptance of responsibility for one's own actions. If the thesis of Ernaux's work is that to speak of choice in relation to women's future is to be guilty of *mauvaise foi*, to deny the existence of choice is surely evidence of a similar *mauvaise foi*. Ernaux's narrator is fully conscious that her oppression is not natural, yet sinks into a – however temporary – state of immanence. Eschewing a more radical existentialism based on an ahistorical voluntarism, Beauvoir *does* acknowledge that, in certain extreme circumstances, women's potential for freedom is rendered immanent, and reduced to a potential possibility by exteriority, in that an oppressive social reality outweighs the force wielded by individual will.

This is clearly not the situation described in *La Femme gelée* where, following Beauvoir's schema, the narrator manifests *mauvaise foi* in preferring a life of security over one of responsibility: she refuses to exercise free volition, presenting herself, instead, as a pawn of external circumstances. It is the simplification of that schema in *La Femme gelée* with the diminution of the power of personal agency from the equation which most undermines the work's feminist potential. While acknowledging the similarities between the two works, the critic Claude Courchay unwittingly points to the inability of Ernaux's narrator to assimilate and act upon the lessons put forward in Beauvoir's work: 'Trente ans après *le Deuxième Sexe*, rien n'a changé. La femme reste un animal domestique.'[37]

PASSION SIMPLE

Ernaux's narrator in *Passion simple* provides perfect illustration of the woman in love described at various points by Beauvoir in *Le Deuxième Sexe II*, a woman who is unable to derive pleasure from independent activity, requiring the lover's presence to give her existence meaning. Despite the masculinist bias which may be viewed as underpinning Beauvoir's existentialist philosophy, a bias which privileges activity, linear progression and transcendence over passivity, circularity and immanence, this chapter argues that to interpret the passive conduct of Ernaux's narrator in *Passion simple* as feminist by whatever criteria one applies remains something of a challenge.[38] The work has generated an ambivalent response among readers, and one which tends to be split along gender lines. While the misogyny and condescension of many male critics are reflected not merely in their denigration of Ernaux's text but also of Ernaux herself, female critics and readers frequently herald the work as a frank portrayal of female passion.[39] If, on the one hand, the narrator is viewed as representing the archetype of feminine frivolity – 'Annie Ernaux parle de la passion dans laquelle la femme devient presque une midinette'[40] – on the other hand, the more common interpretation of *Passion simple* views it as challenging the dominant male discourse by relating physical passion from a woman's perspective, where the Other is not female, but male. Antoinette Fouque, founder of the *des femmes* publishing house and leader of the differentialist *Psychanalyse et Politique* group, praises *Passion simple* for its radical representation of female sexuality:

> Jusqu'à présent, ce sont les femmes qui étaient réduites au rôle d'objet sexuel. Dans *Passion simple*, c'est l'homme qui est presque un homme potiche. Avec ce livre, qui ne prétend pas être exemplaire, Annie Ernaux a simplement réussi à montrer, par sa propre expérience, que les femmes aussi pouvaient surmonter leur passion, la sublimer, avec les mêmes outils que les hommes.[41]

The Barthesian epigraph to *Passion simple* – 'Nous deux – le magazine – est plus obscène que Sade'[42] – can be read as providing indirect justification for this female appropriation of traditionally male terrain, in that it endorses a graphic portrayal of sexual relations over the sanitised, idealised versions of romantic love typically associated with women writers. The mention of Sade in the text's epigraph may also act as a forewarning to the reader that the work's content, its portrayal of sexual relations, may appear unconventional or even misogynous. The opening section of the work develops the theme of pornography intimated in its epigraph through the description of the narrator's first experience of watching a pornographic film on a satellite television channel. Pornography's function as visual stimulus is foregrounded in this description, in that, without a decoder, the narrator is unable to make out the dialogue. It is the explicitness of the gestures, of the act of penetration, which strikes her, an explicitness which, never having witnessed on television before, she finds overwhelming. In other words, it is not the act itself which is disturbing, but the fact that the spectator has never seen the act represented before. The description of both the act and the response of the spectator is clearly related to the content of the work which follows, signalling the narrator's awareness of the reader's potential reaction to the subject matter of *Passion simple*: 'Il m'a semblé que l'écriture devrait tendre à cela, cette impression que provoque la scène de l'acte sexuel, cette angoisse et cette stupeur, une suspension du jugement moral' (PS, p. 12).[43] This first reference to the act of writing reveals the narrator's perception of the innovative and disturbing content of the work, of her unspoken belief that it is likely to provoke an intense reaction in the reader, indeed, that that is partly its aim. Yet, as with the spectator of the pornographic film, this intense reaction will result less from the content of the work per se, than from its novelty for the reader.

The narrator's view of herself as a kind of literary pioneer, as one of the few artists to provide an explicit representation of women's sexuality from a woman's perspective, is suggested later in the work when discussing the visual arts. Attributing the absence of female representation of the male body until recently to 'la condition dominée des femmes' (PS, p. 50), she writes in a footnote (ibid.): 'De la même façon j'ai regretté qu'il n'existe pas, peint par une femme, un tableau provoquant autant d'émotion indicible que la toile de Courbet montrant au premier plan le sexe offert d'une femme couchée, au visage invisible, et qui a pour titre l'*Origine du monde*.' *Passion simple*, then, can be seen to fill a lacuna in literature by its provocative representation of female sexuality, yet one which remains approximate and therefore cannot be fully comprehended, or, more importantly, judged, by the reader. The narrator's belief that language can only approximate 'real-life' experience is reinforced by the fluidity and imprecision of the cinematic images. The reader is therefore implicitly encouraged to emulate the narrator's conduct when watching the pornographic film, to focus on the visceral and physical, rather than on the intellectual or moral. The dialogue-less pornographic film foreshadows the overwhelmingly sexual nature of the relationship portrayed in *Passion simple* and, as this chapter proposes, one in which the role of the female can be interpreted as corresponding to its cinematic equivalent – that age-old stereotype of male sexual fantasy: 'une silhouette de femme en guêpière, avec des bas' (PS, p. 11). Gestures and actions are presented as of greater significance than language in the narrator's account of her sexual passion – unaware what the relationship represents for her lover, it is the physical, the concrete, which provides her sole certainty: 'La seule vérité incontestable était visible en regardant son sexe' (PS, p. 35). This emphasis on the visual, on the physical components of their relationship, is all the more ironic given that the narrative also depicts the psychological repercussions of that relationship on the narrator, a depiction which highlights the infrequency of the lover's presence.

The absence of intellectual union between the parties further explains the importance of the visual. Indeed, the narrator's intellectual activity is shown to all but cease during the sexual affair represented in *Passion simple*, and she responds Pavlov's-dog-like to external stimuli: 'Les mots et les phrases, le rire même se formaient dans ma bouche sans participation réelle de ma réflexion ou de ma volonté' (PS, p. 13). There is little verbal communication between the narrator and her lover, an absence foreshadowed not only by the unintelligibility – and expendability – of the dialogue in the pornographic film, but also by the work's title: 'Je devinais – autant qu'on puisse le faire avec justesse lorsqu'il s'agit d'un étranger – qu'il n'était pas attiré par les choses intellectuelles et artistiques, malgré le respect qu'elles lui inspiraient' (PS, pp. 32–33).[44] If the lover's foreignness in *Passion simple* reinforces the narrator's belief that words can only approximate

'reality', its relevance to her uncertainty as to his interest in art remains unclear: his foreignness may hinder precision in communication, yet his level of French is sufficient to carry out a high-ranking
diplomatic post in France: 'il s'exprimait assez bien en français' (PS, p.
36). The narrator's ignorance may therefore be presumed to stem either from the predominantly sexual nature of the relationship, or from
a deliberate exoticisation of the Other, in which manifestations of class
are rendered more palatable by being read as evidence of national
differences.

While the narrator views her relationship as analogous to her writing, in that she invests herself completely in both, demonstrating the
same concern with minutiae in an endeavour to perfect the finalised
whole, writing – or even verbal accounts of her passion – is seen to
provide an inferior version of her 'real-life' experiences. Indeed, the
intrinsic inferiority of art to life or life's inevitable diminishment at the
hands of art is a *topos* of *Passion simple*. If the metanarrative comments of *La Place* and *Une femme* acknowledge the difficulties in providing a representative portrayal of the narrator's parents, in *Passion
simple* they question the very possibility of accurately reflecting 'reality', endeavouring instead to outline its essential components. When
the narrator looks at the scene left behind in her home following the
departure of A., she describes it as 'un moment, qui composait un
tableau dont la force et la douleur ne seront jamais atteintes [pour
moi] par aucun autre dans un musée' (PS, p. 20).[45] This inferiority, and
art's inability to do more than provide an approximation of 'reality' –
'les signes d'une passion' (PS, p. 31) – can again be viewed as an indirect reinforcement of the narrator's initial suggestion that morality is
irrelevant when judging the work's merits: since art can never capture
the intensity of 'real-life' experiences, including the irrational nature
of passion, the reader does not possess the hermeneutic authority to
assess the work from a moral perspective.

As is the case in *La Place* and *Une femme*, the narrator of *Passion
simple* does not attempt to present the reader with a chronologically
consistent and coherent representation of her liaison or to adopt one
particular literary genre to do so: 'je ne sais pas, maintenant, sur quel
mode je l'écris [her passion], si c'est celui du témoignage, voire de la
confidence telle qu'elle se pratique dans les journaux féminins, celui
du manifeste ou du procès-verbal, ou même du commentaire de texte'
(PS, pp. 30–31).[46] Rather than seek to link or explain certain remarks,
she simply enumerates facts which help convey the significance of her

relationship to the reader. The adoption of this fragmented, impressionistic approach to writing and generic categories in *Passion simple* is appropriate for a number of reasons: the inherently 'irrational' nature of the narrator's experience; the recentness of the events portrayed – having begun to relate them only two months after the end of her relationship, the narrator has yet to assimilate them properly; and her equation of explanation with self-exoneration. We return to the narrator's acute awareness of the impression the text may be making on the reader, and to her recurrent, if circumspect, desire to influence their interpretation of it: 'Les seules données, peut-être, à prendre en compte, seraient matérielles, le temps et la liberté dont j'ai pu disposer pour vivre cela' (PS, p. 32).

Whatever the limitations of the literary medium posited in *Passion simple*, the continuing 'humanist' element in the narrator's approach is evident in this foregrounding of the material and in the rejection of the psychoanalytic as a viable interpretative paradigm to understanding her liaison with A.. However, the narrator's reference to the inappositeness of a psychoanalytic reading of the work somewhat aptly reveals more than it conceals – she qualifies her rejection of such a reading with a parenthetical explanation which undermines that very rejection: '(*Autant en emporte le vent*, *Phèdre* ou les chansons de Piaf sont aussi décisifs que le complexe d'Œdipe)' (PS, pp. 31–32).[47] Ernaux also rejects the validity of a psychoanalytic reading of her work generally, since psychoanalysis does not sufficiently historicise the subject, nor, she argues, can the self-consciously structured nature of literary composition be reconciled with the free association of psychoanalysis.[48] Furthermore, as her latest works demonstrate, writing, unlike psychoanalysis, has not curtailed Ernaux's need to work through the themes of childhood. Ernaux's dismissal of psychoanalysis as an appropriate hermeneutics for her writing may also stem from a belief that it represents another example of middle-class misappropriation of working-class experience: in Ernaux's opinion, before psychoanalysis should be invoked as a productive reading strategy, *conscious* identity-forming structures such as social class merit more serious consideration.

In its immediacy, in its recounting of contemporary events related by the adult narrator, rather than past events firmly grounded in childhood, in its ostensible lack of interest in social class, *Passion simple* would seem to represent a new chapter in Ernaux's writing history. The text incorporates only one explicit reference to class: the narrator describes the differences between her foreign lover and herself as cultural, yet remarks that, had he been French, she would have considered them 'des différences sociales' (PS, p. 33). However, as subsequent works demonstrate, this new beginning is illusory, as is *Passion simple*'s silence on the themes which dominate the earlier works. Rather than signal a break with the past, the passion described in the work serves to reinforce links with her childhood by enhancing the narrator's understanding of it: 'je me suis rappelé les femmes, seules ou mariées, mères de famille, qui, dans le quartier de mon enfance, recevaient en cachette un homme l'après-midi [...]. Je pensais à elles avec une profonde satisfaction' (PS, p. 30). Indeed, it could be argued that it is the very similarity of their origins which attracts the narrator to A.: he too requires material possessions to indicate wealth, as the narrator did when an adolescent, drinks heavily, as did the men who populated her childhood, and watches the same television programmes as her father. Also, both are exiles, she from her class, he from his country. As with all of Ernaux's writing, then, *Passion simple* represents a return to origins, a reiteration of, not a dissociation from, the formative influences of childhood. Like her counterpart in *La Place* and *Une femme*, the narrator expresses a desire to re-establish contact with the past, rather than the drive for severance voiced in *Les Armoires vides* and *Ce qu'ils disent ou rien*, a desire both facilitated and necessitated by the recent death of her mother: 'Dans mes rêves, il y avait aussi ce désir d'un temps réversible. Je parlais et me disputais avec ma mère (décédée), redevenue vivante, mais je savais dans mon rêve – et elle aussi – qu'elle avait été morte' (PS, p. 59).

The narrator maintains that the delay between composition and publication allows her to focus on the act of writing without regard for its consequences – that she makes repeated mention of these potential consequences proves this assertion to be somewhat disingenuous (which the inclusion of her favourite adverb does little to change): 'Je ne ressens naturellement aucune honte à noter ces choses, à cause du délai qui sépare le moment où elles s'écrivent, où je suis seule à les voir, de celui où elles seront lues par les gens et qui, j'ai l'impression, n'arrivera jamais' (PS, p. 42). When she revisits the place where she had an abortion 20 years earlier – a further indication of the narrator's desire to renew links with the past, following the recent departure of her lover – she directly invokes the reader's notion of 'normality', revealing the same susceptibility to the influence of 'normal', 'natural' behaviour paradigms as her counterpart in *La Femme gelée*. The spectre of 'normality' haunts *Passion simple*, in that it is partly the narrator's need to reassure herself of the representativeness of her experience which motivates the production of the text, a need which points to the current paucity of accounts of sexual passion written by women, thereby corroborating the innovativeness of the text's content: 'Je me demande si je n'écris pas pour savoir si les autres n'ont pas fait ou ressenti des choses identiques, sinon, pour qu'ils trouvent normal de les ressentir' (PS, p. 65). She seeks the reader's ratification of the 'normality' of her conduct, echoing the narrator's dialogic relationship with the reader in *La Femme gelée*, and illustrating the drive for representativeness viewed as characteristic of women's auto/biographical writing. The narrator may explicitly adopt a devil-may-care attitude in portraying her relationship, but, as with her predecessor's disregard of social criticism, her defiance is less resolute than it appears. As the work draws to a close, the narrator's bravura is succeeded by a more conciliatory attitude vis-à-vis the reader: 'Ce sont les jugements, les valeurs "normales" du monde qui se rapprochent avec la perspective d'une publication' (PS, p. 69).[49] While such a transformation may be viewed as a consequence of the cathartic effect of the writing process, it foregrounds the narrator's continuing awareness of the presence of the Other and concomitant need for readerly approbation.

'L'Amoureuse'

The lack of intellectual sustenance the relationship brings the narrator is reinforced by the fact that it is the lover's physical presence that is shown to give her existence meaning. In her lover's absence, the narrator is portrayed as a type of automaton, executing the minimum number of functions necessary for everyday life, while perceiving everything in relation to her next meeting with her lover – her mind is only briefly engaged if activities or interests are relevant to him and to their affair: 'A partir du mois de septembre l'année dernière, je n'ai plus rien fait d'autre qu'attendre un homme: qu'il me téléphone et qu'il vienne chez moi' (PS, p. 13). Waiting characterises the narrator's existence in *Passion simple*, her time is spent 'en rêveries et attente' (PS, p. 28), and, while describing her life between meetings as an 'attente indéfinie, douloureuse, jalouse' (PS, p. 16), she would prefer to devote herself completely to the anticipatory pleasure inherent in the act of waiting rather than be distracted by the rest of her life. Indeed, even when the lover has made contact and the narrator is preparing for his arrival, we are told, 'j'entrais dans une autre attente' (PS, p. 17). Waiting similarly constitutes the principal 'activity' of Beauvoir's 'amoureuse', *Le Deuxième Sexe II*, p. 572: 'Pour exister, il lui faut donc que l'amant soit auprès d'elle, occupé par elle; elle attend sa venue, son désir, son réveil; et, dès qu'il l'a quittée, elle recommence à l'attendre.'

The narrator's life takes on an eternally cyclical quality, revolving around the presence or absence of her lover. It comprises an increase in suffering until he telephones, frenetic activity leading up to his arrival, awareness of his imminent departure, followed by an overwhelming sense of lethargy until the cycle begins again. Unable to enjoy the present, the narrator's existence is spent either awaiting A.'s next visit, or, when that visit materialises, dreading the moment he will leave – when the future at last becomes the present, it is projected into the future again. Similarly, in a long-term perspective, the narrator translates the increase in physical pleasure the relationship gives her into a decrease in its potential longevity – she views every sexual encounter as plundering their finite capital of desire. The relationship with A. also affects her long-term perspective of the past as well as of the future, in that all personal and professional landmarks shrink into insignificance compared to the importance of A. in her life: 'j'étais sûre qu'il n'y avait jamais rien eu de plus important dans ma vie, ni avoir des enfants, ni réussir des concours, ni voyager loin, que cela, être au lit avec cet homme au milieu de l'après-midi' (PS, p. 19). While recognising the ephemerality of her existence during this liaison, with the cessation of the relationship the narrator remains unable to focus on the present, on the gaping vacuum of an existence without her lover. This continuing inability to inhabit the present partly accounts for her writing project, as she endeavours to relive what has been, to prolong her relationship through literature, an endeavour reflected in the prevalence of the imperfect tense throughout *Passion simple*:[50] if the future consumes the present during the living of her relationship, it is the past which does so during its writing in her vivid recollections of a period when A. was part of her existence. While writing cannot hope to capture the intensity of a 'real-life' relationship, it can nonetheless fulfil a panacean function by allowing the narrator to re-experience her 'passion simple' in literary form.

In many respects, the narrator of *Passion simple* is portrayed as assimilating the stereotype of the submissive female to a nauseous degree ('prête, maquillée, coiffée, la maison rangée' [PS p. 18]). Unlike the young girl in *La Femme gelée*, the mature woman in *Passion simple* is well-versed in the art of feminine seduction, devoting herself to the perfection of her physical appearance in the hope that she will continue to stimulate and satiate A.'s sexual appetite: 'Les seuls moments heureux en dehors de sa présence étaient ceux où j'achetais de nouvelles robes, des boucles d'oreilles, des bas, et les essayais chez moi devant la glace, l'idéal, impossible, consistant en ce qu'il voie à chaque fois une toilette différente' (PS, p. 22). As Beauvoir remarks in *Le Deuxième Sexe II*, the older woman has learnt from experience that social validation comes through her adherence to patriarchal 'aesthetic' norms of beauty and femininity, rather than the perfection of 'internal' qualities. If the narrator of *Passion simple* can be seen to reflect a stereotypically feminine concern with pleasing her lover, that lover is shown to embody a stereotypical machismo in both appearance and conduct, and is described in Beauvoirean terms as 'en situation dominante' (PS, p. 32). Given the extramarital nature of the affair, the narrator may never initiate a meeting, and appears grateful for whatever scraps of his existence he can spare her. She expends all her energy in predisposing her lover to see her again, and is willing to tolerate any degradation if it guarantees the continuation of the relationship.

Unlike her predecessors, the narrator voices no dissatisfaction with her subjugated position, indeed longs to preserve it. That subjugated position and lack of autonomous agency are demonstrated by her constant wagering with fate – 'Je promettais d'envoyer 200 francs au Secours populaire s'il venait me voir avant une date que je fixais' (PS, p. 28) – and her superstitious conduct. She consults horoscopes, which, with their emphasis on monolithic behaviour paradigms, represent a rigidification of her passive role, and desires to see a fortune-teller when the relationship is over. As the relationship runs its course, the narrator in *Passion simple* does occasionally express the tension viewed by Beauvoir as characteristic of the female erotic experience (and prevalent throughout the early trilogy), a tension which epitomises the subject/object dichotomy of the female condition under patriarchy – and one she associates with the clitoral/vaginal experience of eroticism – and the confrontation between transcendence and immanence. Any movement towards transcendence – as in the narrator's fleeting contemplation of ending her relationship – is short-lived and always occurs in the lover's absence. While Beauvoir's analysis of erotic love argues that this tension in the individual's dual status of subject and object can be resolved successfully in a reciprocal relationship in which each partner is both giver and given, the lack of reciprocity on which the relationship is based in *Passion simple* renders such a resolution impossible. Ernaux's narrator dare not assert herself as transcendent subject for fear that even her status as object will be taken from her.[51]

Unlike those ideological reinforcers in the early trilogy which, having little in common with the 'real-life' experiences they supposedly reflect, are ultimately rejected by the narrators, mediatic representations which endorse and validate her experience are deliberately sought by the narrator of *Passion simple*. As more detached, retrospective observers, Ernaux's earlier narrators perceive various media as ideological crutches, upholding patriarchal representations of femininity, while a narrator in the throes of passion is unlikely to assess the ideological content of these props, instead falling back on the social conditioning which condones them. Like her manner of dressing and behaving, the role played by songs or films can be interpreted as pointing to the stereotypical nature of her experience: 'Les [chansons] plus sentimentales, auxquelles je ne prêtais aucune attention avant, me bouleversaient' (PS, p. 27). Similarly, while the written text of *Passion simple* cannot hope to translate accurately her 'life text', that 'life text' is nonetheless shown to be influenced by previous literary models, an influence which both reinforces the clichéd nature of the narrator's experience and substantiates Beauvoir's numerous remarks on the influential role played by literature in women's lives: 'Tout ce temps, j'ai eu l'impression de vivre ma passion sur le mode romanesque' (PS, p. 30). Indeed, in many respects, the narrator of *Passion simple* appears to relinquish all pretensions to the politically aware behaviour implicitly advocated by her predecessors – the reader can almost sense her relief at no longer having to police her own conduct in order to gauge its degree of feminism. It is as if the narrator has given up trying to fight the effects of social conditioning, an interpretation which would also explain the reader's impression in *La Femme gelée* that behind the narrator's feminist façade lurks a feminine woman longing to give in to her conventional inclinations.

Feminist Readings

The beneficial effects of the relationship on the narrator are less than evident: her confidence undermined, she devotes her time and attention to embellishing her appearance, attempting to delay what she perceives as her lover's inevitable departure. The reader nowhere has the impression that the relationship provides the narrator with an enduring happiness or even that she takes an active role sexually. At most, there is a sort of masochistic enjoyment of the extremes to which her obsession drives her: while aware of the lack of reciprocity in the relationship, the narrator nonetheless appears to relish her dependency on her lover. If Denise's quasi-masochistic behaviour in *Les Armoires vides* has its origins in class difference, in *Passion simple* it seems to stem from the narrator's sense of her privileged situation – that of a middle-aged woman experiencing sexual fulfilment – a sense not easily reconciled with a feminist reading of the text. The narrator's objectification is such, that, even in her lover's absence, she lives her life under his imaginary gaze: 'je déambulais en sueur sous son regard imaginaire boulevard des Italiens' (PS, p. 44). She also refers to herself as 'possédée par l'image de A.' (PS, p. 51), an absence waiting to be filled by her lover's presence, a husk of an existence. When she masturbates after the relationship has come to an end, it is to him that she attributes her orgasm, in other words, she anchors what Beauvoir would consider a more transcendent, clitoral pleasure in the more immanent centre of eroticism, the vagina, which 'ne devient un centre érotique que par l'intervention du mâle' (LDS II, p. 148). It is, however, her desire to have an Aids test in the hope that she will have an eternal reminder of her lover which may be seen as providing the most disturbing evidence of her dependency on him.

The sexual subordination of the narrator – even if it is desired – contravenes a reading of her conduct as feminist. Indeed, such desire can be viewed as demonstrating the efficiency of the socialisation process, in that the individual has internalised the oppressive structures of ideological conditioning, and this, without even the institutionalised restraints of marriage obliging her to do so. In her chapter 'L'Amoureuse', Beauvoir comments on the self-deception inherent in this willed objectification: 'elle choisit de vouloir si ardemment son esclavage qu'il lui apparaîtra comme l'expression de sa liberté; elle s'efforcera de surmonter sa situation d'objet inessentiel en l'assumant radicalement' (LDS II, p. 547). When one of the two members of the couple is so evidently '"sous la main"' (PS, p. 38), it requires a formidable interpretative sleight of hand to consider such a position feminist. Similarly, that a male lover be the object of a female narrator's obsessive passion, a passion related from a first-person female perspective, does not per se corroborate a feminist reading of the narrative: the traditional hierarchical relationship between the sexes has not altered, only its representational perspective – this time we are privy to the oppressed's version of events first-hand. Finally, the account of a passion related in Ernaux's trademark minimalist style, rather than the more effusive and clichéd

language of *romans à l'eau de rose* – which is not to say that the
content of the work escapes cliché – equally has no bearing on the
text's feminism. Indeed, such an interpretation merely reinforces patriarchal binary oppositions by its implicit characterisation of sober,
detached language as masculine and descriptive, 'emotional' language
as feminine.

As this chapter has aimed to demonstrate, the inherent lack of reciprocity in the relationship renders a feminist reading of the work problematic. Ernaux has maintained elsewhere that true feminism lies in
the rejection of norms and stereotypes, in living one's life to the limit
without recourse to politically correct definitions of behaviour. Her
writing aims to describe 'real', representative female experiences rather
than prescribe ideal, feminist modes of conduct, and it is this aim which
explains her ability to incorporate any feminine thorns into her feminist side:

> L'importance, c'est de vivre quelque chose jusqu'au bout, ce que ça apporte.
> C'est l'aventure, la curiosité. Et qu'il y a des siècles que les hommes vivent les
> aventures jusqu'au bout, ils ont presque le privilège de vivre en toute liberté.
> Il y a une chose qui évidemment peut ne pas apparaître dans le livre – je ne
> demande rien à cet homme. Je ne lui demande pas de me venir en charge. Je
> lui demande simplement, en termes crus, qu'on baise. [...] Pour moi le comble
> du féminisme, d'une certaine manière, c'est de vivre quelque chose en dehors
> de se dire 'Ah mon Dieu, c'est un stéréotype'. C'est de le vivre et de l'écrire.[52]

If Ernaux's interpretation of the aims of feminism has distinct
Beauvoirean echoes in its adoption of the male model as normative,
the incorporation of such aims in the form of an individualistic desire
for unbridled sexual expression is surely insufficient evidence for a
feminist reading of *Passion simple*. Rather than posit *Passion simple*
as a feminist text – something the work itself does not do – it may be
more productive to perceive it less as a feminist portrayal of sexual
passion, than, as Ernaux suggests, a representation of the human desire to transgress continually experiential boundaries. The narrator in
Passion simple is grateful to her lover for extending the parameters of
'normality', for introducing her to realms of experience previously
unknown to her. She feels better able to understand the marginal behaviour of others after her relationship, and this greater empathy may
account for the subject matter of Ernaux's next work, *Journal du dehors*. If Ernaux's narrator in *Passion simple* does not behave in a
recognisably feminist manner, she does express common qualities of
individual experience – as reflected in the ease with which readers of

both sexes relate to the narrator's account of her passion.[53] While the text may be read as offering a pessimistic model for feminist hermeneutics, it can be interpreted more positively if viewed in light of the narrator's courageous willingness to surpass the confines of the habitual and the familiar in order to achieve a form of experiential and spiritual growth.

CHAPTER 3

Writing the Auto/biographical Legacies of *La Place* and *Une femme*

La Place and *Une femme* signal a marked evolution in Ernaux's writing project. As Chapter 2 illustrates, that evolution is nonetheless foreshadowed by the transitional status of *La Femme gelée*, a text which can be seen to bridge the emotional intensity of the earlier works and the more reconciliatory attitude towards the past portrayed in *La Place* and *Une femme*. The nostalgia for childhood in *La Femme gelée* and the narrator's ability to perceive her parents' characteristics as resulting from a combination of historical and social circumstances, rather than existing solely to frustrate her desires, pre-empt the greater narrative empathy of the later works. The occasional use of metacommentary in *La Femme gelée* also paves the way for the increasing abandonment of the fictional façade in Ernaux's subsequent writing, as the auto/biographical comes to the fore. The instances of metacommentary first employed in *La Femme gelée* become more prominent in *La Place* and *Une femme* both in their typographical separation from the main narrative and in their explicatory function of the narrator's perception of the role of writing and language generally. While the narrator in *La Femme gelée* occasionally refers to her position as retrospective writer, she does not discuss the act of literary composition. The fictional status of the earlier works renders a description of the writing process extraneous, the narrators' aim being to establish the truthfulness of their theses, rather than digress on the most appropriate literary means of doing so. In *La Place* and *Une femme*, however, the narrator is explicitly portraying her 'real-life' parents, and feels a moral duty to provide an accurate depiction of them, a depiction clearly facilitated by instructing the reader of her 'writerly' intentions throughout.[1] When compared to the early trilogy,

87

La Place and *Une femme* constitute 'more overtly "authentic" narratives' both in their extensive incorporation of auto/biographical details without recourse to a fictional medium and in their representation of the difficulties encountered in achieving an accurate literary transcription of these details.[2]

Ernaux's classification of these two works as *récits* further indicates a reduction in the more explicitly fictional elements of her writing. If the early trilogy can be classed as autobiographical novels or autofiction, the precise generic status of Ernaux's later works is uncertain, and, in Ernaux's opinion, of little importance, her professed aim being to provide an accurate representation of her subject matter 'sans souci d'un genre littéraire défini'.[3] While the narrator in *Une femme* addresses the issue of categorisation directly, commenting on the amalgamation of genres which constitutes her work, Ernaux has also insisted that *La Place* does not adhere to one specific generic category – to consider it a purely biographical work would be to deny, or at least to limit, its representative value: 'ce ne sont pas mes *Souvenirs pieux*, comme l'a fait Marguerite Yourcenar, ce n'est pas une biographie, ce n'est pas le roman de mon père, ce sont des lueurs qu'on peut projeter et qui sont signifiantes'.[4] The generic hybridity of *La Place* and *Une femme* is particularly complex: while presented as a mixture of the ethnographical and the biographical through the inclusion of factual information and 'détails concrets', these works are equally autobiographical. In them, we find a third-person narrated and a first-person narrating subject, leading to a fusion of the biographical and the autobiographical, despite the narrating subject's endeavours to dissociate them. The autobiographical is contained through emphasis on the biographical, which is in turn contained through emphasis on the ethnographical, in that, while the narrator's motivation for writing the work is acutely personal, it is the representative aspects of her parents' existence which she wishes to portray, the characteristics they have in common with those belonging to the same stratum of French society. The narrator's account of her parents focuses principally on external details, on their actions, habits and words, rather than describing their particular psychological characteristics. Through her ethnographical emphasis, she seeks to extend the referential scope of the works, to make the private public and to give the particular life a representative resonance. The titles of both works reflect this concern with representativeness: *La Place* refers above all to her father's inferior position in the social hierarchy, while the use of the indefinite article in the title of *Une femme* situates her mother within a general category, rather than in her familial relation to the narrator – she is an individual in her own right, not simply the narrator's mother. The use of the indefinite article suggests that the work's title may equally be taken to designate the narrator herself, further reinforcing the interdependency of the biographical and the autobiographical in the work.

In both *La Place* and *Une femme*, the narrator provides a genealogical overview of her parents' families in an attempt to situate them within a broader social framework and to present them as representative working-class figures: 'L'histoire de mon père ressemble à celle de ma mère, famille nombreuse, père charretier et mère tisserande, l'école quittée à douze ans, ici, pour les travaux des champs comme domestique de ferme' (UF, p. 36). She retraces the parental histories which History has occluded in order to write working-class experience into literature and to give her parents' lives an enduring significance through literary restitution. This emphasis on the wider social conditions within which her parents, as members of 'la classe dominée', must be portrayed, is clearly expressed in one of the original titles of *La Place*, which was *Eléments pour une ethnographie familiale*, echoing Zola's sociological characterisation of *Les Rougon-Macquart* as an 'Histoire naturelle et sociale d'une famille sous le Second Empire'. Ernaux's ostensive aim in writing these works is not to provide an auto/biographical account of her parents, but to use the biographies of her parents as an archetype on which to base a sociological representation of the common values, tastes, customs and vocabulary of their class – the universal is firmly grounded in the particular and in first-hand experience.[5] Despite the narrator's claim in *Une femme* that her work comprises an historical element, the historical particularities of her parents' lives are subsumed under her desire to foreground their representativeness; it is not their specific historical circumstances which she seeks to capture, but their essential working-class characteristics:[6] 'C'est dans la manière dont les gens s'assoient et s'ennuient dans les salles d'attente, interpellent leurs enfants, font au revoir sur les quais de gare que j'ai cherché la figure de mon père. J'ai retrouvé dans des êtres anonymes rencontrés n'importe où, porteurs à leur insu des signes de force ou d'humiliation, la réalité oubliée de sa condition' (LP, pp. 100–01).[7] History forms an unobtrusive backdrop to both works: specific events, such as the First World War, are of interest to the narrator only insofar as they influence parental development.

A further means by which the narrator increases the objectivity of her account is in her use of initials to designate the principal geographical locations in *La Place*, such as Yvetot or Lillebonne, and her father's real name. If the purpose of this narrative device has traditionally been to safeguard the anonymity of 'real-life' people and places, thereby demonstrating the authenticity and 'realism' of the text, given that Ernaux's narrator provides numerous factual details which enable the reader to identify the towns implied, its role in *La Place* can be understood as reflecting her desire to make people and places representative of a shared social condition by denoting both the particular and the general. In *Une femme*, however, the narrator writes the names of the towns in full. As with the greater prevalence of affective memories in *Une femme*, the narrator's decision to provide the names of towns can be interpreted as an acknowledgement of her intense emotional involvement with the text's subject matter, and the futility of maintaining otherwise.[8] The narrator's frequent recourse to descriptions of photographs may be viewed as a further attempt to increase the representativeness of parental portraits by providing the reader with detailed images of her parents before she was born. Yet the very infrequency with which photographs were taken – as highlighted by the ubiquitous serious expressions and awkwardness of her parents in them – and the fact that they tend to be taken on special occasions, undermine any claim to their representativeness.

If the auto/biographical and ethnographical elements of these works point to their endemic generic instability, the numerous self-reflexive interventions throughout *La Place* and *Une femme* both illustrate and elucidate another important aspect of their creation, and one which further increases that instability. That is, the literary or fictional dimension to the narrator's representation of her 'real-life' subject matter – these works are also about their own composition.[9] The modification in narrative approach represented by *La Place* and *Une femme* is addressed in numerous metanarrative interjections; both narratives are interspersed with remarks explicating the writerly objectives – and, by implication, the desired readerly interpretations – of the works.[10] These metanarrative comments express the narrator's aims in navigating the narrative complexities of *La Place* and *Une femme*, yet their existence also betrays her awareness of certain tensions within her literary project. Paradoxically, the first-person interventions, which continually remind the reader of the presence of the narrating subject and of the artificial, constructed nature of the works, highlight the narrator's determination to provide an 'innocent', representative portrayal of her parents.[11] They express the narrator's desire to move beyond the subjective and the personal to the typical.

If this personal drive for representativeness throws into relief the tensions at the heart of Ernaux's literary project, as we have seen it also helps account for the composite position occupied by *La Place* and *Une femme* in terms of genres: the narrator's recurrent emphasis on objectivity originates in the intrinsically subjective nature of the accounts. In *La Place*, the narrator aims to adopt an inventory-like approach when describing the constituents of her father's life in an attempt to increase the objectivity of the account, an approach reflected in the numerous brief paragraphs separated by page breaks and the absence of transitional explanations. It is, however, in *Une femme* that such an approach is most visibly incorporated in the text, in the series of descriptive memories of the narrator's mother and segments of information about her mother's childhood. The inclusion of these lists, which frequently contain sociological indicators, enables the narrator to restrict the subjective vagaries of memory by presenting information in a series of self-contained vignettes with little or no narratorial comment. The pared-down, 'classic' language employed by the narrator in the carefully constructed portraits of her parents can be seen to minimise further the texts' emotional resonance for her.

In an interview with Jean-Jacques Gibert, Ernaux acknowledges that the novelistic aspect of her writing continues to exist in the inevitable degree of fictionalisation, of distortion, inherent in a literary transcription of her parents' 'real-life' existences: 'la fiction passe où elle veut [...] *La Place* est de l'ordre du fictionnel dans la mesure où j'ai donné un destin à mon père'.[12] In *Une femme*, the narrator expresses her belief that there exists an ideal, definitive order of narrative which will best capture her mother, a belief which explains her unwillingness to integrate supplementary information into the existent maternal portrait as her narrative draws to a close: 'Maintenant que ma mère est morte, je voudrais n'apprendre rien de plus sur elle que ce que j'ai su pendant qu'elle vivait' (UF, p. 105).[13] In other words, the narrator acknowledges the inevitable bias of her account by editing out what does not appeal to her. This editorial censorship makes clear the work's subjective, selective element, and the narrator's need for a panacean product above a factually comprehensive one, even when it may produce a heightened understanding of her mother's circumstances. The personal motivation behind the act of writing, the restitutive function of the works, prohibits the incorporation of this information in the narrative. Earlier in *Une femme*, the narrator also refuses to provide an account of her father's death, since *La Place* has already done so: 'Je ne peux pas décrire ces moments parce que je l'ai déjà fait dans un autre livre, c'est-à-dire qu'il n'y aura jamais aucun autre récit possible, avec d'autres mots, un autre ordre des phrases' (UF, p. 73). While this notion of a definitive literary transcription of 'reality' is revised in subsequent works, its articulation in *La Place* and *Une femme* foregrounds the importance of the act of literary composition in these texts: having pieced together in writing the disparate elements of her mother's existence and sought to impose on these elements 'un ordre idéal' (UF, p. 43), the narrator is unwilling to disturb the integrated portrayal of her mother by the inclusion of further 'factual' information – her fictionalisation extends beyond the inevitable distortion inherent in the act of writing lives.

In the same interview, however, Ernaux rejects a purely, or mainly, novelistic status for *La Place*, a rejection stemming from her politicised perception of novel-writing and from her equation of fiction with falsehood:

> Des écrivains, issus du même milieu que le mien, ont aussi le sentiment que le roman est un genre faux. On ne peut pas; parce que précisément, comme disait mon père, 'c'est du roman'. Ce qui nous arrête c'est peut-être que – comme le veut Lukács – le roman est vraiment d'essence bourgeoise.

In *La Place*, the narrator perceives a fictionalised version of her father's life as having a potentially more emotive effect on the reader than a factually accurate one. Ernaux's narrator appears to seek a type of Brechtian *Verfremdungseffekt* in writing, engaging the reader's intellect while keeping them emotionally distant from the subject matter of the work – indeed, the repeated scissions in the narrative effectively prevent the reader from establishing prolonged contact with its subject matter. The narrator's desire in *La Place* and *Une femme* to make amends for what she views as her previous disparagement of her parents' lives further accounts for her eschewal of all deliberate fictionalisation: having been guilty of fictionalising them in their absence ('Au loin, j'avais épuré mes parents de leurs gestes et de leurs paroles, des corps glorieux' [LP, p. 97]; 'Étudiante à la fac de lettres, j'avais d'elle une image épurée, sans cris ni violence' [UF, p. 66]), when that absence becomes permanent, the narrator feels obliged to provide an accurate testimony to their lives in *La Place* and *Une femme*.

As the Introduction remarks, Ernaux's containment of the fictional elements of these works and her explicit engagement with factual material also stem from her retrospective perception of the earlier publications, the form and content of which she views as inherently contradictory: while the content of the early trilogy offers a critique of the bourgeois value system which considers all things working-class as 'de mauvais goût', its fictionalised form indirectly endorses such a value system. Ernaux interprets this embellishment of her working-class subject matter as an implicit avowal that it cannot be presented in unadulterated form. The literary transcription of her parents' existence, an existence which centres on the fulfilment of life's basic essentials, should equally limit itself to the essential and avoid deliberate fictionalisation. From *La Place* onwards, the narrator considers her subject matter as worthy of literary representation without the poeticised trimmings to make it more palatable for bourgeois consumption. However, the interventionist stance of the narrating subject throughout these works, and the dogmatic aspect to many of her assertions, particularly in *La Place*, reveal a continuing need to explain and justify the biographical subject vis-à-vis her bourgeois readers.

The recurrent presentation, indeed, justification, of her writing project as highlighting the typicality of her parents' existence can be seen to undermine the narrator's professed conviction that such an existence merits literary representation. For it to constitute a culturally viable product, worthy of the bourgeois reader's time and effort, it appears that her parents' existence must be sanctified by sociological representativeness rather than presented in a unique or idiosyncratic manner, despite the narrator's personal desire to do so. The narrator's determination to contain the highly subjective nature of the account through her adoption of the scientifically detached role of ethnologist, sociologist, or historian – whatever the generic permutations of *La Place* and *Une femme*, such permutations tend to be anchored in 'objective' discourses – may be viewed as an endeavour to increase the gravitas of Ernaux's literary project by giving it a form of scientific validation, and indicates to her bourgeois reader that her relation to her subject matter is as much intellectual as emotional. The narrator may express allegiance to her father through the use of the pronoun 'nous' and its possessive form, and deny complicity with her bourgeois readership, yet her interventions repeatedly draw attention to her current 'outsider', as well as previous 'insider', status. Indeed, despite adopting the 'nous' form throughout the work, the narrator claims to have stopped employing it in 'real life'. Whatever the empathy and solidarity with her working-class origins expressed in various metacommentaries, the very presence of these metacommentaries foregrounds her desire to dialogue with the bourgeois reader and to reassure them of her aims.[14] The metanarrative comments throughout *La Place* and *Une femme* reveal a narrator striving to reconcile personal loyalties with professional requirements: she seeks to be faithful to her class origins, to demonstrate her in-depth knowledge of them, and yet to avoid alienating her reader by providing them with recurrent explanations of her aims and objectives, to highlight that she is nonetheless 'one of them' by constantly taking care to distance herself from the world of her parents.[15] The narrator's ambivalence towards her culture of origin can be seen to encompass the different attitudes of her parents: while her father remains proud of his working-class culture, her mother aspires to the acquisition of bourgeois values and status. Indeed, the title of *La Place*, while denoting her father's awareness of his position in the social hierarchy, can also be taken to signal the narrator's acknowledgement of the complexities of her own position as writer.

Ernaux may perceive the classification of literature as little more than an exercise in middle-class intellectualisation, yet the narrators in both *La Place* and *Une femme*, by their repeated narrative interventions, clearly do view it as essential to justify the particular generic framework they adopt in the works and to instruct the reader of their writerly intentions in order to aid – or, more bluntly, to manipulate – them in their interpretation of the texts. As I have argued elsewhere, Ernaux's narrator attempts to influence the reader by a variety of means, not least by the existence of such comments in the first place, which flatter the reader by their confessional nature, inducing a sense of intimate dialogic exchange.[16] The narrator may 'share' her literary objectives with the reader, yet the narrative hierarchy remains firmly in place, with the narrator striving to control readerly interpretation of the works. The examiner's comment to the narrator after sitting her Capes – '"Vous les avez traînés, vos élèves"' (LP, p. 11) – could equally be applied to certain explicatory interventions made by the narrator in *La Place*. As the Introduction suggests, the coercive nature of many of the elucidations may be responsible for a tendency in some Ernaux criticism to accept their validity unquestioningly. While these elucidations can evidently be rejected by the reader and their interpellatory position resisted, the auto/biographical framework of the texts, the more 'real' space they inhabit, as well as their often emphatic tone, make such resistance harder. The narrator's ongoing concern with detailing her writerly motivations would suggest that it is not so much the endeavour to clarify the objectives of her writing project through an examination of its various genres to which Ernaux objects, but that the endeavour is undertaken by someone other than the narrator herself.

LA PLACE

The narrator strives to convince the reader of the accuracy of her metacommentaries on the generic nature of *La Place* and its principal aims through the employment of a subtly didactic vocabulary which discourages dissent. She appeals to the reader's common sense and emphasises the transparency of the project through the use of adverbs such as 'Naturellement' and 'Simplement' (LP, p. 46). By signalling the self-evident nature of the comments she makes regarding the writing process, the narrator characterises the reader as someone with sufficient literary sensitivities to endorse her remarks without requiring further clarification of them. The narrator also highlights the continuous effort demanded to produce the text she desires: in other words, while the reasons behind her eschewal of a fictionalised framework or her use of language in *La Place* are presented as straightforward, the realisation of her aims in literary form is fraught with difficulties, difficulties which can only be overcome through great determination on the part of the narrator. Much of the vocabulary employed in the metacommentaries points to the laborious aspect of writing, to the obstacles to be surmounted – 'm'efforçant', 'm'arrache' (LP, p. 45) – and to the personal pleasure to be abdicated in favour of the greater good: 'Naturellement, aucun bonheur d'écrire, dans cette entreprise où je me tiens au plus près des mots et des phrases entendues' (LP, p. 46). The reader is encouraged to equate the narrator's arduous effort with the realisation of her aims. Her references to the act of writing throughout *La Place* implicitly foreground the narrator's 'superiority' in taking up the challenge of providing a factually accurate representation of her father's condition rather than simply playing to the reader's preconceptions of working-class life.

Much of the narrator's effort is expended in reducing the subjective desires she understandably harbours to produce a personal portrait of her father and to focus on the emotional links uniting father and daughter. She seeks to portray herself as a neutral chronicler of working-class life, yet one aware of the moral obligation underlying her writing project: 'Le déchiffrement de ces détails s'impose à moi maintenant, avec d'autant plus de nécessité que je les ai refoulés, sûre de leur insignifiance' (LP, p. 72). The narrator wishes neither to idealise nor to dramatise the conditions of existence experienced by her father, but to strike a balanced representation of them. She strives to avoid the poeticisation or miserabilism of previous writers, to avoid in a certain respect the extremes reflected in her own early admiration of, and later condescension towards, her father.[17] The narrator must strike the correct representative note, portraying both the petty rivalries which characterised her father's existence and the pleasure he obtained from everyday activities – whether light-hearted exchanges with customers or working in his garden – without evoking pathos on the part of the bourgeois reader. She does not wish to write a hagiography of her father – too positive a portrayal focusing on the 'simple pleasures' of working-class life risks diminishing the work's political potential. Such a portrayal is associated with middle-class writers, with those whose literary romanticisation of working-class and rural conditions originates in their own privileged social status. For the narrator, the working-class world portrayed by such writers is one viewed through a prism of middle-class conceit, utterly removed from the harsh realities of her father's childhood: 'Quand je lis Proust ou Mauriac, je ne crois pas qu'ils évoquent le temps où mon père était enfant. Son cadre à lui c'est le Moyen Âge' (LP, p. 29). This remark is the first in the work to intimate the literary significance of the narrator's representation of working-class culture from an 'insider' perspective.[18]

As we have seen, however, *La Place*'s existence may stem less from the narrator's desire to fill a literary lacuna through the portrayal of working-class experience than an emotional lacuna enduced by guilt at her previous conduct vis-à-vis her father. The text can be construed as a posthumous tribute acknowledging the paternal qualities which the narrator failed to appreciate while her father was alive. The epigraph to the work by Jean Genet indicates the subjective impetus to the composition of *La Place* and represents a clear avowal of *La Place*'s exculpatory function, in that it is the narrator's wish to make amends for her absence of effort during her father's lifetime which motivates its writing: '"Je hasarde une explication: écrire c'est le derniers recours quand on a trahi."' The narrator hopes to reconstitute the sense of wholeness she enjoyed as a child (and which she fleetingly experiences shortly before her father's death, referring to it as 'un moment qui ressemblait à un rachat' [LP, p. 103]), a wholeness which disintegrated following her class ascent to the bourgeoisie: 'Je me sentais séparée de moi-même' (LP, p. 98). In this respect, *La Place* seeks to fulfil the conventional function of auto/biography and of narrative in general – that of providing coherence to what is inherently disparate. This personal impetus underlying the act of writing has profound implications for the professed neutrality of the text. The narrator may repeatedly signal her intention to focus on the 'public' rather than the personal and highlight the constant vigilance required to separate the idiosyncratic from the representative, but the details provided are still those selected by her. The die are cast in advance, and, as scriptwriter for both parties, the narrator can orchestrate the outcome she desires. It is not during her father's lifetime that the narrator feels an overwhelming need to make amends, but after his death, effectively giving herself free rein to rewrite their relationship, without fear of interruption or contradiction. To have done so during that lifetime may not have produced the same cathartic effect.

Metacommentaries serve not merely to explicate her aims in writing *La Place*, but equally to outline the narrator's, and her parents', attitude to language and to justify her adoption of a particular linguistic register in the work. These metacommentaries point to the narrator's perception of written language – particularly the detached, understated language of *La Place* and *Une femme* – as rendering a more objective portrayal of her parents than spoken language, a perception which may explain her use of italicisation when inserting elements of parental discourse in the narrative: by emphasising the 'writerly' or literary aspect of her work, the narrator seeks to increase the objectivity of her account, an objectivity which a greater emphasis on the text's oral elements would undermine.[19] The use of italics or inverted commas signals a clear divide in the text between the standard written French of the bourgeois narrator and the popular spoken French of her parents. The inclusion of these typographical signposts, particularly italicisation, serves to distance both narrator and reader from the oral components of the text, and therefore to increase the representativeness of her father's portrayal in that such components are not anchored in a specific interlocutor.[20] However, it also results in the very narrator/reader complicity the narrator supposedly wishes to avoid, turning her parents' speech into linguistic museum pieces to be studied by the bourgeois reader. (The use of italics to designate working-class

language is not present in *Une femme*, indicating the greater confluence of the narrator's language and her mother's: the mother makes a
conscious effort to employ her daughter's vocabulary and phrases.)

The oral component to the narrative of *La Place* is also intimated
in certain metanarrative remarks, as in the inclusion of the verb 'dire'
in the narrator's explicatory introduction to the work: 'Je voulais dire,
écrire au sujet de mon père, sa vie, et cette distance venue à l'adolescence
entre lui et moi' (LP, p. 23). Later in the text, she again implicitly
acknowledges the indeterminacy of the boundary separating 'des mots
et des phrases entendues' (LP, p. 46) from their literary transcription
in the work. This reference to her father's speech, as with her use of
italics, serves to segregate the narrator's own language use from the
working-class speech of her childhood. Ernaux's narrator must surely
have employed this vocabulary herself, as well as heard it spoken by
others, and, indeed, examples of popular French repeatedly infiltrate
the narrative.[21] While much of the textual language of *La Place* is oral
in nature, it is subsumed under the general emphasis on the 'written',
echoing the narrator's attitude to language discussed in Chapter 1 in
relation to *Les Armoires vides*: the narrator may foreground the 'written' aspect of *La Place*, claiming its minimalist style is based on letters
she wrote to her parents, yet working-class speech, whether in the
form of direct quotations or general colloquialisms, punctuates the
narrative at regular intervals.[22] The narrator's remarks on language
use, while highlighting the generational and class differences between
her parents and herself – and, even more so, between her grandpar-
ents, who could only speak *patois*, and herself – also seek to distinguish her from earlier middle-class authors writing about the working
class. The narrator's association of middle-class writers with an aesthetics detached from experiential 'reality' is apparent in her criticism
of Proust, whose elevated social status allows him to record the unusual speech patterns of Françoise with no conception of the everyday
shame experienced by those who make 'mistakes' in spoken French.
As we have seen, despite the narrator's privileged epistemological position as 'diasporan subject', her italicisation of her parents' speech
can be viewed as promoting a similar detachment to that for which
she condemns Proust.

As is the case throughout Ernaux's writing, language use is the
principal source of conflict and distress throughout the narrator's childhood in *La Place* due to its pivotal role in indicating social class: 'Tout
ce qui touche au langage est dans mon souvenir motif de rancœur et

de chicanes douloureuses, bien plus que l'argent' (LP, p. 64). Her parents may endeavour to protect her from class discrimination by satisfying her material needs, yet linguistic differences are less easily eradicated. A particularly strained period in father/daughter relations coincides with the advent of the narrator's adolescence, in that her burgeoning sexuality and concern with appearances – we return to the 'good taste' and value judgements of the early trilogy – further distance her from her origins, and she begins to despise the taste, beliefs and language of her milieu. The narrator's increasing assimilation of the French taught at school hinders dialogue between father and daughter, as she grows to resent her father's inability to speak 'correct' French, a resentment which may be viewed as evidence of her own class insecurity.[23] The narrator gradually turns into a spokeswoman for the bourgeoisie in front of whom her father is frightened to express himself. The censorship the narrator encounters at school which prohibits her from discussing her home life is duplicated in her relation with her father: 'Il n'osait plus me raconter des histoires de son enfance' (LP, p. 80).[24]

Like the narrator, her father is keen to improve his French and to lose the *patois* of his parents, since, while proud of his working-class culture, he does not wish to make himself unnecessarily vulnerable through an inability to converse with members of the bourgeoisie. Indeed, his criticism of the narrator's use of school slang presumably stems from his association of it with an inferiority her education is intended to remove. Language use outside the domestic domain always costs her father a conscious effort: he endeavours to speak correctly with others, yet his 'mother tongue' continues to break through, just as, whatever the narrator's differentiation between written French and the popular language of her working-class origins, unacknowledged examples of spoken French pepper her narrative. The pressure endured by the narrator at school to efface all traces of the spoken French associated with her home environment in order to improve her social status may account for the general validation of written language over oral language throughout Ernaux's writing, and for her narrators' frequent claims to have forgotten the language of childhood following their class migration to the bourgeoisie. It is as if the narrator, like her father, cannot let herself go either emotionally or linguistically in the presence of the bourgeois reader; her self-reflexive narrative is indicative of her desire to achieve readerly approbation.

Social Positions

The epigraph to *La Place* appears to indicate an evolution in the narrator's attitude towards her parents, in that it acknowledges her own role in contributing to the estrangement between parents and child. While the first two texts of the trilogy, despite occasional moments of culpability on the part of the narrator, tend to incriminate both parental attitude and, above all, the bourgeois education system for that estrangement, the older narrator of *La Femme gelée* displays a more considered understanding of her situation, yet, as we have seen in the previous chapter, one which still reveals a reluctance to assume responsibility for it. The epigraph of *La Place* and the work's opening section would seem to testify to the narrator's greater willingness to recognise previous deficiencies in her conduct. This willingness to shoulder more responsibility for the father/daughter separation may partly stem from the narrator's association of the death of her father with her entry into adulthood: 'Plusieurs fois, en marchant dans les rues, "je suis une grande personne"' (LP, pp. 21–22).[25] The avowal that her former behaviour played its part in the breakdown in communication between father and daughter carries enormous emotional resonance: 'J'aurais eu honte de lui reprocher de ne pas pouvoir m'envoyer en vacances, j'étais sûre qu'il était légitime de vouloir le faire changer de manières. Il aurait peut-être préféré avoir une autre fille' (LP, p. 82). If such guilt is only rarely made explicit in the main body of the text, its acknowledgement leaves the reader in no doubt of its acuteness: 'J'écris peut-être parce qu'on n'avait plus rien à se dire' (LP, p. 84).

The narrator's alienation from her father, intimated in the epigraph of *La Place*, is contextualised in the text's opening section, which relates the narrator's successful completion of the Capes teaching examination, a completion which further distances the narrator from the world of her parents, and, in particular, from her father, who was always less at ease with her evolving social status than her mother. The mature narrator associates her passing of the Capes with the death of her father – an association reinforced by the use of the term 'cérémonie' to describe both the examination and her father's funeral which occurred two months later, and by her occasional confusion as to the chronology of events – since both serve to increase the distance between father and daughter: retrospectively, the narrator perceives her professional achievement in the Capes as the last major event which separates her from her father by ensconcing her more deeply in the bourgeoisie, a separation rendered final by his death.[26] Given that the separation is shown to be initiated by the narrator's attendance at the *école libre*, it is logical that her success in the Capes examination – the pinnacle of her educational trajectory – symbolises the definitive severance between father and daughter. The sense of class betrayal epitomised by her passing the Capes nonetheless remains imprecise and unarticulated until the death of her father. An accumulation of minor events, ranging from her mother's need to continue working throughout the funeral arrangements, to the absence of any non-family member of the bourgeoisie at his funeral, to her own husband's evident alienation from events, relentlessly exposes the differences between the narrator's past and present worlds.[27] That her husband's awkwardness and peripherality to the proceedings stem from his social class is made clear: 'Plus que jamais, il a paru déplacé ici' (LP, p. 19).[28] Such awkwardness governs relations between husband and father-in-law from their first meeting, as well as relations between the narrator's father and her university friends. The very effort her father makes at such meetings signals his inferior social 'place' by pointing to the increased significance with which a middle-class presence endows it.

In many respects, the narrator's experience of the examination in which she is little more than a passive pawn whose fate is decreed by her 'superiors' mirrors her father's experience of hierarchical relations in society. *La Place* supplies various examples of that experience, whether in her father's embarrassment at having travelled first class with a second-class ticket or in his being instructed which books to read on his first visit to a public library; the guardians of middle-class culture, in the form of two library employees, dictate the extent of his access to it. Indeed, it could be argued that by making her father the subject of *La Place*, the narrator has guaranteed him posthumous access to the cultural domain of literature from which he felt excluded during his lifetime – if his finances procured her access to the middle class through education, she procures him access to it through literature. The narrator's feelings of humiliation after the examination may be fuelled by childhood memories of the hierarchical teacher/pupil relations at school, relations aggravated in the narrator's case by her class origins. Whatever her resentment of the belittling treatment she receives at the hands of the examiners, she remains in her 'place', not daring to express criticism of the system. Throughout *La Place*, her father is shown to behave in a similar manner: from his first job as cowherd at the age of 12, he submits to the poverty of his existence, rather than endeavour to eradicate it through political activity. As the narrator remarks with reference to a muted complaint made by one of her father's fellow farmworkers: 'Ce n'est pas le *Cuirassé Potemkine*' (LP, p. 32).[29]

The narrator's father does not seek to better his social position, merely to preserve it. Throughout Ernaux's writing, it is the mother who is the driving force behind the couple. When the narrator's father has a fall while working as a roofer in *La Place*, it is she who suggests that they start their own business in order to enable him to change profession and to increase family prosperity.[30] Her father's lack of ambition and his general conformism equally affect his hopes for the narrator. While proud of her academic success – as manifested by the list of examination results he carries in his wallet – he cannot comprehend her desire to leave a paid-for post as a trainee teacher: since the state has decreed what his daughter's 'place' should be, he sees no reason for her to change it. An explanation for this lack of ambition is provided by the key phrase of the text, and one which serves to elucidate its title: 'La peur d'être *déplacé*, d'avoir honte' (LP, p. 59).[31] Having grown up in a rigidly hierarchised society and had his education curtailed at the age of 12 by the narrator's illiterate grandfather, her father's respect for authority and the status quo is hardly surprising. This lifelong resignation towards social betterment fails to corroborate the narrator's comment near the work's conclusion that her father gradually loses ambition with age, a comment which may reveal the inevitable embellishment in the narrator's retrospective portrayal of him. Her father's strategy in life is one of risk minimisation: if he keeps quiet and limits his exposure to the bourgeoisie – which accounts for his resolute non-attendance at all the narrator's school activities – he reduces the likelihood of making a social faux pas. Such caution characterises relations not merely with those higher up the social hierarchy but equally with his peers, as illustrated in his reluctance to confirm that the narrator is still at school at the age of 17; just as his daughter does not wish to portray his existence as either too positive or too negative to the reader, so her father does not wish his daughter to appear either too privileged or too deprived to his customers: 'Toujours cerné par l'envie et la jalousie, cela peut-être de plus clair dans sa condition' (LP, p. 92). Indeed, throughout Ernaux's corpus, the working class is shown to be characterised by backbiting and rivalry rather than the idealised solidarity frequently attributed to it in earlier middle-class representations.[32]

The narrator mentions her father's favourite book, *Le tour de la France par deux enfants*, by way of indirect explanation for his absence of social aspirations. This book comprises a variety of clichéd sayings aimed at instilling a sense of resignation in the working class by lauding moral qualities, promoting a rigorous work ethic, and generally encouraging acceptance of the political status quo. Her father appreciates the 'realness' of the work – which is somewhat ironic, given that the remarks it contains are above all examples of bourgeois propaganda – an appreciation which may have contributed to the narrator's decision to abandon all fictional pretence in *La Place*. Her father's lack of drive may partly be attributed to his internalisation of the moralising sentiments expressed in the work. Indeed, the italicised examples of her father's speech in *La Place* reflect exactly the resignation preached by his favourite book: '*On était heureux quand même. Il fallait bien*' (LP, p. 32) or '"*Il y avait plus malheureux que nous*"' (LP, p. 44). The clichéd nature of certain remarks is highlighted by the narrator enclosing them in inverted commas in addition to italicising them. The reiteration of such commonplaces by her father can also be construed as a form of self-defence, enabling him to tolerate his living conditions, or, as the text draws to a close, his approaching death – a death given symbolic prefiguration in the opening of the first supermarket in Yvetot: 'La mort, allusivement, sous forme de maximes, on sait bien ce qui nous attend' (LP, p. 91).

The narrator's depiction of her father's life before her birth may be taken as evidence of her desire for objective accuracy. In order to illuminate her own father's character traits, the narrator's discussion initially centres on her grandfather, foregrounding the power of environmental conditioning, both in the form of broader historical circumstances and more constrained domestic ones. Her father shares his own father's suspicion of the pleasures to be gained from reading, albeit in a less virulent form. While the narrator's grandfather dislikes people reading because it reminds him of his own illiteracy – although, significantly, given his poverty, he does know how to count – her father's limited education and the overwhelmingly physical nature of his working experience produce a similar reaction: 'Il s'énervait de me voir à longueur de journées dans les livres, mettant sur leur compte mon visage fermé et ma mauvaise humeur' (LP, p. 80). His intolerance, the narrator suggests, may also be due to displacement: books become the focus of his frustration at the father/daughter divide in view of education's fundamental role in initiating that divide. The importance of the physical and the manual in defining her father's sense of self – 'En se promenant, il n'a jamais su quoi faire de ses mains' (LP, p. 88) – is also reflected in his language use. Just as he employs the term *culture* solely to refer to agriculture, he does not consider 'work' other than in physical terms: 'Travailler, c'était seulement travailler de ses mains' (LP, p. 81).[33]

If the narrator's mention of her grandfather's illiteracy and her father's distrust of the intellectual serves to highlight the distance travelled in only two generations, since she not only reads works of literature, but writes them as well, it also points to her belief in the formative influence of environment, an influence to which she too is subject and which cannot be eradicated at will. Despite reiterating her objective detachment from her working-class subject matter, the narrator's approach to representing that subject matter – the detailed description of its genealogical origins by way of historicisation – implicitly acknowledges the formative influence her working-class background continues to exert on her. In other words, while the epigraph to *La Place* may be read as indicating a willingness to acknowledge responsibility for the parent/ daughter estrangement, the work's emphasis on the conditioning power of environment partly absolves the individual from such responsibility. By providing the sociological framework in which to understand her father's subsequent behaviour, the narrator also contextualises her own conduct: it is above all the vast economic and cultural differences separating generations – differences allowing her father and the narrator to become the first family members to own property and to attend university respectively – which account for the narrator's previous alienation from her parents and the communication difficulties between parents and daughter.

As *La Place* draws to its conclusion, the narrator intervenes – as she does in *Une femme*, *Passion simple* and *La Honte* – to discuss the 'real time' elapsed since beginning her work, a period of seven months. The narrator attributes the length of time required to write the work (which does not seem unduly long)[34] to the challenge of the task she set herself – that of having to recall actual events rather than inventing imaginary ones. As with the account of her mother's senile dementia in *Une femme*, the narrator wishes to postpone the final pages of the work, pages which deal with the deterioration and demise of her father, yet is propelled by the narrative chronology to relate the circumstances surrounding her father's death. In a manner characteristic of Ernaux's writing, the narrative of *La Place* is circular, beginning and ending with a description of the death of the narrator's father, a description enclosed by accounts of two incidents from her own existence. Mirroring the content of the opening section of *La Place*, the work's conclusion details her father's final days, reiterating the announcement made by her mother on her father's death. At the work's opening, we read: 'Elle a dit d'une voix neutre: "C'est fini"' (LP, p. 13). Towards the end of the text, the narrator's description of the same event points to the interdependency of the biographical and the autobiographical by revealing the emotional catharsis writing the work has had for her: 'Juste au tournant de l'escalier, elle a dit doucement: "C'est fini"' (LP, p. 110). Re-membering the past in the form of her working-class parental heritage, striving to unify its disparate elements through her adoption of different genres, leads to greater self-integration for the narrator.

At the work's conclusion, the narrator returns to the principal subject of her metanarrative comments – her endeavour to provide a representative portrayal of her father's 'reality' – in her reference to Philippe Sollers's *L'Expérience des limites* and the work's final vignette:[35] the principal role of literature, she suggests, lies not in providing a medium in which to expound theoretical or philosophical arguments – which may partly account for Ernaux's indifference to literary categorisation and her narrator's sense of the 'unreality' of her job as university teacher – but in providing a medium for the representation of 'real life'. The work ends with the narrator in a supermarket – she too has joined 'les méchants' (LP, p. 75), as her parents called them, and is now shopping in a large store – being served by a former pupil, who presumes that the narrator remembers her, returning the reader to the opening themes of educational authority and class distinction. However, what constitute major events for some – the professional opportunities of the checkout girl – are not even remembered by others – the narrator – instead destined to become, like so much working-class experience, 'la réalité oubliée'. The narrator's sense of unease and betrayal in front of this girl, her perception of herself as a class defector, echo her feelings on passing the Capes. The narrator may now occupy the position of authority, yet could easily have been in the position of the checkout girl – while she has escaped the material constraints of her class, others have been less fortunate.[36] This meeting acts as a timely reminder that the narrator's social progess is at the expense of others, that the 'rachat' writing represents for her is always ephemeral, and must continually be reclaimed in an endeavour to combat middle-class 'forgetfulness' of the underprivileged.

UNE FEMME

With its distinct echoes of the opening sentence in *L'Etranger*, the first sentence of the work reveals a degree of precision absent from *La Place*: 'Ma mère est morte le lundi 7 avril à la maison de retraite de l'hôpital de Pontoise, où je l'avais placée il y a deux ans' (UF, p. 11).[37] This accuracy, which immediately foregrounds the importance of her mother's death for the narrator, continues throughout the work, and can be understood as a measure to help contain the emotional resonances of her subject matter by placing emphasis on the factual or objective. Dates are supplied to inform the reader of, amongst other events, the year of her mother's birth (UF, p. 24), that of her grand-mother's death (UF, p. 27), and that of her parents' marriage (UF, p. 37). With the exception of her father's date of birth and death as in-scribed on his tombstone in *La Place*, the narrator's limited use of dates in the earlier work relates solely to historical events, while, in *Une femme*, they are used to signal personal landmarks in her parents' lives, including significant developments in their social ascent: 'En 1931, ils ont acheté à crédit un débit de boissons et d'alimentation à Lillebonne' (UF, p. 39). Throughout *Une femme*, the narrator sup-presses the personal repercussions of what she is recounting less easily than in *La Place*, in part because she begins writing the work a mere 13 days after the death of her mother, while *La Place* is written 16 years after the death of Ernaux's father.[38] The narrator recognises the potential 'writerly' benefits in allowing a longer period of assimilation 'afin d'avoir la distance qui facilite l'analyse des souvenirs' (UF, p. 22), yet feels compelled to write about her mother as soon as she is able, further indicating her greater emotional involvement with the work's subject matter. If the opening sentence of the work may reveal a ves-tige of the narrator's guilt at putting her mother in a retirement home – an interpretation intimated in the work's epigraph and made explicit at the text's conclusion, '(Culpabilité de l'avoir placée là, même si, comme disaient les gens, "je ne pouvais pas faire autrement")' (UF, p. 102)[39] – such guilt is less acute than in *La Place*. Not only were any tensions between mother and daughter less pronounced than those between the narrator and her father, but the narrator of *Une femme* has had significantly longer to resolve previous differences with her mother before her death.

    In a manner analogous to the narrative structure of *La Place*, the narrator describes her dead mother at the beginning of the work (unlike

La Place, however, she is not present throughout her final hours) before going on to provide her biographical details. In these texts, the death of the parent is at the forefront of both the writing and reading process. The description of her mother's hospital bed, which resembles a cot with its 'barres destinées à l'empêcher de se lever' (UF, p. 12), testifies to her regression to a childlike state, a regression graphically documented in '*Je ne suis pas sortie de ma nuit*', in which the narrator has to assume the role of nurturer to her mother in the advanced stages of Alzheimer's disease. That the bars remain raised even after her mother's death may be taken as denoting the hospital's desire to prevent intimate contact between mother and daughter. The existence of bars not only points to her mother's continuing physical resilience at the end of her life, whatever her psychological deterioration, but also the enforced inhumanity of her living conditions. If the opening section of *Une femme* mirrors that of *La Place* in its description of the death of a parent – and in the presence of the narrator's (now ex-) husband after that death and his similarly negligible contribution to events – it differs in its portrayal of the impersonal perfunctoriness surrounding that death. The work's opening section highlights the clinical approach of the hospital staff and the ruthless inflexibility of the bureaucratic machine: the narrator's wishes are shown to come second to the speedy disposal of her mother's body. All opportunity for the expression of individual grief is swept aside as the high-speed bureaucratic process conveys her mother relentlessly to her burial: the narrator receives the telephone call informing her of her mother's death at 10 o'clock, and by 12 o'clock has returned home, having undertaken all the necessary preparations for the funeral. The proceedings following her mother's death illustrate society's desire to minimise disruption to the smooth functioning of 'normality' – even the entrance to the morgue is unmarked – and to dispense with the unpleasantness of death as quickly as possible while safeguarding its commercial viability. The bureaucratic indifference to the narrator's personal needs contrasts with the solidarity shown by the family, who accompany her to her parents' grave in Yvetot and who, however clumsily, endeavour to communicate with her. The concern shown by relatives mirrors that displayed in *La Place*, in which the family deals with the father's death with dignified efficiency.

The rapidity with which her mother's funeral takes place is particularly distressing for the narrator, whose every gesture, including the act of writing, demonstrates her longing to retain contact with the maternal body: 'J'aurais voulu que cela dure toujours, qu'on fasse encore quelque chose pour ma mère, des gestes, des chants' (UF, p. 17). For the narrator, indirect contact in whatever form is preferable to its cessation, just as her mother alive with Alzheimer's disease, however debilitated, is preferable to her deceased: 'Pour tous, il était mieux qu'elle soit morte. C'est une phrase, une certitude, que je ne comprends pas. Je suis rentrée en région parisienne le soir. Tout a été vraiment fini' (UF, p. 19). The desire for the eternal prolongation of the maternal presence, even in a purely literary form, finds its most poignant expression at the text's conclusion. As the narrator writes *Une femme*, so overpowering is her sense of that presence that the narrator is transported back to a period when her mother was still alive, while remaining fully conscious of her death. This illusory maternal presence points to the ambivalent role of writing in the work, in that while it progressively aids the narrator in accepting the irredeemable loss of the mother, writing can equally delay that acceptance by its creation of a literary doppelgänger.[40] The emotional consolation the narrator derives from such vicarious communication with her mother accounts for her wish to defer publication of the work: 'Dans ces conditions, "sortir" un livre n'a pas de signification, sinon celle de la mort définitive de ma mère' (UF, p. 69). The narrator's use of birth imagery to illustrate the revitalising effect of her literary conception of the maternal is particularly appropriate, given the mother's regression to a childlike state at the end of her life and the narrator's own adoption of the mothering role. The creative replaces the procreative, as the narrator reciprocates her mother's gift of life by giving her a posthumous literary rebirth: 'Il me semble maintenant que j'écris sur ma mère pour, à mon tour, la mettre au monde' (UF, p. 43).[41] The narrator's sense of giving birth to the maternal highlights the extent of the mother/daughter reconciliation in *Une femme* when compared to earlier works such as *Les Armoires vides*, in which the abortion can be viewed as the narrator's metaphoric expurgation of all remaining ties with her working-class childhood. A positive re-evaluation of the maternal heritage has replaced the desire to exorcise its influence. If the narrators in the early trilogy seek to escape the confines of their working-class background, from *La Place* onwards they are engaged in an antithetical quest: to re-establish contact with it through the portrayal of others, whether parents, a lover, or ordinary men and women.

The narrator's unwillingness to sever links with the maternal is manifested in her contentment that the weather throughout the month following her mother's death is similar to that at its beginning, that there remains a metereological connection between past and present. This desire to abolish the effects of time and her visceral need simply to focus on her mother rather than contextualise or analyse her existence are reflected in the narrator's initial inclination to perceive her in a series of timeless images. That inclination is tempered by the narrator's awareness that the emotional onslaught of these very personal images must be contained if she is to achieve a degree of representativeness in her portrayal: 'Je voudrais saisir aussi la femme qui a existé en dehors de moi, la femme réelle, née dans le quartier rural d'une petite ville de Normandie et morte dans le service de gériatrie d'un hôpital de la région parisienne' (UF, p. 23). As this quotation demonstrates, the expression of the narrator's intentions in *Une femme* has become less dogmatic than in *La Place*, as if recognising the impossibility of producing a purely objective portrayal of her mother – the use of the term 'aussi' signals this recognition, as does the verb 'espérer' in the following remark: 'Ce que j'espère écrire de plus juste se situe sans doute à la jointure du familial et du social, du mythe et de l'histoire' (ibid.). The impression is of a narrator more realistic about the aims of her literary project. Similarly, in her use of terms such as 'familial' and 'mythe', the narrator admits to the inevitable degree of fictionalisation involved in the writing process, stemming from the emotional proximity of mother and daughter.[42] Throughout Ernaux's corpus, the mother/daughter relationship dominates all others, and the more conciliatory tone of *Une femme*'s metanarrative remarks can be seen as an acknowledgement of the emotional significance of that relationship: the narrator can only hope to contain or neutralise – rather than eradicate – the subjective elements in the narrative by providing two accounts of her mother, one public, the other private.

The greater sense of reconciliation which permeates *Une femme* when compared to *La Place* originates in the narrator's profound affinity with her mother, an affinity based on their common gender – 'Je croyais qu'en grandissant je serais elle' (UF, p. 46)[43] – and on a mother/daughter complicity in their love of literature and erudition from which her father was excluded. While her father's world is grounded in the physical and the pragmatic, it is the mother who responds to her daughter's intellectual needs and who thereby approximates the paradigm of adulthood encountered at school in the form of her schoolteachers. In her 'public' portrayal of the mother, the narrator seeks to moderate the subjective component of *Une femme* by emphasising her detachment

from the task of documenting her mother's family history, a detachment reinforced by the substantial progress which has taken place over
only two generations. If progress is represented in pedagogical terms
in relation to her father's family in *La Place*, in *Une femme* generational
differences are shown to be above all economic: her grandmother's
recycling rituals in order to minimise waste are quite alien to her middle-class granddaughter. In the manner of nineteenth-century realists
and naturalists, the narrator presents herself as a neutral medium
through which her mother's *histoire*, and that of other members of the
working class, can find articulation: 'Ce savoir, transmis de mère en
fille pendant des siècles, s'arrête à moi qui n'en suis plus que l'archiviste'
(UF, p. 26).[44]

As in *La Place*, the narrator provides a brief biographical overview of her mother's genealogy. However, in contrast to the paternal
grandfather, the maternal grandmother, who is the dominant grand-
parent, is a keen reader, a trait she too passes on to her daughter and
granddaughter in turn. Both women are portrayed in analogous terms:
while her grandmother 'faisait la loi' (UF, p. 25), her mother is described as 'la figure dominante, la loi' (UF, p. 59). Indeed, these references to a gynocentric 'loi' may be interpreted as a ludic rejection of
the Lacanian paradigm of the child's entry into the Symbolic and subjection to male dominance in the form of the 'Nom-du-Père'. The narrator provides a series of images describing key aspects of her mother's
childhood in an attempt to reflect its essential characteristics and to
achieve a more balanced representation of its positive and negative
elements by the eschewal of direct narrative intervention. The information conveyed in these images reveals the influence of past generations on the narrator herself, an influence apparent in her tomboyish
behaviour of early childhood as described in the trilogy – her mother,
we are told, had 'les mêmes savoir-faire que les garçons' (UF, p. 28) –
as well as in the taboo status of female sexuality throughout Ernaux's
corpus, which can be traced back to the maternal grandmother's fear
of 'l'enfant naturel pour les filles' (UF, pp. 26–27). Further notational
impressions describe her mother in early and late middle age, and this
impressionistic approach is reinforced by the numerous page breaks
and narrative discontinuities, pointing to both the lacunae of memory
and the narrator's disinclination to analyse them. Despite a youth circumscribed by alcoholism and poverty – out of six children, only her
mother and one other sister did not suffer from alcohol abuse[45]– her
mother's irrepressible *joie de vivre* continues to nourish her dream of

social advancement, a dream which lies behind her choice of the narrator's abstemious, hard-working father as a husband. Once married, her mother's job as shopkeeper and bookkeeper of the family's accounts brings her into regular contact with the outside world, increasing her self-assurance and unwillingness to accept the limitations of her working-class condition. Her determination not to be defined by social class translates itself into a burning ambition for her daughter's social betterment, the repercussions of which form the subject matter of the early trilogy. The account of her mother's married life in *Une femme* concurs with the representation of the same period in *La Place*, as do subsequent events in the work – whether the Franco-Algerian war or her father's stomach operation – reinforcing versimilitude through reiteration.

The mother/daughter relationship in *Une femme* is portrayed in an ambivalent light: the narrator's mother may at times be violent or vulgar towards her daughter, yet is also extremely loving and generous, as exemplified in the sacrifices she makes to guarantee her daughter the success and social status which eluded her: 'En écrivant, je vois tantôt la "bonne" mère, tantôt la "mauvaise"' (UF, p. 62).[46]Only in retrospect does the narrator comprehend the full extent of these sacrifices – both financial and intellectual – which allowed her to attend university: 'Les gisants de la cathédrale, Dickens et Daudet au lieu de *Confidences*, abandonné un jour, c'était, sans doute, davantage pour mon bonheur que pour le sien' (UF, p. 58). As in *La Place* and throughout the early trilogy, the 'mauvaise' mother is felt most acutely in the realm of sexuality, provoking extreme hostility on the part of the adolescent narrator: 'Quelquefois, je m'imaginais que sa mort ne m'aurait rien fait' (UF, p. 62). The mother's silence on sexual matters originates in a quasi-pathological fear of the possible consequences any expression of her daughter's sexuality will entail.[47] This fear also manifests itself in a subconscious desire that her daughter remain in childhood: 'Elle essayait de me conserver enfant, disant que j'avais treize ans à une semaine de mes quatorze ans, me faisant porter des jupes plissées, des socquettes et des chaussures plates' (UF, p. 61). The narrator's perception of her mother's sexual oppressiveness as a form of betrayal in its collusion with phallocentric norms is starkly conveyed in the work: 'je confonds la femme qui a le plus marqué ma vie avec ces mères africaines serrant les bras de leur petite fille derrière son dos, pendant que la matrone exciseuse coupe le clitoris' (UF, p. 62). That the narrator continues to experience this conflation in the present points to the ongoing sense of mutilation she feels at the maternal censorship on sexuality. The damage caused by such censorship is further illustrated in the mature narrator's failure to cast off its negative repercussions in language use: 'Ainsi, j'écris de la manière la plus neutre possible, mais certaines expressions ("s'il t'arrive un malheur!") ne parviennent pas à l'être pour moi' (UF, p. 62). The example provided in parentheses is the same euphemistic threat the narrator associates with her mother in *Les Armoires vides*.

It could be argued that, just as the mother seeks to insulate the daughter in the realm of childhood, the mature narrator's profound and continuing identification with the mother indicates a corresponding daughterly desire to inhabit that same realm of attachment, demonstrating a reluctance, or, perhaps, inability to move on and assume the mother's death. The narrator's desire to return to the halcyon days of mother/daughter symbiosis may be attributed to the resolution of earlier conflicts or to the real-life death of the mother. Indeed, the recurrent image the narrator has of her mother posthumously can be viewed as confirming this desire for regression. That it is not the real 'three-dimensional' mother figure anchored in a specific historical moment whom the narrator imagines, but a type of visceral ersatz, may account for the image's continuing intensity: 'Son image tend à redevenir celle que je m'imagine avoir eue d'elle dans ma petite enfance, une ombre large et blanche au-dessus de moi' (UF, p. 105).[48] The narrator frequently dreams of her mother as she composes *Une femme*, and, on one occasion, her dream can be taken to illustrate both the narrator's unarticulated desire to regress to the mother/daughter symbiosis of childhood and the significance of sexuality throughout that childhood: 'Une fois, j'étais couchée au milieu d'une rivière, entre deux eaux. De mon ventre, de mon sexe à nouveau lisse comme celui d'une petite fille partaient des plantes en filaments, qui flottaient, molles. Ce n'était pas seulement mon sexe, c'était aussi celui de ma mère' (UF, p. 104). This image, which also occurs in *'Je ne suis pas sortie de ma nuit'*, provides the most striking description of the physiological links uniting mother and daughter, and reinforces the narrator's impression of giving literary birth to her mother through the writing of *Une femme*. Its appearance at the end of the text points to the narrator's sense of reconciliation with the mother following the writing process, in that it is in the domain of sexuality – the greatest cause of conflict between them – that it takes place. Unlike *La Place*, which employs a 'public' framework to elucidate the narrator's relationship with her father in the incidents related in its opening and concluding sections, the first and final images of the mother in *Une femme* are personal ones.

The intimacy which characterises the mother/daughter bond in *Une femme* has heterosexual echoes in both parties' perception of their relationship to the other: 'Même vivant loin d'elle, tant que je n'étais pas mariée, je lui appartenais encore' (UF, p. 69). Its similarities to the heterosexual model are most clearly articulated in the implicit parallel the narrator draws between the mother/daughter relationship and her father's relationship with her mother: 'Il me semble que nous étions tous les deux amoureux de ma mère' (UF, p. 46). It is in '*Je ne suis pas sortie de ma nuit*' that the mother/lover analogy is most fully developed. As Chapter 2 demonstrates, the traditional Oedipal scenario of daughterly separation from the mother and attachment to the father does not find illustration in Ernaux's writing, in that the mother's dominant character beyond earliest infancy leads to a prolonged daughterly identification with her and her consequent projection into the paternal role. The sense of union which permeates the narrator's relationship with her mother also stems from their geographical proximity throughout much of the narrator's adulthood. When her mother returns to Yvetot after a period of living at her daughter's house in Annecy, it is the first time that the narrator has never, at some point, shared her home: 'Une fois, j'ai pensé, "ce studio est le seul lieu que ma mère ait habité depuis ma naissance sans que j'y aie vécu aussi avec elle"' (UF, p. 83). Indeed, there is a sense in which the narrator never really leaves home, in that her mother continues to play an important role in her domestic universe throughout adulthood, a role which may further contribute to the narrator's difficulty in coming to terms with the loss of her mother. When her mother moves in with the narrator for the last time, her presence can be viewed as filling the role vacated by the narrator's husband, who has separated from her. Having lost the male partners in their lives, mother and daughter can now devote themselves fully to one another.[49]

As the narrative chronology approaches the period of her mother's life afflicted by Alzheimer's disease, the narrator would prefer to defer indefinitely the description of her mother's condition. Her aim to provide an 'authentic' portrait of her mother – an aim which also lies behind the decision to publish '*Je ne suis pas sortie de ma nuit*' – nonetheless obliges her to document her mother's traumatic decline. While the representation of that decline is prerequisite to her being able to integrate, and come to terms with, the different facets of her mother's personality, it also corresponds to Ernaux's belief that literature must challenge 'representative' norms – in both senses of the term – through the portrayal of marginalised or neglected subjects. Psychological illness is one such subject: 'Je parlais d'elle à des gens qui ne la connaissaient pas. Ils me regardaient silencieusement, j'avais l'impression d'être folle aussi' (UF, p. 93). Towards the text's conclusion, the narrator returns to the dangerous intolerance of the belief that, given the severity of her mother's degeneration, she would be better off dead, a belief mentioned earlier in the work and again alluded to in '*Je ne suis pas sortie de ma nuit*'. For the narrator, the pleasure she considers both parties to derive from the mother/daughter relationship until her mother's death is grounds enough for its continuation. The closing stages of her mother's life allow the narrator the opportunity to reciprocate, albeit on a smaller scale, the mother's self-sacrifice for the daughter, to provide whatever comfort or gratification she is able; in the absence of verbal communication, it is the emotional and the physical which unite mother and daughter.

If the metanarrative comments in *Une femme* foreground both the narrator's objectives in writing the work and her means of realising them, they equally attest to the 'real-life' healing process of the narrator. The narrator can only bring herself to write that her mother is dead approximately three weeks after the funeral, and, two months later, to read that same sentence with detachment, yet is unable to visit the area in which the retirement home is located. Later, however, she reports being able to return to the hospital where her mother died, signalling a progressive coming-to-terms with the death of her mother as her narrative takes shape. Whatever her longing to regress to her childhood role and to withdraw into a private cocoon surrounded by images of the maternal, the narrator is fully aware of the benefits of a more 'public' form of writing: by allowing others to share in her mother's life and death through literary representation and by establishing the representative components of that life, the narrator helps mitigate the sense of abandonment she feels following her mother's death. As in *La Place*, the impetus behind the narrator's desire for greater objectivity is a highly subjective one.

At the text's conclusion, the narrator has finally acquired the psychological strength to relate the events of the day preceding her mother's death. In an assertion which echoes the unificatory purpose of *La Place* ('je me sentais séparée de moi-même'), the importance of which is highlighted by its typographical separation, the narrator states calmly: 'Maintenant, tout est lié' (UF, p. 103). Writing has had a cathartic effect on the narrator, allowing the daughter to establish communication with the Other, not only in the form of the reader, but also of the mother, with whom verbal communication had ceased some time before her death. In contrast to the rapidity of the bureaucratic procedures described at the work's beginning, the writing process has enabled the narrator to give expression to her own sense of grief. This dual role of the Other, encompassing both mother and reader, and its significance to the remedial effects writing the text has had on the narrator are expressed at its conclusion: 'Il fallait que ma mère, née dans un milieu dominé, dont elle a voulu sortir, devienne histoire, pour que je me sente moins seule et factice dans le monde dominant des mots et des idées où, selon son désir, je suis passée' (UF, p. 106). For the narrator to achieve a restored sense of 'uterine' wholeness, it would appear that her mother has to be presented to the bourgeois readership of *Une femme* on its terms. This conclusion finds strong echoes in *La Place*, in which the narrator is only able to achieve a sense of restitution and reconciliation when the working-class subject matter of her text has been assimilated into the predominantly bourgeois medium of literature, an assimilation garlanded by the accolade of the *Prix Renaudot*: 'J'ai fini de mettre au jour l'héritage que j'ai dû déposer au seuil du monde bourgeois et cultivé quand j'y suis entrée' (LP, p. 111). Despite inveighing against the numerous shortcomings of bourgeois culture, the narrator's ultimate submission to it is demonstrated by her need to have it attest to the validity her parents' existence through literary representation.

CHAPTER 4

Self/representation through the M/other in the Diaries of '*Je ne suis pas sortie de ma nuit*', *Journal du dehors* and *La Vie extérieure*

This chapter examines two very different examples of the diary form in Ernaux's writing; '*Je ne suis pas sortie de ma nuit*' and *Journal du dehors/La Vie extérieure*. While the first work is a highly personal account of the physical and psychological degeneration of the narrator's mother through Alzheimer's disease, the latter two comprise a more objective series of literary snapshots, capturing everyday life in a *Ville Nouvelle* in the Paris suburbs. The adoption of the diary form in '*Je ne suis pas sortie de ma nuit*' is presented as more than mere literary convention: the narrator claims to have had no intention of publishing the diary when she wrote it. That the projected readership of the diary was apparently limited to its author may account for the uncharacteristically subjective nature of Ernaux's writing in it. The narrator's originally private conception of the act of writing in '*Je ne suis pas sortie de ma nuit*' may also be discernible in her portrayal of that act as a visceral, rather than intellectual, exercise: the diary is presented as a channel through which she can voice her thoughts and feelings 'uncensored'. The narrator's claim to have published the diary unaltered is supported by the appearance of repetitions, chronological errors – 'Je dois me tromper de date' (JSN, p. 57) – as well as the names of individuals. '*Je ne suis pas sortie de ma nuit*' constitutes the most explicitly auto/biographical text in Ernaux's corpus, in that, for the first time, we are provided with the real names of Ernaux's sons and of her ex-husband, names which first appeared in the dedication to *Ce qu'ils disent ou rien* and *La Femme gelée* respectively. It is also here that the nominal identity of the narrator's mother appears in full, unlike its more elusive counterpart 'Madame D.', whom we encounter in *Une femme*.

Where '*Je ne suis pas sortie de ma nuit*' was conceived as a diary for the narrator's personal expression and centres on the mother/daughter relationship within the confines of a hospital, both the temporal and focal scope of *Journal du dehors* and *La Vie extérieure* is significantly broader. As the titles of the works indicate, rather than provide a daily account of events within a narrowly circumscribed domesticity, *Journal du dehors* and *La Vie extérieure* can be read as the diaries, if not of Everyperson, then of the working class or socially excluded – and of the narrator herself – each work documenting the existence of suburban inhabitants over a period of six and eight years respectively, as they commute to work or go shopping. *Journal du dehors* and *La Vie extérieure* combine the representation of experiential ordinariness with the desire for greater self-knowledge characteristic of diary writing, yet generate such knowledge through the observation of the lives of others. The diary is clearly an important medium of self-expression for Ernaux, who has kept a diary since the age of 16. Her mother destroyed the first few years' entries – the maternal censorship and concern with the opinion of *autrui* invaded the author's most private domain – and the earliest surviving entries now begin from the age of 22.[1] While it is possible to view '*Je ne suis pas sortie de ma nuit*' as a continuation of that diary, the work may also be interpreted as a retributative measure against the earlier transgression of Ernaux's privacy by the mother. The woman who above all else feared the judgemental gaze of the Other on her private life, whose conduct was contained by the 'civilising' influence of the *qu'en-dira-t-on*, has that life exposed in all its intimate detail during its most vulnerable period.[2]

'JE NE SUIS PAS SORTIE DE MA NUIT'

Ernaux's narrator provides a brief introduction to her diary, which, by describing the circumstances of its composition, signals her awareness that readers may find its graphic treatment of her mother's degeneration disturbing. The distressing aspect of that degeneration and the reader's potentially negative reaction to it are later intimated in the narrator's conjecture that others may compare her mother to a witch, foregrounding both her mother's unkempt appearance and mainstream society's inability to accommodate her Otherness. This judgemental presence of the Other is typified in the attitude of a salesman the narrator encounters – a man whose own mother suffers from Alzheimer's disease – and implicitly justifies the need for her introduction: 'Sa mère aussi est atteinte de la maladie d'Alzheimer, il en parle à voix basse, il a honte. Tout le monde a honte' (JSN, p. 49). The normalising gaze of the Other is given allegorical representation in the form of the mirror in the lift the narrator takes when visiting her mother, a lift which transports her from the outside world of a smooth-functioning French society to the marginalised world of the hospital. The mirror also highlights the key role played by cultural paradigms of female beauty and the corporeal in defining female self-worth, paradigms which aggravate the narrator's apprehension of her own physical degeneration. Indeed, '*Je ne suis pas sortie de ma nuit*' can be read not only as the narrator's endeavour to reconcile herself with the death of her mother, but also to confront her own fear of ageing through the portrayal of the mother's decrepit body and the physiological mirroring of mother and daughter. As the content of *Passion simple* suggests, the narrator's awareness of the ageist conventions surrounding the sexually desirable female becomes understandably more acute as she moves beyond middle age. The role played by the mirror in the work may further be interpreted as a Lacanian prefigurement of the physical severance between mother and daughter following the former's death. The death of the mother is seen to bring with it the death of the child.

Despite the contextualising function of the introduction, the narrator claims to be indifferent to the reception of her writing as she produces it: 'Cette inconscience de la suite – qui caractérise peut-être toute écriture, la mienne sûrement – avait ici un aspect effrayant' (JSN, p. 12). As this study has suggested, however, the predominance of metanarrative comments throughout Ernaux's writing signals her narrators' perpetual awareness of the judging Other – whether in the form of the reader or the mother – and anxiety as to the interpretative strategies to be adopted by these 'invisible presences'.[3] As her narrator remarks in '*Je ne suis pas sortie de ma nuit*', 'Ma mère, sa force, son angoisse perpétuelle aussi. J'ai la même tension, mais dans l'écriture', adding in a revelatory remark: 'Mon père disait d'elle avec admiration: "Tu n'auras pas le dernier mot avec elle!"' (JSN, pp. 71–72). This narratorial anxiety also finds expression in *Journal du dehors*: 'Est-il possible de dissocier le sens présent et individuel d'un acte de son sens futur, possible, de ses conséquences?' (JDD, p. 71). Indeed, as the Introduction remarks, it was partly Ernaux's wish to contain the influential role of the readerly Other – a role she viewed the early trilogy as promoting through its more 'palatable', fictionalised subject matter –

which prompted a change in generic format in works following *La Femme gelée*. If the graphic treatment of non-mainstream subjects increases the likelihood of a hostile reception for her writing, the self-reflexivity of texts from *La Place* onwards nonetheless allows her narrators to engage explicitly with the politics of reception. The main text of '*Je ne suis pas sortie de ma nuit*' may not display the same 'proactive' resolve in setting forth the conditions of composition and, consequently, of reception as earlier works, yet its introduction can be viewed as playing a role analogous to that of the metacommentaries in *La Place* and *Une femme*, in that the narrator seeks to influence the reader's response to the work which follows. It may be the narrator's awareness that the diary format will limit her metanarrative interventions in the main body of the narrative which explains her unusually explicit interpellation of the reader in the introduction: 'En aucun cas, on ne lira ces pages comme un témoignage objectif sur le "long séjour" en maison de retraite, encore moins comme une dénonciation (les soignantes étaient, dans leur majorité, d'un dévouement attentif), seulement comme le résidu d'une douleur' (JSN, p. 13).

The narrator's decision to publish '*Je ne suis pas sortie de ma nuit*' points to Ernaux's revised perception of the role of literature, a perception, as Chapter 2 illustrates, first articulated in *Passion simple*. The desire for a definitive literary representation of 'real life' has been replaced by a recognition of the potentially infinite possibilities of re-presentation, by a characterisation of auto/biographical writing as an endlessly revisionary undertaking. The static coherence of the maternal portrait presented in *Une femme* renders it inauthentic for the narrator of '*Je ne suis pas sortie de ma nuit*':

> Peut-être désirais-je laisser de ma mère et de ma relation avec elle, une seule image, une seule vérité, celle que j'ai tenté d'approcher dans *Une femme*. Je crois maintenant que l'unicité, la cohérence auxquelles aboutit une œuvre – quelle que soit par ailleurs la volonté de prendre en compte les données les plus contradictoires – doivent être mises en danger toutes les fois que c'est possible. En rendant publiques ces pages, l'occasion s'en présente pour moi. (JSN, pp. 12–13)

The narrator's acknowledgement of the artificial homogeneity of the earlier maternal portrait, and her readiness to document aspects of her mother's existence previously unrepresented may also be indicative of an increase in narratorial confidence. After the publication of a substantial body of writing, all of which, in some respect, represents a return to origins, the need for 'une seule image, une seule vérité' is rendered obsolete. '*Je ne suis pas sortie de ma nuit*' supplements the narrative of *Une femme* – begun three weeks after the death of the narrator's mother – by providing the reader with additional perspectives on the mother/daughter relationship, a role *La Honte* fulfils in relation to Ernaux's corpus as a whole.[4] The revelation of the source of the narrator's shame in *La Honte* and its positing as the catalyst to Ernaux's entire writing project invite the reader to reassess previous works, to participate in a revisionary process of reading analogous to that which characterises the narrator's modified perception of the act of writing.

The work's composition is governed by the narrator's immediate emotional needs on returning from visits to her mother. The disordered day-to-day spontaneity which is presented as structuring the narrative of '*Je ne suis pas sortie de ma nuit*' finds correspondence in the mother's increasing psychological confusion and childlike inability to see beyond the present moment. The corporeal quality which comes to define the mother/daughter relationship as physical intimacy replaces verbal communication is reflected in the writing of the text: 'J'écrivais très vite, dans la violence des sensations, sans réfléchir ni chercher d'ordre' (JSN, p. 11). The narrator displays a visceral need to express herself – the act of writing, as much as what she writes, is cathartic for her. In '*Je ne suis pas sortie de ma nuit*', Ernaux gives free rein to the desires her narrator expresses in *Une femme* to wallow in the affective images of her mother and to abandon the 'balance' provided by a more objective account of her life.[5] It is as if, having fulfilled her 'public' duty in *Une femme* by drawing attention to the hierarchical social conditions and oppressive ideology to which her parents were subject, the narrator can now address her own needs more fully, and concentrate on the personal repercussions of the mother/daughter relationship. The earlier focus on social class, while occasionally visible in the narrator's account of her mother's behaviour in '*Je ne suis pas sortie de ma nuit*', is replaced by gender-related concerns.[6] These concerns underline the narrator's growing consciousness of the female ageing process, as her mother comes to embody a future version of the narrator herself.[7] If the narrators of *La Place* and *Une femme* strive to endow the parental subject with representative value in terms of social class, it is the mother's sexual identity which has representative force in the symbiotic blurring of mother and daughter in '*Je ne suis pas sortie de ma nuit*'. This work provides the clearest illustration of the Chodorowian relationality between mother and daughter in Ernaux's writing – a relationality touched upon in Chapter

1 – and of the narrator's sense of self as symbiotically linked to the maternal, rather than characterised by a more 'masculinist' separatism.[8] The narrator of *'Je ne suis pas sortie de ma nuit'* may not consciously seek to present her mother in a representative light, yet her gender-based affinities with the maternal body are fundamental to her self-perception.

The Reproduction of Mothering

The first diary entry is simply marked December 1983, yet, as the work progresses, the narrator begins to supply the precise date of her entries. Unlike Ernaux's other publications in diary form, *Journal du dehors* and *La Vie extérieure*, which signal only the year of entry, in *'Je ne suis pas sortie de ma nuit'* chronological precision is paramount in recording her mother's regression: if a few days can bring about a rapid deterioration in her mother's condition, one day is the difference between her being alive or dead. At the beginning of the work, when the narrator's mother can still be looked after at home, she addresses her daughter as 'Madame', displaying a civility which would appear to be characteristic of the early stages of Alzheimer's disease, in that many of the patients the narrator encounters in the hospital behave in an excessively polite manner. Earlier works foreground the determination with which the narrator's mother learns the rules of social etiquette, and, in *'Je ne suis pas sortie de ma nuit'*, clichéd forms of politeness appear so ingrained that they manage to surface from the psychological shambles of her mother's mind. This politeness may represent her mother's subconscious attempt to counter the degradation which makes up her daily life by employing socially-recognised forms of civilised behaviour in a manner similar to the dying father's effort to speak in order to demonstrate his continuing vitality in *La Place*.[9] The degeneration of the mother's intellectual faculties as the work progresses further accounts for its more subjective focus, in that, as the verbal becomes increasingly meaningless, it is the physical and affective which predominate. The narrator is gradually projected back into the mother/child relationship of early childhood, yet, this time, is forced to assume the role of mother alongside that of daughter, a role she is neither willing nor able to relinquish: 'Tout est renversé, maintenant, elle est ma petite fille. Je ne PEUX pas être sa mère' (JSN, p. 29).

As nurturer to her mother, the narrator has to feed and dress her, tasks which she undertakes gladly in that they reinforce the mother/daughter fusion of childhood. If the narrator's mother reverts to a childlike state, the narrator similarly reverts to the passionate emotions she felt for her mother in earliest childhood. Indeed, it may be that, as a non-sexual, non-threatening Other, the mother's dependence on her daughter allows the narrator to give full expression to the intensity of their relationship, rather than seek the metaphorical obliteration of her mother in order to usurp her role.[10] Eating remains one of her mother's few pleasures, and her predilection for sweets and yoghurts testifies to her regression to the world of childhood. As Chapter 1 suggests, her mother's lifelong valorisation of food and association of it with social affluence, an association originating in her impoverished working-class origins and one which may have influenced her career as shopkeeper, may further explain her focus on it at the end of her life. '*Je ne suis pas sortie de ma nuit*' also reveals the narrator's own eating disorder in the form of bulimia, a disorder intimated in *Une femme*: 'Loin de son regard, je suis descendue au fond de ce qu'elle m'avait interdit, puis je me suis gavée de nourriture, puis j'ai cessé de manger pendant des semaines, jusqu'à l'éblouissement, avant de savoir être libre' (UF, pp. 65–66).[11] This quotation encapsulates the complexities of the mother/daughter relationship in Ernaux's writing by its foregrounding of the censorious power of the maternal gaze and the narrator's subsequent need to transgress interdictions – in this case through deprivation and excess in relation to food – in order to contain maternal influence. If certain eating disorders may be attributed to the individual's need to exert control over one area of an existence which they feel escapes them, the omnipresent maternal censorship characteristic of the narrator's childhood and adolescence and the general dominance of the mother figure in the works surely contribute to the narrator's own need to do so. The narrator's love for her mother is presented as all-consuming at the time of her bulimia in '*Je ne suis pas sortie de ma nuit*', intensifying her need to break free from the confines of the parental home and assert her autonomy.

As she reverts more and more to childhood, the narrator's mother loses the ability to converse, then to walk, and finally to eat independently. When her mother can no longer eat solids, the regression is complete, and the narrator witnesses her mother's existence – and, by extension, her own – rewound to its point of departure: 'Les yeux vagues, la langue et les lèvres suçant, sortant, comme le font les nouveau-nés' (JSN, p. 83).[12] The gradual deterioration of the mother conversely mirrors different phases in the maturation process of the narrator, as she is continually transported back to events from her own childhood:

'Elle s'est levée ce matin et d'une petite voix: "J'ai fait pipi au lit, ça m'a échappé." Les mots que je disais quand cela m'arrivait dans mon enfance' (JSN, p. 19). During the early stages of her stay in hospital, her mother's oppressive attitude to sexuality – an attitude to which Ernaux's corpus repeatedly bears witness – is symbolised in her wearing two bras, an act which, once again, serves to galvanise the narrator's memory of an earlier incident from her own childhood: 'Je me suis rappelé le jour où elle avait découvert que j'en portais un sans que je le lui aie dit. Ses cris. J'avais quatorze ans, c'était en juin, un matin. J'étais en combinaison et me lavais la figure' (JSN, p. 16). The detail with which the narrator recalls such incidents – and there are numerous examples throughout the text – highlights the pervasiveness of the mother's formative influence on the daughter's sexuality.

The childlike behaviour of the patients, their identical mode of dressing and the institutionalised routine in the hospital inevitably lead both narrator and reader to draw comparisons between the hospital and school: 'je la reconduis à la salle à manger (j'allais écrire "réfectoire", comme au pensionnat)' (JSN, p. 56). The patients are like children playing at being grown-ups, whose exaggerated civility lapses into childish bullying. The patients' childlike attitude is reflected in their short-term perspective, as exemplified in the old man who telephones daily without ever contacting the right person, yet who remains perpetually hopeful: like the narrator's mother, he never loses the desire to communicate with others. The routine stasis of hospital life extends to the temperature which remains constant throughout the year, just as time, in the form of various clocks all set at different times, appears to cancel itself out. Indeed, the narrator partly attributes her mother's imaginative ramblings to a desire to compensate for the utter predictability of hospital life. The lift, which represents the journey between two segregated worlds – that of mainstream society and the peripheral hinterland of the hospital – and is consequently the scene of numerous guilty farewells for the narrator, can be viewed as fulfilling the role played by her father in earlier texts, who transports the narrator on his bike between home and school. This interpretation of the analogous function of the father/school in childhood and the lift/hospital in adulthood reinforces the Lacanian reading mentioned earlier, in that both initiate the narrator's entry into the 'Symbolic' through a parallel severance with the mother: if the young narrator's attendance at school contributes to the mother/daughter separation in childhood through her assimilation of bourgeois values, the mature narrator's visits to the hospital foreshadow a subsequent separation following the death of the mother. The similarities between the world of the hospital and the narrator's school life are reinforced when her mother responds to her daughter's arrival at the hospital in the same joyful manner as the young narrator greeted her mother's infrequent appearance outside the school; now, however, it is the mother who is confined to the closed universe to which the narrator only has superficial access. The narrator associates the slamming of the lift doors with her mother slapping her as a child, yet, as the dominant member of the partnership, it is now she who feels guilty at this symbolic rejection of the other.

The inverted nurturing roles portrayed in *'Je ne suis pas sortie de ma nuit'* and the narrator's projection of her frustrations at her mother's earlier behaviour towards her on to her own role as mother shed light on the mother/daughter relationship depicted elsewhere in the corpus. The 'bad mother' of *Une femme* and the early trilogy resurfaces, but its self-designatory aspect enables the narrator to confront the negative elements of her mother's previous behaviour: 'Je me sens sadique, comme elle l'était autrefois à mon égard. Elle me hait encore' (JSN, p. 51). The ambivalence of the mother/daughter relationship is manifested in the narrator's acute awareness of her mother's shortcomings in the past, yet fear of falling short of maternal expectations in the present, as reflected in her guilt at having put her mother in a home or at not having detected signs of her mental deterioration early enough. That ambivalence is further highlighted in a rare negative interpretation of the mother/daughter symbiosis: while mother and daughter communicate quasi-telepathically, such closeness can be felt by the narrator as a usurpation of her own personality, a usurpation intimated in *Une femme*: 'elle a poursuivi son désir d'apprendre à travers moi' (UF, p. 57). In *'Je ne suis pas sortie de ma nuit'*, the narrator perceives herself as a void, an ersatz for her dead sister, and one which has subsequently been filled by her mother, leading her to the stark conclusion, 'Je n'ai donc pas de moi' (JSN, p. 42). Having been negatively compared to her sister as a child – '"elle est bien moins gentille que l'autre"' (JSN, p. 77) – the narrator feels that her sole means of rivalling her sister in her mother's estimation is through death.

Body Doubles

In *'Je ne suis pas sortie de ma nuit'*, her mother embodies for the narrator the entire spectrum of femaleness, from earliest childhood to adolescent interest in the opposite sex through motherhood to old age and decay: 'Elle est le *temps*, pour moi. Elle me pousse aussi vers la mort' (JSN, p. 74). The female maturation process personified by her mother finds illustration in a recurrent image the narrator experiences:

> Image persistante: une grande fenêtre ouverte, une femme – moi dédoublée – regarde le paysage. Un paysage ensoleillé d'avril, qui est l'enfance. Elle est devant une fenêtre ouverte sur l'enfance. Cette vision me fait toujours penser à un tableau de Dorothea Tanning, *Anniversaire*. On voit une femme aux seins nus et derrière elle des portes ouvertes à l'infini. (JSN, pp. 49–50)

When interpreted in light of the Tanning painting, this image unites the narrator's childhood past with her sexually active present and unknown future. The title of the painting evokes the passing of time and the consequent process of physical degeneration, pointing to the role played by the narrator's age in her revisionary perspective.[13] This pictorial combination of looking back to the past and forwards to the future is echoed in the text in the narrator's memories of key incidents from childhood and in her contemplation of her own future in the form of her mother's degradation ('moi dédoublée'). As she approaches the menopause, she reassesses her own mother's experience of it, an experience which she now considers central to an understanding of the key event of childhood portrayed in the opening of *La Honte*.[14] The sense of physical specularity between mother and daughter may intensify the narrator's awareness of the imminence of her own menopause: she is one year younger than her mother was when her maternal grandmother died, an event which was shortly preceded by her mother going through the menopause. In '*Je ne suis pas sortie de ma nuit*', the narrator relates her need for eroticism with A. to the decay of the maternal body: an active sexual relationship constitutes a type of immunisation, a *défi*, against the ageing process by providing evidence of her continuing sexual attractiveness. As a middle-aged woman, she is fully cognisant of the social norms which govern women's sexual behaviour and determine what constitutes a sexually attractive woman – what the narrator refers to as 'images inchangées: beauté, jeunesse, aventure' (JSN, p. 91). While the narrator's resolve to live her life to the full is shown to stem from her acute consciousness of her mother's physical degeneration and her own maturity, it is no doubt further fuelled by the fact that she undergoes a life-threatening operation in the course of the narrative.

The narrator's enjoyment of the physical expression of her sexuality contrasts with the oppressive attitude of her mother, for whom religion acted as a form of self-censorship. It is only in its current non-sexual state that the narrator finally gains access to the maternal body. If the omnipresent eye of the divine curtailed the mother's sexual liberty, so the mother attempted to curtail the daughter's. The narrator's continuing association of religion with maternal censorship in its specific form of the gaze is highlighted when the sight of a nun reminds the narrator of her mother: 'C'était le visage de l'Inquisition. J'ai pensé avec malaise à ma mère' (JSN, p. 42). It is the nun's piercing eyes which strike her, connoting both the all-seeing eyes of the mother, as well as the oppressive role played by the narrator's Catholic education: 'Souvenir du regard de ma mère, quand j'étais enfant: elle, le confesseur' (JSN, p. 46). If the maternal gaze formed a ubiquitous feature of the narrator's childhood, it continues to penetrate her adult existence in the look of others and in the narrator's irrational belief that her mother continues to visually police her behaviour. (The narrator of *Passion simple* similarly imagines herself under the gaze of A. in his absence.) As the introduction to this chapter suggests, subjecting her mother's life to close scrutiny through writing can be interpreted as a means of countering the perceived power of the maternal gaze. Equally, the mother's gradual loss of sight at the end of her life may facilitate the narrator's candid representation of her: the far-seeing gaze and its concomitant censorship have finally been contained.

If the narrator focuses so persistently on the physical in '*Je ne suis pas sortie de ma nuit*', it is not merely because the psychological is scarcely recognisable in her mother, but, crucially, because the maternal body forms the locus of autobiographical identity for the narrator. As in *La Place* and *Une femme*, the generic demarcations separating biography from autobiography are blurred in the narrator's pluralising of the work's subject matter. The frail and decrepit maternal body of the present, so far removed from the dynamic, physical presence of the narrator's childhood, is fundamental to the narrator's own sense of identity in '*Je ne suis pas sortie de ma nuit*': 'Son corps est blanc et mou. Après, je pleure. C'est à cause du temps, d'autrefois. Et c'est aussi mon corps que je vois' (JSN, p. 20). An intertextual reference to one of the narrator's nicknames for her mother provides further evidence of her concern with the ageing process. In '*Je ne suis pas sortie de ma nuit*', the narrator reveals that she used to call her mother 'Vanné' as a child, an appellation which appears in *Les Armoires vides*, along with an explanation of its derivation: 'Vannée [sic], je voulais l'appeler Vannée, à cause de sa peau poudrée, fanée déjà, de sa robe beige en cloqué, lourde de seins' (LAV, p. 181). The sight of her mother's ageing

body – 'Cette horreur de la voir nue' (JSN, p. 24) – graphically reinforces the finiteness of the narrator's own sexual attractiveness, as conveyed by the incongruous use of the adjective 'obscène' in the following description: 'L'espace entre les lèvres et le bas du visage s'allonge,
ses lèvres s'amincissent de façon obscène' (JSN, p. 60). The severity
with which the narrator judges the physical features of older people
repeatedly foregrounds her own fear of growing older, a fear clearly
reflected in her description of one of the hospital carers as 'âgée,
effroyablement laide' (JSN, p. 70). It is difficult to conceive of a male
writer experiencing such anguish when confronted with physical degeneration.[15] If Virginia Woolf's belief that it is important for women
to think back through their mothers finds ample illustration in Ernaux's
writing, *'Je ne suis pas sortie de ma nuit'* demonstrates that they also
think forward through them, in that the valorisation of female youth-
fulness leads women to perceive loss as a future, as well as a past,
event.

The physical identification between mother and daughter is at times
so intense in *'Je ne suis pas sortie de ma nuit'* that the narrator is
unable to distinguish between the maternal body and her own: 'Jamais
femme ne sera plus proche de moi, jusqu'à être comme en moi' (JSN,
p. 22). This convergence of mother/daughter identity can also be construed as a type of coping mechanism on the part of the narrator, in
that the mother will live on in the daughter after her death, a
generational continuation of gender also touched upon in *Une femme*.
The narrator's longing for a form of continuous maternal present is
reinforced by the general absence of the pluperfect tense in Ernaux's
writing, even when portraying events in the distant past such as her
mother's childhood. However severe her mother's physical and psychological deterioration, the narrator would rather she continue to
live: 'J'ai peur qu'elle meure. Je la préfère folle' (JSN, p. 20). Her mother's occasional moments of lucidity, when she employs familiar phrases
or appears to comprehend the gravity of her situation, are sufficient to
elicit filial desire for continuing contact with her. This desire for the
eternal presence of the mother is reiterated throughout Ernaux's writing, a writing her narrator describes as motivated by 'ce désir de sauver,
de comprendre, mais sauver d'abord' (JSN, p. 103). The predominance
of the perfect tense in Ernaux's corpus can also be viewed as illustrating
her narrator's determination to defer indefinitely the petrification of
the past through its temporal connection with the present. Both this
deferral and the fluidity of mother/daughter identity account for the

lack of finality which characterises the mother's death in Ernaux's writing, a lack which belies the sentiment expressed in a remark quoted from the humorist Zouc in '*Je ne suis pas sortie de ma nuit*': '"Il faut que les gens soient morts pour être sûre de ne plus être sous leur dépendance"' (JSN, p. 26).

That the prevailing impetus behind Ernaux's writing project is preservation explains her narrators' eternal return to the subject of childhood and, in particular, to the mother figure. Analogous to the role played by the narrator's dreams in '*Je ne suis pas sortie de ma nuit*' which evolve in an atemporal framework, the literary text allows her to revitalise her mother posthumously, to return to the refuge of the maternal which characterises childhood and adolescence. Indeed, so overpowering is the narrator's desire for her mother to remain alive that she may displace her own wishes on to her: '"Je suis allée sur la tombe de papa, mais je n'ai pas pu y arriver, on me conduisait en sens inverse" (bien sûr, elle veut vivre, elle ne veut pas le rejoindre)' (JSN, p. 62). Rather than testify to her continuing determination to live, her mother's remark could equally indicate that she is being kept alive against her will. This longing for the indefinite perpetuation of the maternal is reflected in the narrator's wish to preserve her mother's clothes 'comme dans un musée' (JSN, p. 45). Similarly, the narrator would like to keep a record of her mother's phrases – a function partly fulfilled by the narrative which incorporates various examples of them and employs one in its title – and she repeatedly highlights the significance of her mother's voice, whatever its sense-making limitations. As in the young narrator's valorisation of the 'pre-Symbolic' maternal voice in *Ce qu'ils disent ou rien*, it is not the content of her mother's speech which is important to the narrator of '*Je ne suis pas sortie de ma nuit*', simply its existence: 'Il y a pour moi, toujours, sa *voix*. Tout est dans la voix. La mort, c'est l'absence de voix par-dessus tout' (JSN, p. 80). If feminist theory perceives the female's relationship to the prelinguistic mother/child fusion as stronger than the male's due to the female child's inability to identify with the father/phallus, the mother's dominant role in Ernaux's writing may further intensify the significance of the mother's voice for the daughter.

The emphasis on the physical and emotional synthesis between mother and daughter throughout '*Je ne suis pas sortie de ma nuit*' provides strong echoes of the dream recounted by the narrator in *Une femme*, a dream also evoked in this work. (Interestingly, given the 'noncensored' diary form, on this occasion the narrator does acknowledge the dream's subliminal relevance when she remarks 'Oser creuser cela' [JSN, p. 54].) As Chapter 3 argues, the confluence of genitalia portrayed in the dream can be interpreted as reinforcing the birth analogy employed in *Une femme*, an analogy which the inverted nurturing roles of '*Je ne suis pas sortie de ma nuit*' sustain. That analogy also finds expressìon in the narrator's perception of writing as a form of giving – a further type of present – a perception reiterated in both *Une femme* and *Passion simple*: 'Est-ce qu'écrire, et ce que j'écris, n'est pas une façon de donner?' (JSN, p. 79). As in *Une femme*, this characterisation of writing as offering her mother the gift of literary rebirth intimates the narrator's sense of guilt at the perceived shortcomings in her relationship with her mother, as well as her desire that writing serve to preserve and revitalise the maternal. The narrator's continuing, coterminous identity with the mother would appear to be fundamental to her creativity.

The physical specularity of mother and daughter is duplicated in other female relationships in the hospital. The narrator's mother inhabits a predominantly female universe, in which the women resemble one other physically – and sartorially, in that they all dress the same, wearing that quintessential female index, the apron – and behave in a similar, somewhat stereotypical, manner (which, given their obligatory recourse to years of social conditioning, is hardly surprising): 'À côté, la vieille refait indéfiniment son lit, pliant la couverture, la dépliant. Femmes' (JSN, p. 30). An atmosphere of complicity unites these women; communication takes place not through conventional channels, but through a more primitive means: 'Une immense agitation, mystérieuse' (JSN, p. 31). Verbal exchanges are, in every sense, meaningless – the women simply require the reassuring presence of another. Female identity in '*Je ne suis pas sortie de ma nuit*' is portrayed as interchangeable, as characterised by a constant relational displacement, in that the narrator resembles her mother, who resembles other women, who resemble the narrator: 'Comme cette petite vieille, je me recroquevillais autour de mon ventre douloureux' (JSN, p. 47). The narrator views herself as forming one link in an infinite chain of womanhood, a chain which is both synchronic in that she projects her own female identity and that of others onto other women, and diachronic, in that older women are seen to embody her own future degeneration: 'je suis maintenant un être dans une chaîne, une existence incluse dans une filiation continuant après moi' (JSN, p. 86). That physical approximation between women extends beyond the mother–daughter dyad is foregrounded when the narrator uses the condition of the other female patients to gauge her own mother's deterioration. The fluidity underlying female identity is further reinforced when, on two occasions, the narrator projects her mother into the ancillary role of domestic helper, once in the hospital and once in a dream set in her own home, a projection which may reveal her continuing guilt at her mother's subservient role when living with the family in Annecy, a role described in both *La Femme gelée* and *Une femme*. (The references to dreams throughout '*Je ne suis pas sortie de ma nuit*' can be seen to undermine Ernaux's repeated invalidation of psychoanalytic readings of her work.) Just as displacement in the form of role inversion enables the narrator to confront the more negative aspects of the mother/daughter relationship, so dreams fulfil a similar function.

The role of intertextuality in the work, as elsewhere in Ernaux's writing, reinforces the bona fide auto/biographical nature of events portrayed in that they find confirmation in earlier works, particularly *Les Armoires vides* and *Passion simple*: 'Pensé à la chatte qui est morte quand j'avais quinze ans, elle avait uriné sur mon oreiller avant de mourir. Et au sang, aux humeurs que j'avais perdus avant d'avorter, il y a vingt ans' (JSN, p. 20).[16] Familiarity with Ernaux's corpus increases the significance of remarks made by the narrator, particularly in a work such as '*Je ne suis pas sortie de ma nuit*', in which the conditions of composition limit the inclusion of parenthetical explanations. The narrator's earlier abortion is mentioned in both *Les Armoires vides* and *Passion simple*, forms the principal subject matter of *L'Evénement*, and is implicit in the reference to her university bedroom already quoted. Not only does the sight of her mother's naked body in hospital, particularly her genitalia and stretch marks, give rise to thoughts of her abortion by reminding the narrator of the birth process, but the cat she refers to was carrying kittens which also die. The fact that, until *L'Evénement*, *Les Armoires vides* and *Passion simple* were the only texts in Ernaux's corpus to treat the subject of abortion may explain their importance in this work as implicit or explicit terms of reference: the narrator may subconsciously associate her experience of abortion with her mother's regression to earliest infancy, with her own unwilling adoption of the maternal role and consequent guilt following the death of the mother/child.[17] A further link is established after her mother's death: 'Je sais que je n'ai été dans cet état que deux ou trois fois dans ma vie, après un chagrin d'amour, après l'avortement' (JSN, p. 102).

In '*Je ne suis pas sortie de ma nuit*', the recurrent juxtaposition of the mother/daughter relationship and the narrator's heterosexual relationship with A. confirms the intensity of the daughter's physical and emotional passion for her mother portrayed in *Une femme*; the mother/daughter fusion is compared to an erotic alliance. As Chapter 3 suggests, the mother's dominant and, in many ways, conventionally 'masculine' character, which can be viewed as replacing the paternal role in the traditional Oedipal scenario, may explain the narrator's adoption of a heterosexual paradigm when describing her complicitous love with her mother, a love from which her father is excluded. That the beginning of her mother's decline and her relationship with A. coincide reinforces the parallels between these relationships. The narrator compares her mother's need of love from her to her need of love from A.: 'J'ai envie de pleurer en voyant cette demande d'amour qu'elle a envers moi, qui ne sera jamais plus satisfaite (je l'ai tant aimée dans mon enfance). Je pense à ma propre demande d'amour vis-à-vis de A. maintenant, alors qu'il me fuit' (JSN, p. 32). She also attributes similar behavioural manifestations and motivations to these amorous Others: if her mother tidies up constantly to compensate for her lack of psychological order, A.'s accumulation and classification of books compensate for his lack of education.[18] As the work draws to a close, the narrator makes explicit the analogy between the strength of the physical and emotional love she feels for her mother and her sexual relationships: 'Mon enfance revenait, les dimanches après-midi où nous dormions ensemble [the narrator and her mother]. Et puis Sées, 1958, quand j'avais froid sur mon lit, obsédée par Claude G., et à cause de A. en 84. Un seul et même amour' (JSN, p. 107). The intensity of the narrator's grief at the death of her mother is illustrated by her apathy towards future amorous developments: where she had previously wagered with fate in an endeavour to influence the course of events – events which, it is presumed, related to her liaison with A. – she is now numb with indifference, evidence that, whatever the comparisons she draws, her sexual relationships pale into insignificance when compared with the strength of the mother/daughter bond.[19] The final pages of the work present the death of the mother as the summation of all the narrator's previous hardships – her past life is reduced to little more than a parenthesis, subsumed under her present suffering: 'Toutes les peines vécues n'ont été que des répétitions de celle-là' (JSN, p. 104).

In a comment which echoes the dichotomised perception of pain and pleasure underlying the narrator's sexuality in *Les Armoires vides*,

the narrator of '*Je ne suis pas sortie de ma nuit*' points to the representativeness of the emotional and physical consequences of both her mother's
illness and her relationship with A. – however personal the account of her
suffering in the work, its ultimate value lies in its representative function:
'C'est par cela, la maladie de ma mère, puis la rencontre de A., que j'ai
renoué avec l'humanité, la chair, la douleur' (JSN, p. 49). The experience
of her mother's death is presented as humbling, in that the narrator is
reminded of the relativity of past hardships and obliged to confront the
triviality of previous concerns. Somewhat paradoxically, the very intensity of the narrator's grief can be seen as revivifying, in that it reinforces
her essential humanness by situating her experience within a more global
perspective, a perspective fundamental to Ernaux's other 'diaries', *Journal
du dehors* and *La Vie extérieure*. It is in her connection with others, in her
sharing of basic life experiences, that she perceives the possibility of consolation. This focus on the Other, in default of the mother, this shift in
emphasis from the personal domain of the diary in '*Je ne suis pas sortie de
ma nuit*' to its public domain in *Journal du dehors* and *La Vie extérieure*
may also have been facilitated by the location of the private diary in the
public space of the hospital. While published several years apart, the content of these two different diary forms and their act of composition are
contiguous: not only do both serve to elucidate the self through the medium of the Other, but the private diary finishes in 1985, the year its
public counterpart begins, as if to confirm that the death of the mother
necessitates a desire to seek self-representation elsewhere.[20]

JOURNAL DU DEHORS AND *LA VIE EXTERIEURE*

Ernaux's disregard of conventional generic boundaries and her desire to
transgress established forms as highlighted in the Introduction find illustration in her use of the diary form in *Journal du dehors* and *La Vie
extérieure*, a diary form which, to employ Michel Tournier's phrase, is
more of a 'journal extime' than a 'journal intime'. The works' titles and
the epigraph by Rousseau in *Journal du dehors* – 'Notre *vrai* moi n'est pas
tout entier en nous' – immediately suggest to the reader that the quintessentially private genre of diary writing has undergone substantial modification in the works. Ernaux takes a genre characterised by subjective self-
scrutiny within a narrowly defined environment, and turns that scrutiny
on the general public of a Paris suburb to produce works rivalled only
by *La Honte* for their objectivity. If the texts' explicit focus on non-

personal relationships differs from that of earlier works, *Journal du dehors* and *La Vie extérieure* continue to incorporate a tenet fundamental to Ernaux's writing since *La Place*: the role of the Other in promoting self-understanding; *Journal du dehors* and *La Vie extérieure* perpetuate Ernaux's ethnological belief in the detailed observation of others as a basis for self-knowledge.

JOURNAL DU DEHORS

For many readers, the publication of this work provided confirmation of Ernaux's increasing resistance to the lure of writing about family relationships in the past: from *Les Armoires vides* to *Journal du dehors*, Ernaux's corpus can be seen to reflect a gradual extension of referential horizons, moving from a focus on the narrator and her childhood in the early trilogy, to her parents as she reconciles herself with her past in *La Place* and *Une femme*, to a non-family relationship in the present in *Passion simple* before describing the lives of anonymous people she encounters in contemporary urban society in *Journal du dehors*. However, the subsequent publication of '*Je ne suis pas sortie de ma nuit*', *L'Evénement* and, above all, *La Honte*, by their return to the familial – and familiar – subject matter of earlier works, testifies to the continuing power that lure holds for her. If the sheer number of *dramatis personae* and their relationship to the narrator in *Journal du dehors* differ significantly from previous texts in Ernaux's corpus, many of the individuals portrayed endure the same social exclusion as the customers and family members in the early works, just as a similar political motivation to extend the boundaries of literary representation, to include the excluded, fuels the writing of *Journal du dehors*. That the sense of social exclusion experienced by a working-class narrator in a small Norman town in the 1950s finds duplication in the lives of the inhabitants of a Parisian suburb in the 1980s and 1990s highlights the continuing relevance of the political impetus behind Ernaux's literary project. The formative role played by the narrator's past is also apparent in the choice of vignettes which constitute the work: 'D'autres fois, j'ai retrouvé des gestes et des phrases de ma mère dans une femme attendant à la caisse du supermarché' (JDD, p. 106). (Interestingly, her mother is given the 'superior' role of client in this recollection, rather than her usual one of shopkeeper.) A remark made in '*Je ne suis pas sortie de ma nuit*' corroborates this interpretation of the 'outside' focus in *Journal du dehors* as partly reflecting the narrator's continuing endeavour to engage with the past in the form of the m/other: 'Comme si au-dehors je la [her mother] cherchais. Dehors, c'est le monde. Avant, elle était quelque part dans le monde' (JSN, p. 108). The opening sentence of *Journal du dehors* offers further evidence of the subjective drive behind the narrator's selection of vignettes, in that it can be read as underlining the central role played by her mother's Alzheimer's disease in 1985, the year of the first entry: 'Sur le mur du parking couvert de la gare R.E.R. il y a écrit: DÉMENCE' (JDD, p. 11).

Ernaux's narrator in *Journal du dehors* provides transitory impressions of the contemporary urban landscape of a Parisian suburb through her fragmented documentation of exchanges between individuals participating in everyday activities, whether shopping or commuting; to employ a de Certeauian turn of phrase, *Journal du dehors* depicts how 'les pratiquants de l'ordinaire' consume public spaces.[21] While such activities do not habitually form the subject matter of literary representation, they nonetheless make up a significant proportion of most people's day-to-day existence. Consequently, the material infrastructure on which these daily trajectories depend is shown to play a fundamental role in the individual's biographical trajectory in *Journal du dehors*: 'Neuf années de ma vie vont se refermer par un changement de parcours Cergy-Paris, il y aura le temps du train Cergy-Saint-Lazare et le temps du R.E.R. A.' (JDD, p. 75).[22] It is the very ordinariness of the surroundings the narrator records which is their most striking feature, and her familiarity with them is made clear from the work's opening: this narrator is part of, as well as apart from, the landscape she portrays; she is both participant and observer, remarking on the arrival of a new saleswoman in one of the shops she frequents or on the length of time another has been employed. The people who populate *Journal du dehors* – the 'petites gens' of Mitterrand's patronising reference (JDD, p. 39) – are individuals with their own life history, yet that history is shared in part by the narrator. In many of the scenes described, the narrator's pronominal usage intimates her sense of solidarity, as well as familiarity, with her subject matter: 'Il chante toujours les mêmes chansons, qu'on a apprises à l'école ou en colonie de vacances' (JDD, p. 20); 'Nous sommes devant le distributeur de billets du centre commercial' (JDD, p. 28). It may be that the void left by the death of the mother in '*Je ne suis pas sortie de ma nuit*' fuels the narrator's desire to ensconce herself in the familiar world of those same 'petites gens' who populated her childhood landscape.

As in *La Place* and *Une femme*, the narrator's evident familiarity with the universe she portrays, a familiarity stemming from both her shared social origins and prolonged contact with the people she is describing, reinforces the veracity of her accounts. The narrator in *Journal du dehors* is, however, markedly less interventionist than her counterparts in *La Place* and *Une femme*. The narrator may select and describe the entries, but generally avoids imposing her own interpretative grid on them: the fragmented format of the work and the disparateness of the entries it provides, as well as the narrator's desire to let others speak for themselves, work against the explicit formulation of a unifying, coherent thesis. The greater narratorial neutrality of this work is facilitated by the prevalence of third-person rather than first-person accounts, in that the cinematic quality and brevity of these self-contained entries introduce a distance between text and reader. This sense of detachment which permeates the reading process in *Journal du dehors* is given allegorical illustration in an entry which describes a seductive male voice-over urging customers in a shop to purchase particular products. When the narrator sees the man to whom this previously free-floating 'third-person' voice belongs, she is struck by the incongruity between the impression given by his voice and the unattractive real-life individual. Unless confronted with the 'first-person' source of the utterance, the reader need never revise their preconceptions but can remain cocooned within their own palliative version of 'reality'.

This account precedes an important comment by the narrator – one of the few direct interventions in the work – in which she contrasts her occasional use of the first person as a means of embarrassing or shaming the reader, of making them confront 'la réalité oubliée' (LP, p. 101) of working-class, suburban life through direct implication in it, with the greater impartiality inherent in the use of the third person, an impartiality which may result in an inaccurate impression on the part of the reader/shopper. In other words, while the use of the third person reflects the narrator's desire to give the reader greater hermeneutic freedom, a possible consequence of that freedom is a reduction in the work's 'political' potential in that it does not oblige the reader to engage fully with its content. Such a reduction is apparent in the narrator's account of visitors' reaction to Imelda Marcos's wealth when visiting a museum in which its acquisitions are displayed; they appear more interested in her vast array of underwear than in the political regime which allowed it to be accumulated in the first place. Like the museum, *Journal du dehors* displays a tendency to subsume the political in the personal in its use of anecdotal evidence to document social exclusion. That the narrator occasionally makes explicit her criticism of social hierarchies may stem from her belief that the reader, like the visitors to the Marcos museum, needs to be reminded of the political subtext to the work.[23]

The 'dehors' of the work's title further corroborates a political reading of its content in that it can be taken to designate not only the work's more detached manner of representation in the third person but also its general subject matter, referring both to the public domain and the socially excluded who inhabit it – and who remain outside the parameters of literary representation. While the opinions of 'la classe dominante' are public currency, those of 'la classe dominée' are not sollicited: 'Dans *Libération*, Jacques Le Goff, historien: "Le métro me dépayse." Les gens qui le prennent tous les jours seraient-ils dépaysés en se rendant au Collège de France? On n'a pas l'occasion de le savoir' (JDD, p. 47). On the rare occasion when the socially excluded or members of 'la classe dominée' do acquire mediatic representation, its anodyne form simply perpetuates the status quo by playing to the prejudices of 'la classe dominante'. In extreme cases, those unable or unwilling to participate in mainstream society are either removed from it and reduced to living on the streets or else accommodated in purpose-built seclusion in institutions such as the 'Maison de Nanterre' which features on a television programme reassuring 'la classe dominante' of the social benefits of marginalisation.[24] The media are shown to play a key role in formulating public response to contemporary events, as in their support for the strike of predominantly middle-class students over that of working-class railwaymen. Those inhabiting the social periphery in *Journal du dehors* include the racially marginalised, and their experience is equally subject to misrepresentation by the media, when it is represented at all. With reference to two children who die of starvation, the narrator remarks: 'Personne ne pense à dire, ne veut dire que le médecin, inconsciemment, n'examinait pas ces enfants d'un couple du quart monde avec la même attention qu'il portait à ceux d'une famille de cadres moyens' (JDD, p. 60).[25]

If Ernaux's narrator criticises the misrepresentation of the socially excluded in a variety of media, ranging from journalistic articles to television programmes, *Journal du dehors* implicitly validates the literary representation of working-class experience by presenting it directly to the reader with neither a discursive nor fictional framework to justify it. The content of *Journal du dehors* aims to redress such mediatic bias by allowing the socially excluded to express themselves rather than have a reader-friendly voice-over speak for them. For Ernaux's narrator, the resultant fragmentation or diminution of the work's political impact is clearly preferable to a coherent representation in which the individuals portrayed are little more than ventriloquists' dummies. Through the presentation of apparently insignificant encounters or dialogue involving the socially excluded, the narrator endeavours to capture contemporary French society from the perspective of the underside rather than the usual 'Le Goffian' angle.[26] It is the disparity between the prevalence of social exclusion in French society and its absence in literary representation which *Journal du dehors* seeks to remedy. As the Introduction highlights, for Ernaux, literature's role is not to reinforce the reader's preconceptions by portraying the '*déjà-vu, déjà-lu, déjà-fait*',[27] but to disturb, to give permanent inscription to subjects, which, while representative of human experience, are deemed unsuitable for literary representation. With reference to an account of Ania Francos's cancer, she writes: 'On ne peut pas *lire* cela, nous pensons habituellement tout par rapport à la vie' (JDD, p. 40). *Journal du dehors* displays this same democratic desire to expand the conventional range of literary subject matters to include the typically non-, under- or misrepresented.[28]

The work's emphasis on the public domain, on outside spaces, also explains why its principal recurrent characters are the homeless – indeed, an entire range of beggars and begging techniques is portrayed.[29] While the narrator is critical of the conformity which drives individuals to display the material attributes or cultural indicators deemed appropriate to their social status – and she is particularly scathing of middle-class intellectuals whom she portrays as out-of-touch and elitist – the marginalisation of the excluded partly isolates them from such conformity. Many of the individuals depicted appear as distilled versions of humanity in that, having renounced their allocated role, they are no longer dependent on the usual social props to convey their status and are more truly themselves. The narrator's interest in beggars may also stem from an implicit association between her role as writer under constant public scrutiny and the lack of privacy which characterises the lives of the homeless: just as they must become indifferent to the judgemental eye of the Other if they are to lead an existence in the public domain, so the writer must endeavour to contain the influence of the omnipresent gaze of the readerly Other.

Social exclusion in *Journal du dehors* is not limited to the homeless or poor, but is shown to characterise many everyday situations, in which 'minority' participants are made aware of their marginal status. At the butcher's, for example, people who are single, and who neither have nor desire the standard version of 'domestic bliss' – and the meat consumption which accompanies it – are clearly marginalised, as are lone travellers at railway stations. Society is presented as stigmatising those who do not possess the conventional symbols of social success and integration, whether in the form of established heterosexual relationships or material wealth. If the narrator's social origins account for her empathy with the poor and destitute, her current financial and cultural capital allows her to witness instances of marginalisation at the upper end of the social spectrum: in *Journal du dehors*, an account of a blind beggar is followed by a vignette set in an art gallery. The exclusiveness of the gallery is reflected both in the money required to buy a painting and in the cultural codes required to participate in an appreciation of its content. Whatever the milieu, social exchanges are presented as rigidly hierarchised, whether between a customer and checkout woman, or a university lecturer and her students.[30]

By her representation of events which involve the verbal exchanges and anecdotes of others (resulting in a *mise en abîme* of narration in which the narrator narrates others narrating), the narrator signals the omnipresence of storytelling in everyday life. Whether describing an advertisement which employs a range of narrative approaches to promote a particular service or product – 'Un échantillon de fiction' (JDD, p. 30) – or overhearing a conversation between passengers on a train, the narrator points to the incorporation of literary techniques in day-to-day language use. Communication is shown to comprise the standard components of narrative, including character, plot, digression, and eventual dénouement, as individuals endeavour to confer a sense of order on the spontaneity of day-to-day occurrences.[31] Even in the butcher's, the manner in which a woman orders a piece of meat is given a literary slant: 'poème de la vie domestique se récitant avec satisfaction, agrémenté de détails descriptifs' (JDD, p. 42).[32] Throughout *Journal du dehors*, there is a sense of life reflecting art, with people skilfully manipulating their oral narratives in order to arouse interest in the interlocutor and, indeed, anyone else within hearing distance. This process of consciously transmitting a private exchange to a public forum is inverted when Marguerite Duras and Jean-Luc Godard have a televised tête-à-tête as if on their own; both types of exchange are portrayed as equally disingenuous. In *Journal du dehors*, as in the opening section of *Passion simple*, the narrator perceives the act of narration – whether oral or written – as comprising an erotic value, a value linked to the narrator's dominant role in influencing readerly reaction: 'Façon impudique de raconter, exhibition du plaisir de la narration, ralentir le processus qui mène à la fin, augmenter le désir de l'auditoire. Tout récit fonctionne sur le mode de l'érotisme' (JDD, p. 46).[33] This Barthesian perception of the eroticism inherent in the act of writing is linked to the writer/lover's acute, if veiled, awareness of the Other in the narrator's description of a young couple who behave as if they were alone: 'Mais c'est faux: de temps en temps ils regardent les voyageurs avec défi. Impression terrible. Je me dis que la littérature est cela pour moi' (JDD, p. 91). This avowal confirms not only the fundamental importance Ernaux attributes to literature's provocative function, but, more significantly, that the imaginary presence of the Other is a constant in the act of writing.

Throughout the work, the narrator highlights the absence of meaningful interaction between people, their reluctance to engage with one another and the consequent individualism which expresses itself through the association of material wealth and self-worth.[34] The relationship between financial capital and social exclusion accounts for the work's focus on the commercial – money and shopping are recurrent themes. Commercialism has become the new religion, as conveyed in the narrator's comparison of an autobank to a confessional,[35] of a hypermarket to 'une cathédrale de verre' (JDD, p. 50), and by her reference to 'un certain ordre social et commerçant' (JDD, p. 43), as if the two are indissolubly linked. Shopping's allure is in part attributable to the importance of material possessions in constructing a successful social persona. *Journal du dehors* highlights the quasi-hypnotic seductiveness of the shopping environment, which, through a range of advertising techniques, creates a sense of need in customers, which subsides as soon as they step outside the commercial environment. The manipulative power of consumerism is disguised behind an educative façade, as voice-overs explain the origin of particular festivals, before detailing the multifarious products required in order to celebrate them. The influence of the commercial is also apparent in the conflation of innovation and social progress, and in society's general valorisation of novelty throughout *Journal du dehors*, whether it take the form of the *Ville Nouvelle* in which the narrator lives, the constant incitement to buy new and fashionable possessions, or even her new commuter route in the RER, which reflects 'Le vingt et unième siècle après le XIXe de la gare Saint-Lazare' (JDD, p. 87).[36]

While most of the fragments in *Journal du dehors* relate a class-based exclusion, whether portraying those who exercise it or, more commonly, those who suffer from it, others centre on aspects of female sexuality. In a highly disturbing account, the narrator provides a detailed description of clitoridectomy, an act given symbolic representation in *Une femme* when describing her mother's sexual oppressiveness. In other vignettes, this focus on sexuality appears deliberately provocative, as in the following remark: 'on ne voit aucun inconvénient à insulter Dieu mais rares sont ceux qui acceptent de cracher sur le crucifix (sans doute moindre encore aurait été le nombre de ceux qui se serviraient de celui-ci comme d'un godemiché)' (JDD, p. 77). Similarly, when a pickpocket attempts to steal from the narrator, her reaction is unexpected: 'Plus humiliée encore que tant de maîtrise, d'habileté, de désir, ait pour objet mon sac à main et non mon corps' (JDD, p. 102). These examples make clear the role played by the narrator's personal history in governing the selection process and in influencing her interpretation of the scenes she observes. They point to the traumatic curtailment of all sexual expression throughout the narrator's childhood; the fundamental role played by religion in reinforcing that curtailment; and the mature narrator's insecurity about her sexual attractiveness. Yet, whatever the imbrication of the personal and the political, the narrator also highlights her narrative role as impartial vehicle or facilitator: 'Je suis traversée par les gens, leur existence, comme une putain' (JDD, p. 69).[37] The projected role of the first-person pronoun throughout Ernaux's writing echoes this analogy, in that it implicates the reader, obliging them to take up and fill the subject position it designates.

The fragmented format of *Journal du dehors* reflects the transitoriness and lack of sustained human contact characteristic of suburban living.[38] Individuals are shown to perform essential tasks with minimum interactive requirements in an increasingly functional environment: 'Le ramasseur de caddies des Linandes n'est plus là. Maintenant il y a des chariots à pièces' (JDD, p. 39). The world portrayed is an anonymous one, where communication is infrequent and isolation usual. When describing an underground car park, the narrator remarks: 'On n'entendrait pas les cris en cas de viol' (JDD, p. 29). The shopping centres portrayed are soulless, featureless masses of concrete which can only be reached by car. However, just as the narrator is able to detect beauty in this modernised, commercial environment, so too the consequences of such existential fragmentation are not perceived as wholly negative. If the urban environment has aggravated social exclusion by reducing opportunities for interaction and, therefore, for collective responsibility, it has nonetheless allowed the narrator to provide a more objective selection of snapshots, to attain the emotional distance she views as prerequisite to representativeness: 'Aucune description, aucun récit non plus. Juste des instants, des rencontres. De l'ethnotexte' (JDD, p. 65).[39]

The narrator may enjoy the freedom the suburban landscape allows her, yet the existence of *Journal du dehors* testifies to her desire to diminish the sense of alienation experienced by those who inhabit it, including herself. That alienation is conveyed in the repeated references to people avoiding eye contact with one another – 'On réussit à éviter, sans les regarder, tous ces corps voisins de quelques centimètres' (JDD, p. 14) – an avoidance given symbolic significance in the number of blind people who figure in the text. Indeed, just as her counterpart in *'Je ne suis pas sortie de ma nuit'* endeavours to combat the power of the maternal gaze by focusing on the mother, the narrator's constant turning of her gaze on the world around her can be viewed as an endeavour to combat suburban anonymity.[40] The narrator attributes her selection of vignettes to the need to locate her own character traits in the people she is describing in order to feel closer to them. The concluding remarks of *Journal du dehors* echo an earlier comment in *La Place*, in which the narrator seeks aspects of her father in the anonymous individuals around her:

> C'est donc au-dehors, dans les passagers du métro ou du R.E.R., les gens qui empruntent l'escalator des Galeries Lafayette et d'Auchan, qu'est déposée mon existence passée. Dans des individus anonymes qui ne soupçonnent pas qu'ils détiennent une part de mon histoire, dans des visages, des corps, que je ne revois jamais. Sans doute suis-je moi-même, dans la foule des rues et des magasins, porteuse de la vie des autres. (JDD, pp. 106–07)[41]

This image – which further recalls the birth analogy used in *Une femme*, where the inscription of the maternal is perceived as a form of giving birth – points to the narrator's fundamental belief in the representativeness of individual experience, whatever the existential isolation of modern society, a representativeness founded on the past's contiguity with the present.

LA VIE EXTERIEURE

Annie Ernaux's most recent publication in diary form, *La Vie extérieure, 1993–1999* constitutes both a chronological and thematic continuation of her earlier diary, *Journal du dehors*. Like its predecessor, the work's emphasis is on the revelatory function of the Other – whether human or material – a function which similarly privileges the interconnectedness of individuals over the anonymity of their surroundings. This interconnectedness is again reflected in the representative role of the 'je transpersonnel' in *La Vie extérieure*, in that the diary entries portraying the narrator's environment are selected both in order to gauge particular developments in her personal trajectory and to provide sociological documentation of a segment of contemporary French society. Time passing is conveyed not through an inner existentialist or metaphysical anguish, but through alterations in the material and human composition of her urban landscape, which act as potent reminders of how rapidly the present becomes history:

> La sensation du temps qui passe n'est pas en nous. Elle vient du dehors, des enfants qui grandissent, des voisins qui partent, des gens qui vieillissent et meurent. Des boulangeries qui ferment et sont remplacées par des auto-écoles ou des réparateurs de télés. Du rayon de fromage transféré au bout du supermarché, lequel ne s'appelle plus Franprix mais Leader Price. (LVE, pp. 21–22)

Whether relating the end of Mitterrand's presidency or the advent of the euro, the narrator repeatedly foregrounds the imbrication of the personal and political, of the local and inter/national, in her interpretation of events as signposting stages in her own maturation process.[42]

La Vie extérieure demonstrates a more acute awareness of the passing of time than *Journal du dehors*, an awareness entirely fitting with the historical period it records, a period directly preceding the third millennium. Subtending the work is the desire to preserve the present in writing, to leave a trace of, and for, history, in an endeavour to counter what the narrator perceives as the classist distortion in the representation of contemporary French society by the media. If earlier narrators fail to relate to the working-class experience portrayed by middle-class male writers, the narrator of *La Vie extérieure* condemns the mediatic bias which ignores the everyday 'reality' of the socially marginalised, a bias which the unrepresented have no power to challenge. In a remark which provides close echoes of the narrator's description of her objectives in writing *Une femme*, she states: 'Mais l'art n'est pas cette chose au-dessus de l'humanité' (LVE, p. 19).[43] The narrator repeatedly condemns the valorisation of the purely artistic over the human, and the purported superiority of the eternal and universal qualities of art over the mortal and individualistic nature of humans – *La Vie extérieure* posits 'real' human beings as the most interesting and significant vestiges of civilisation, not their fictional version in literature or painting.[44] Ernaux's narrator signals the narcissistic insularity required to engage intellectually and emotionally with a work of art while ignoring the social exclusion of one's fellow citizens: 'La vie extérieure demande tout, la plupart des œuvres d'art, rien' (LVE, p. 128). The narrator may express uncertainty as to the power of art to reduce human suffering and exclusion – there is no doubt that a depressing sense of helplessness pervades the work – yet unless art represents 'real' people and places and is about, rather than above, ordinary humanity, it has little hope of doing so.[45]

La Vie extérieure documents the contemporary urban environment, an environment presented as centring on the commercial – as in *Journal du dehors*, there are a number of scenes set in shopping centres, or relating people travelling to and from them by public transport – and on the mediatic.[46] This work highlights the tenuousness of a community sentiment founded on shared modes of transport or material requirements.[47] The absence of disinterested interaction with, or altruism towards, the Other and the predominance of commercial materialism are epitomised in a checkout girl's perfunctory greeting to the narrator when she is about to make a purchase: the narrator is perceived solely in terms of her potential buying power. However, as in *Journal du dehors*, the depiction of the commercial environment incorporates positive elements. In its emphasis on the similarities between past and present epochs, *La Vie extérieure* can be seen to present an optimistic picture of the shared components underlying and unifying human experience.[48] This representation of the 'global fusion' of individuals at both a local and inter/national level equally encompasses the environments they inhabit: 'Insensiblement, la gare de Cergy-Préfecture s'est mise à ressembler, en modèle réduit, à toutes les gares du monde où il y a du monde, Marseille, Vienne, Bratislava' (LVE, p. 66). The fundamentally specular relationship uniting the individuals and habitats portrayed in the work can be seen as a further manifestation of the drive for representativeness expressed in earlier works such as *La Place* and *Une femme*. Indeed, the frequent inclusion of the quintessentially 'Ernausian' term 'signe(s)' draws attention to the 'transpersonal' significance of the components of the narrator's environment, components which comprise 'les signes d'une époque, rien d'individuel' (LVE, p. 88).

While located in the contemporary suburban environment, *La*

Vie extérieure repeatedly foregrounds the recurrence of age-old human traits and dramas within it. The past remains present, whether in its artistic rendition in songs or paintings – as is the case throughout Ernaux's corpus, songs constitute a particularly emotive form of representation for her narrator – or in people's manner of behaving.[49] Modernity and social progress have done little to eradicate the prejudiced exclusion of peripheral figures, as signalled by the narrator's descriptions of an incest victim ostracised by the local village population as 'une héroïne antique face à un chœur en furie' (LVE, p. 17); of a deceived husband as tainted by the 'insulte anachronique' (LVE, p. 59) of cuckold; and of a beggar as 'plus pauvre et plus malheureux qu'un paysan du temps de Molière' (LVE, p. 77). If the quasi-ritualistic behaviour paradigms uniting past and present are given positive expression in the account of a bride-to-be's wedding preparations or in young women's primitive sexual excitement when they experience 'quelque chose de la chasse ancestrale, des yeux fauves du mâle guettant la femelle au travers des feuillages' (LVE, p. 46), the ongoing exclusion of those who fall outside social norms points to a fundamental lack of humanitarian progress: the plague victims of the past have become the Aids sufferers of the present. In other words, if the diary entries of *La Vie extérieure* posit the existence of archetypal human traits as evidence of the potential for greater social integration, the 'realised' examples of human conduct they portray frequently undermine such potential. This emphasis on present manifestations of past forms of behaviour and *mœurs*, on the ahistorical aspects of human experience, imbues the work with biblical echoes – echoes again reflective of the proximity of the historical moment being recorded – as conveyed in the narrator's perception of an early morning trip to the supermarket as taking place 'au bord de l'Éden, premier matin du monde' (LVE, p. 27). The biblical associations inherent in the recurrent representation of supermarkets as bountiful terrestrial paradises are reinforced by the narrator's perception of shopping centres as partly duplicating the role of the Church in earlier times.

The sense of helplessness or, more pessimistically, indifference towards the Other which pervades the work informs the individual's response both to international events – as manifested in the narrator's repeated frustration with the general public's lack of concern for the fate of the Bosnians[50] – and to the presence of a multifarious array of beggars in the work.[51] As in *Journal du dehors*, *La Vie extérieure* seeks to make visible a segment of the population whose lack of conformity to mainstream social values renders them invisible to the public at large. Indeed, beggars are portrayed as literally having to shout at passers-by to make them confront the 'reality' of social exclusion.[52] In both texts, beggars adopt a range of different techniques in an endeavour to engage the public's attention – in an age characterised by novelty, they too must display an entrepreneurial spirit. However, even their willing adherence to a mainstream work ethic through the selling of newspapers for the homeless fails to produce greater social integration – the valorisation inherent in the gaze of the Other continues to be denied them: the unemployed or socially excluded are both too familiar and too prevalent to arouse visual interest. In a manner analogous to the narrator's attribution of values in *Les Armoires vides*, 'la classe dominante' in *La Vie extérieure* epitomises the normative 'vrai' from which the marginalised are excluded: 'De plus en plus, ces journaux de la charité – que personne ne considère comme de "vrais" journaux, ni leur vente comme un "vrai" travail – apparaissent comme une mesure dérisoire pour accommoder la pauvreté, voire empêcher qu'elle ne devienne dangereuse' (LVE, pp. 40–41).

The greater pessimism in *La Vie extérieure*'s portrayal of social relations when compared to *Journal du dehors* is further exemplified in the more prominent role played by racism in the work. While Africans and 'Beurs' populate the numerous diary entries as members of the Parisian public, the narrator makes clear her concern about the growing racism affecting French society both through the provision of statistics – 'Quarante-cinq pour cent des gens trouveraient bon qu'il y ait des députés du Front national à l'Assemblée' (LVE, p. 73) – and specific examples of racist crimes, as in the murder of Imad Bouhoud. *La Vie extérieure* points to the state's tacit sanctioning of racist conduct among its employees in its depiction of a social security employee's treatment of those unable to speak French (LVE, p. 98), or of the CRS's refusal to let any non-white schoolchildren participate in a demonstration (LVE, p. 106). The narrator also comments on the racism implicit in such euphemistic terms as '"les jeunes des banlieues"' (LVE, p. 118), and intimates that the French public's sympathy for the Kosovans stems less from political empathy than from their relatively non-threatening Otherness: 'Et les femmes portent des fichus et des jupes longues comme nos paysannes d'autrefois' (LVE, p. 125).[53] As in *Journal du dehors*, those confined to the social periphery are shown to possess an awareness of, and engagement with, the human condition which materialism has anaesthetised in others. *La Vie extérieure* portrays the political involvement of mainstream society as limited to the verbal, as paying lip service to an egalitarian social agenda, while endeavouring to disguise the less pleasant aspects of human existence more efficiently. A law forbidding mendicity is the logical conclusion to this desired conflation of the invisible with the non-existent. Beggars constitute an annoying reminder that the Panglossian representation of modernity promoted by the media has yet to infiltrate 'real life': 'Vision qui nie la civilisation et le progrès' (LVE, p. 59). However much individuals may seek to appear politically or racially correct, their concern for the Other is revealed as superficial – solidarity in *La Vie extérieure* is an ephemeral affair, originating in an egotistic desire to improve one's self-image rather than the quality of life of the Other: social inequalities and indifference to their eradication characterise the French society represented in the work.

Like *Journal du dehors*, *La Vie extérieure* is particularly scathing of middle-class intellectuals, whom it represents as a self-selecting and self-satisfied elite, concerned above all with the social status which accompanies their professional success rather than its deservedness in the first place.[54] In stark contrast to the narrator, the conduct of the writers and intellectuals portrayed in the work highlights their belief in 'la supériorité du monde des idées sur le monde réel' (LVE, p. 107), and in the distinct separation of the two. When given the occasion to engage in dialogic exchange with the Other in an endeavour to eradicate social inequalities, they seek either to display their own erudition – as in the audiences who attend a talk by the writer Taslima Nasreen or a presentation by the academic at the *Ecole normale supérieure* – or perceive their mere presence at political events as evidence of their philanthropic intent: no further action is deemed necessary. The writers who protest against the 'loi Debré' are ironically shown to indulge in the same form of social exclusion as they have come to denounce, only interacting with those who form part of their literary coterie. The work repeatedly criticises the condescension and political naivety manifested by the 'dominants' towards the socially excluded, whether on the part of the Mercedes-driving 'socialist' schoolteacher or the politician Alain Madelin, whose ignorance of everyday 'reality' is illustrated in his conviction that the obvious solution to being unemployed is to become self-employed. Whatever the revolutionary sentiments of France's past, *La Vie extérieure* paints a depressing picture of the conservatism at the heart of contemporary French society. Individualistic indifference to the Other reinforces the stultification of the current social order, which promotes consumerism over humanism: 'En clair, cela veut dire que des hommes sont rayés d'un trait pour que d'autres, les actionnaires, s'enrichissent' (LVE, p. 80).

The commercialisation and class divide subtending French society are further aggravated by the politically biased representation of the media. If television is criticised in *Journal du dehors* for its blatant appeal to middle-class sensitivities, *La Vie extérieure* is even more condemnatory of the media's lack of neutrality and political conscience. A radio broadcast announcing the deaths of six people, including immigrant children and two homeless people who froze to death, is followed by a remark from the prime minister, stating '"l'économie semble repartir du bon pied"' (LVE, p. 36). Such classist disregard for the subaltern – and, it is intimated, the foreign Other – is further illustrated in the media's deification of, and inexhaustive interest in, the aristocratic Princess Diana while ignoring the barbaric murder of hundreds of innocent working-class Algerians. The narrator attributes the overwhelming response to Diana's death both to the media's portrayal of her as an individual to whom the public can relate – she is paradoxically seen to embody the key 'Ernausian' value of representativeness – and the French people's emotional indulgence in an 'apolitical' death which does not call into question their general absence of social conscience: the nature of Diana's death merely endorses the public's lack of political will by its exemplification of the arbitrariness of fate.[55] The media in *La Vie extérieure* in no sense provide representation of the lives of ordinary French people, of '[les] voix d'en bas' (LVE, p. 76), but constitute a vehicle for vacuous political rhetoric, bolstering the ideological hold of the dominant. In a manner similar to the 'innocence' of Mitterrand's condescending reference to 'petites gens' (JDD, p. 39) in the earlier 'journal extime', even the pronunciation of public figures reflects the hierarchical nature of social relations: 'Cette prononciation politico-médiatique ressemble à celle des instituteurs lisant une dictée à leurs élèves. Chirac, Juppé et les autres semblent vouloir éduquer le peuple, lui apprendre l'orthographe et le bon usage de la langue' (LVE, p. 64).[56]

Paradoxically, while television can play a principal role in bringing individuals together through its reinforcement of intercultural links, the spectator's consciousness of the televisual medium is seen to trivialise the most serious of events, to highlight the performative aspect of representation above all else, thereby affecting his/her ability to empathise fully with its content. The spectator's familiarity with the on-screen projection of international disasters such as warfare leads to a decrease in sensitivity towards them as the fictional and real become blurred. This misrepresentation and trivialisation by the media is a key theme in the work: if individuals such as Princess Diana or Bill Clinton are normalised through their mediatised portrayal, so too are traumatic events, which further accounts for the general lack of social conscience portrayed in *La Vie extérieure*. The public's ability simply to ignore unpleasant aspects of existence is highlighted when Parisians appear swiftly to forget the murder of civilians as a result of the bombing campaign in 1995 or when the French public fails to acknowledge its collective responsibility for the death of a young child – the artistic is again valorised over the human: 'Cela ressemble au début du roman de Toni Morrison, paru au printemps, *Paradis*. Ici, comme c'est la réalité, personne n'a envie d'en parler' (LVE, pp. 104–05). Thus, *La Vie extérieure* foregrounds the negative consequences of the predominance of storytelling and narrative techniques in everyday life portrayed in *Journal du dehors*.[57] The mediatisation of 'real life' is apparent in both the ham acting of Chirac who has not been president long enough to improve his televised performance and in the TV documentary about incest.[58] In the latter, the predictability of the spectator's misogynistic response – the woman/witch should be destroyed for her supernatural powers of seduction, while the helpless man is absolved of all responsibility – further points to the repetitious structure of storytelling, to the comfort sought from reinforcing prejudices rather than calling them into question: the television programme illustrates society's desire to minimise disruption to the status quo rather than endeavour to comprehend the reasons behind a father's rape of his daughter. Whatever the infringement of individuals' rights, the social order must be seen to function smoothly. If *La Vie extérieure* suggests that both the isolation characteristic of existence in contemporary society and the mediatisation of human suffering contribute to the ephemerality and fragmentation of intersubjective relations at both the local and inter/national level, it also intimates that this detachment from the Other is aggravated by the sense of 'unreality' permeating certain events due to the biblical – and, consequently, allegorical – associations of the particular historical period in which they take place.

If mediatic representation is shown to distort and misrepresent the lives of ordinary individuals, in a manner characteristic of Ernaux's writing *La Vie extérieure* points to its own role in redressing that imbalance by its portrayal of both *faits divers* which take place in Cergy-

Pontoise and inter/national political or humanitarian events: 'Ecrire cette histoire n'est peut-être pas la pire façon de ne pas oublier la guerre en Bosnie' (LVE, p. 65).[59] As in *Journal du dehors*, the narrator seeks not only to dismantle subject hierarchies - describing Chirac in one vignette and a beggar in another – but equally aesthetic hierarchies in her valorisation of non-elitist forms of pictorial representation such as the poster: however seemingly banal, posters provide a valid source of information about the everyday in contemporary French society. The narrator also values grafitti as an articulation of '[les] voix d'en bas' in that its general dismissal as 'serious' art means that it remains untainted by mediatic representation.[60] These forms of expression constitute the visual equivalent of earlier narrators' desire to avoid 'literariness' in their writing, and their incorporation in the text may be viewed as reflecting the same democratic drive to increase accessibility and objectivity as the role played by photographs in previous works. In *La Vie extérieure*, Ernaux's narrator employs commercially successful forms of mediatic representation – indeed, *La Vie extérieure* constitutes one such form – in order to combat the elitist exclusiveness of 'la classe dominante' and to increase both the artistic and social integration of the outsiders the work represents.

Ernaux's use of the diary form in '*Je ne suis pas sortie de ma nuit*' and *Journal du dehors/La Vie extérieure* points to her belief in the fundamental contiguity of self and Other. If the subject matter of these works is ostensively the Other, the selection process and nature of the diary entries clearly correspond to the needs of the self. All three texts are driven by the desire to reinforce the connection between self and familiar Other, whether in the form of the mother or, more broadly, the narrator's childhood community. Similarly, in all texts, that drive to relocate the refuge of the familiar fulfils both a personal and political aim. If the representation of the maternal in '*Je ne suis pas sortie de ma nuit*' aids the narrator in coming to terms with the death of the mother – as well as with the ageing process – it also obliges her to re-engage with the world around her, averting her to the presence of a 'dehors'. In *Journal du dehors* and *La Vie extérieure*, the narrator's representation of the socially excluded originates in that same need to diminish her sense of isolation by renewing contact with her environment, while simultaneously testifying to her desire to extend the parameters of literary inscription to include the 'petites gens', the marginalised among whom her mother figured – particularly during the period of her life represented in '*Je ne suis pas sortie de ma nuit*'. In these texts, the diary constitutes a means of promoting the self/Other fusion by transforming the typically monologic discourse of diary writing into a form of dialogic exchange.

CHAPTER 5

The Return to Origins:
La Honte and *L'Evénement*

The final chapter of this study focuses on Ernaux's two most recent non-diary works, *La Honte* and *L'Evénement*. If *La Honte* and *L'Evénement*'s chronological position makes them appropriate texts with which to conclude a study of Ernaux's writing, they equally represent a culmination of the many 'Ernausian' themes and techniques discussed in previous chapters, yet a culmination which is oddly circular. By way of conclusion, then, the following analyses of *La Honte* and *L'Evénement* will incorporate references to earlier works. As this study has highlighted, the narrative structure of Ernaux's texts is typically circular, in that a female narrator provides retrospective analysis of past events before returning to the present at the works' conclusion: 'Tous mes livres sont des univers clos, hélas! Il n'y a pas d'issue.'[1] This circularity is apparent in the thematic content of even the most linear works – the 'diaries': the beginning of *Journal du dehors*, for example, can be read as containing an implicit reference to the mother and her deterioration from Alzheimer's disease in its description of a graffito reading 'DÉMENCE', while the work ends with an explicit reference to her; similarly, '*Je ne suis pas sortie de ma nuit*' begins and ends with the death of the mother, a thematics which informs Ernaux's entire writing project. If circularity characterises the intratextual structure of Ernaux's writing, *La Honte* and *L'Evénement* bring the corpus itself round full circle: while *La Honte* represents the ultimate return to origins in its positing of the 'primal scene' as the ur-source of all subsequent shame and alienation experienced by Ernaux's narrators, *L'Evénement* brings her writing trajectory back to its original point of departure in that it supplements her first text, *Les Armoires vides*, in its account of the narrator's abortion. Viewed consecutively, *La Honte* and *L'Evénement* reflect the progressive stages in the maturation process of the narrator in Ernaux's corpus and the class divide which distinguishes childhood from adulthood: while *La Honte* projects the narrator back to the world of childhood and depicts the principal event in initiating estrangement between parents and daughter, *L'Evénement* can be seen to portray its ultimate realisation in the act of abortion, the life-changing event which symbolises the narrator's severance with her working-class childhood and the definitive advent of both adult consciousness and bourgeois status.

LA HONTE

As Chapter 4 remarks, *La Honte*'s return to the themes which dominate Ernaux's writing before *Passion simple* may have confounded certain readerly expectations in its relinquishment of both the increasing narrative focus on the Other and the contemporary chronological framework of more recent texts.[2] However, that the focus on the Other in these interim texts has as its impetus the narrator's characteristic drive for greater self-knowledge makes the return to childhood origins in *La Honte* less surprising. While *La Honte* can be viewed as a return to origins in its re-presentation of the constituents of social class in the narrator's childhood and of the shame associated with her working-class upbringing, its content does not simply duplicate the subject matter of existent texts but leads to a reappraisal of it. *La Honte* claims to disclose the pivotal event of the narrator's childhood, an event which has been omitted from earlier familial representations. This event is presented as provoking the parent/daughter estrangement which subtends Ernaux's corpus, indeed, which the very existence of that corpus can be seen as an endeavour to reduce. If the recurrent intertextuality of Ernaux's writing – what Philippe Vilain refers to as the 'caractère spéculaire' of her work[3] – encourages the reader to re-engage with previous representations, resulting in a revisionary interpretative process in which definitive readings are repeatedly deferred, the dramatic nature of the revelation with which *La Honte* opens cannot but cast much of the content of earlier works in a different light. While works preceding *La Honte* attribute the narrator's shame at her working-class origins to the bourgeois indoctrination of the education system, *La Honte* locates the genesis of this shame in an 'internal' rather than 'external' source: the narrator's schooling may aggravate her sense of alienation from her working-class environment, but it is her parents who are portrayed as the catalyst for it. The narrator is almost 12 when the 'scene' takes place in *La Honte*, which is also the age at which the narrators of the early trilogy begin to experience difficulties in inhabiting their parallel domestic and educational universes.[4] Unable to reveal the original source of shame, these narrators may have exaggerated the role played by schooling in distancing them from their working-class milieu.

The work's epigraph by Paul Auster signals Ernaux's revised, more 'postmodern' perspective on the relationship between language – and, by extension, literature – and 'reality'. In this perspective, first articulated in *Passion simple*, literature can never provide more than an approximation of 'reality': 'Le langage n'est pas la vérité. Il est notre manière d'exister dans l'univers.' The narrator rejects the possibility of a linguistically stable or absolute notion of 'vérité', foregrounding instead the functional, remedial role of language – language is presented as a tool with which to mediate between 'reality' and the self. The epigraph suggests that it is not merely the inevitable disparities between language and the extra-linguistic world it denotes which account for the repeated attempts of Ernaux's narrators to capture that world in their constant return to origins, but language's panacean function further justifies that return: the linguistic re-presentation of the past through literature constitutes a type of umbilical cord which continues to nourish and sustain the narrators in the present. As Chapter 4 suggests, Ernaux's revised perspective vis-à-vis the aims of the literary text may be related to her expanding corpus, to the fact that, despite repeated treatment of what is often ostensibly the same subject matter, each act of writing reveals nuances distinguishing the subject both from the narrator's recollection of it and its previous presentation in literature. In *La Honte*, this perspective is conveyed in the narrator's characterisation of literature as a consciously constructed linguistic edifice based on a prototypical 'reality', rather than a transparent reflection of the world: 'Me servir de ces mots, dont certains exercent encore sur moi leur pesanteur, pour décomposer et remonter, autour de la scène du dimanche de juin, le texte du monde où j'ai eu douze ans et cru devenir folle' (LH, p. 38). Her comment on 'le texte du monde' is quintessentially postmodern – as is her emphasis on fragmentation rather than continuity throughout *La Honte* – and echoes the remark made in *Passion simple* quoted in Chapter 2, note 46, in which the narrator makes reference to the 'text' of her life and to its written version: 'De ce texte vivant, celui-ci n'est que le résidu, la petite trace' (PS, p. 69).[5]

The work begins with what will surely become a well-known opening sentence, expressed with trademark Ernaux laconism: 'Mon père a voulu tuer ma mère un dimanche de juin, au début de l'après-midi' (LH, p. 13). The narrative timescale of *La Honte* resembles that of *Ce qu'ils disent ou rien* in that it centres on one summer, in this case, the summer of 1952. The narrator of *La Honte* recalls the date of the attempted murder – 15 June 1952 – as representing the first important date of childhood. The account of this traumatic event serves to illuminate the significance of the mother figure throughout Ernaux's writing: the attempted or metaphorical murder of the mother as the narrator enters adolescence and, later, her actual death, form the pre-text of Ernaux's writing, and partly explain the daughter's continuing need to construct a textual discourse with the maternal. A footnote clarifying the young narrator's verbal response to her father's action – '"Tu vas me faire gagner malheur"' (LH, p. 15) – underlines this significance: 'En normand, gagner malheur signifie devenir fou et malheureux *pour toujours* à la suite d'un effroi' (LH, ibid.; emphasis added). Rather than seek to provide an explicit explanation of, or justification for, her father's conduct in *La Honte*, the narrator places it in its sociological context by enumerating the components of both the domestic universe in which the attempted murder took place and, subsequently, her educational universe. The narrator is less concerned with understanding the circumstances which gave rise to the 'scene' – a particularly problematic task given her age at the time and the nebulousness of her memories of it – than in relating its repercussions, repercussions which form the subject matter of the corpus preceding *La Honte*.[6] The absence of anecdotal accounts of events or individuals and the presence of objects or topographies in *La Honte* foreground the fundamentally ethnographical nature of the work and contribute to the objectivity of the account, despite the narrator's anguish at witnessing the 'scene'.

The descriptive details which furnish *La Honte*'s opening section reflect the recurrent thematics of Ernaux's corpus in their emphasis on the role played by religion in the narrator's home life and on the constant bickering which typifies parental communication, and in which the mother adopts the dominant role. While earlier works generally portray such maternal dominance in a positive light – it is above all '*Je ne suis pas sortie de ma nuit*' which intimates its more detrimental effects – its destructive consequences on the father in *La Honte* are clear: his wife's relentless nagging in the claustrophobic atmosphere of the kitchen – the sole room of the house enclosed on all sides – spurns him into violent action. It is as if, having been metaphorically emasculated by his wife's conduct, the gentle dreamer of past texts, who never even raises his voice – let alone a hand – is driven to reassert his masculinity. The wording of the opening sentence is significant, in that it could suggest that the narrator's father did not intend to kill her mother, but only desired to. Indeed, the vagueness of the narrator's memory as to his precise actions leaves them steeped in ambiguity (which further blurs the 'vérité' of the situation, in that she both does and does not represent what happened). Equally, it may have been the daughter's intervention at the site of the crime which saved her mother's life, an intervention which can be seen to symbolise the mother/daughter complicity of earlier works in the daughter's literal coming between the parents. If, as Chapters 3 and 4 argue, the daughter's intense intimacy with the mother evokes parallels between the mother/daughter relationship and the heterosexual paradigm, *La Honte* reinforces such parallels by pointing to the similarities subtending the mother's treatment of father and daughter, similarities which foreground her authoritarian, 'masculine' conduct: 'Comme ma mère était plus chrétienne que mon père, qu'elle s'occupait de l'argent et rencontrait mes maîtresses, je devais considérer comme naturel qu'elle crie après lui de la même façon qu'après moi' (LH, p. 18).

The text can be seen to fall into five parts: the recollection of the 'scene'; a brief analysis of significant personal objects and public events in 1952; an examination of the spatial and cultural indicators of class in relation to the narrator's home life; a similarly deconstructive reading of her school life; and an account of events which took place in the summer following the 'scene', including a trip to Lourdes with her father. The final section once again highlights the intratextual circularity of Ernaux's writing, in that it provides a chronological continuation of the work's opening. Yvetot forms the basis of both home and school life for the narrator, and is designated in the work by 'Y.'. The metanarrative explanation for this designation foregrounds Yvetot's significance as an affective rather than geographical locus. However, the affective significance attributed to its role as a 'lieu d'origine sans nom' (LH, p. 43) in *La Honte* is surely equally pertinent to *Une femme*, where it is named in full. The narrator's unwillingness to name the town in *La Honte* is all the more puzzling, given that its physical features and layout are related in much greater detail than elsewhere in the corpus. The narrator's comprehensive description of her domestic geography starts from the relatively broad vantage point of the town, closes in on her area and street, before concluding with a depiction of the *café-épicerie* itself. Indeed, the text supplies exhaustive directions on how to locate the narrator's house in Yvetot and – unlike other works – names her street correctly, when it is surely also home to her 'lieu d'origine'.[7] This gradual reduction in narrative scope is mirrored in the subsequent section of the text which details her school life, heightening the atmosphere of claustrophobia which characterises the narrator's universe, and which is acutely felt on the day of the 'scene'. Such claustrophobia is intensified by the predictability of her parents' daily routine and the omnipresence of customers throughout childhood, a presence which may partly account for the narrators' self-reflexive awareness of the readerly Other throughout Ernaux's writing. If the judgemental gaze of the Other may be detected in the constraining presence of metanarrative remarks, it is also apparent in the religious indoctrination to which Ernaux's narrators are subject, an indoctrination which *La Honte* represents as particularly coercive: 'L'enseignement et la religion ne sont séparés ni dans l'espace ni dans le temps. Tout, sauf la cour de récréation et les cabinets, est lieu de prière' (LH, p. 76).[8] The narrator's unquestioning religious beliefs in pre-adolescence and her impression of having been indelibly corrupted at witnessing the 'scene' lead to her implicit association of the latter with the Fall.[9] Echoing the restorative function of earlier works such as *La Place* and *Une femme*, *La Honte* can be read as a form of confessional, in that the narrator hopes, by avowing her 'sin', to reduce its emotional hold over her.

The religious sentiments propagated at school are reinforced by the narrator's mother in *La Honte*, and by the literature the narrator reads.[10] The narrator quotes an excerpt from the preface of *Brigitte jeune fille* – as she quotes from *J'élève mon enfant* in *La Femme gelée* – to prove the oppressiveness of the idealised model of womanhood it promotes: '*la vraie femme de France est encore et toujours une femme qui aime son foyer, son pays. Et qui prie*' (LH, p. 105). The hypocrisy of a Catholic ideology which validates a bourgeois way of life, while simultaneously advocating the heroine's rejection of all material goods, is unambiguous. As elsewhere in the corpus, the content of books and magazines is shown to encourage the narrator in her fabrication of imaginary universes, in her willing assimilation of the stereotype of feminine beauty portrayed in advertisements: 'je construisais mon corps et mon apparence, jolies dents (avec Gibs), lèvres rouges et pulpeuses (rouge Baiser), silhouette fine (gaine X), etc.' (LH, p. 127).[11] The narrator's description of this adolescent activity is fuelled by an implicit desire to reduce her earlier sense of solitude: 'C'était une activité secrète, sans nom, et je n'ai jamais cru possible que d'autres s'y livrent' (LH, p. 129). It may be that, throughout Ernaux's corpus, the loneliness characteristic of the narrators' cross-cultural locus accounts for the strength of their recurrent desire to confirm the representativeness of their experience: as the only person from her working-class area to attend private school, the narrator occupies a superior position in the educational hierarchy of her domestic universe, while, at school, her association with the unfashionable 'rural' contingent places her at the bottom of the class hierarchy. Having spent her adolescence unable to disclose the contents of the 'scene' and its traumatic ramifications either to members of her home or school environments, the older narrator in *La Honte* may feel particularly driven to have aspects of her experience normalised by the Other, resulting in the contradictory impulse which underlies much of Ernaux's writing: while her narrators profess a disregard of the consequences of writing, that disregard is constantly tempered by the normalising force of what Chapter 4, quoting Virginia Woolf, terms 'invisible presences'.

While the narrator has never recounted the 'scene' in writing before, she has mentioned its existence to lovers. This revelation implicitly posits the reader in the role of the male lover in the case of *La Honte*, indicating both the narrator's awareness that, like her lovers, the reader may be shocked by her account of the 'scene' and consequent endeavour to contain its negative ramifications through her intimate characterisation of the narrator/reader relationship. This indirect attempt to forestall potential readerly reaction recalls the opening section of *Passion simple*, in which the narrator's discussion of a pornographic film contains implied reading paradigms.[12] If the narrator of *La Honte* can only recount this memory to men with whom she is sexually involved – reminding the reader of the narrator's portrayal of the erotic nature of writing in *Passion simple* and *Journal du dehors* – it may be that a similarly close relationship with her readership has had to be established before the narrator feels able to surrender this particular depiction of her origins to the public domain. That the 'scene' has never before been subject to literary representation points to the taboo-breaking purpose with which Ernaux invests literature. By describing the 'scene' which has previously remained at an affective level of her memory, the narrator partially relinquishes ownership of it, not only in that the 'scene' becomes public currency and somehow normalised – the act of narration increases its representativeness for the narrator – but she feels distanced from her own description of it. Apart from its brief acknowledgement in the presence of lovers, it has only ever existed in a non-verbal, visual form for her. Her subsequent inability to relate to her own representation of it further ratifies the sentiments expressed in the work's epigraph: the inevitable distortion in any linguistic representation of 'reality' – and we return once again to a theme articulated in *Passion simple* – undermines the reader's authority to judge that representation. The superstitious conduct of Ernaux's narrators, a conduct above all evident in *Ce qu'ils disent ou rien* and *Passion simple*, here finds illustration in the narrator's fear that the public articulation of this long-kept secret will have apocalyptic consequences. As in previous texts, such superstitiousness is undoubtedly aggravated by the narrator's religious education, an education which threatens divine retribution for any manifestation of 'abnormal' conduct and posits passive prayer as the key to a happy future: 'La prière est l'acte essentiel de la vie, le remède individuel et universel' (LH, p. 77). The portrayal of working-class life in *La Honte* as comprising a series of rigidly defined, chronologically predictable stages to which the individual acquiesces unquestioningly – whether in the weekly short term or 'existential' long term – may further account for the narrators' recurrent recourse to superstition rather than individual agency in Ernaux's writing.

Objectifying the Past

The work's ethnological emphasis on the objects and values which make up the narrator's childhood universe may also stem from the fact that, apart from a few concrete details, her memory of the 'scene' remains vague. The events of 15 June 1952 may denote a watershed between childhood and adolescence, fundamentally altering the narrator's worldview, yet she is unable to recall them vividly. The 'scene' is presented as 'un filtre' (LH, p. 18), a distorting prism which colours her interpretation of all remarks and actions subsequent to that Sunday in June. The absence of precise recollection is partly due to repression – she is able to remember events which took place earlier in childhood – and to the 'scene''s uniqueness, in that it is the recurrent components of childhood which remain clearest in her memory. Retrospectively, the narrator recognises the transitional function of the 'scene', attributing her loss of childhood innocence to it, a loss foregrounded by its sexual symbolism, in that she is on the threshold of adolescence when the 'scene' takes place. This allegorical reading is substantiated by the father's evident need to brandish his masculinity; by the fact that, prior to publishing *La Honte*, the narrator only mentioned the 'scene' to men with whom she was sexually involved; and by her comparison of the 'scene' to an orgasm in that both constitute rare reinforcers of continuity in her fragmented sense of identity.

The 'scene''s transitional role in the narrator's development is also reflected in her description of two photographs, one taken just before, the other, just after, its occurrence. The first photograph, in which the narrator is pictured renewing her vows a year after her first communion, portrays her as a type of sexless, celestial being dressed in white, an angelic picture of innocence before the Fall. The narrator appears markedly older in the second photograph, pictured alongside her father in Biarritz on the return leg of the trip to Lourdes: 'Dans cette tenue, je ressemble à une petite femme' (LH, p. 24).[13] While the narrator's self-designation as 'une petite femme' may intimate her enforced maturity following the 'scene', its marital connotations are inescapable in that she is photographed as part of a couple: if, in the first photograph, she is the 'bride of Christ', in the second she is projected into a similar role vis-à-vis her father. Given the intensity of the mother–daughter symbiosis throughout Ernaux's writing and the sexual symbolism of the father's murderous gesture in *La Honte*, it is tempting to speculate that the father's desired removal of the mother may have partly been a subconscious reaction against such symbiosis, privileging the younger, sexually inexperienced daughter over the older, maternal 'castrator'. Furthermore, as *Une femme* and '*Je ne suis pas sortie de ma nuit*' reveal, the mother stopped menstruating shortly before the summer of 1952, while the narrator began menstruating very soon afterwards.[14] When father and daughter go travelling together, the maternal 'displacement' desired by the father is felt uneasily by the daughter: 'Au fur et à mesure que nous descendions vers le sud, le dépaysement m'envahissait. Il me semblait que je ne reverrais plus ma mère' (LH, p. 115).

These two photographs act as points of reference throughout *La Honte* and endow the narrator's otherwise fragmented sense of self with a degree of coherence. As the narrator delves further into her past, she revises her initial assessment of them, once again highlighting the transformative role of the perceiver in the act of interpretation (and therefore the inevitable inaccuracies of any readerly interpretation of events, in that, despite actually witnessing the 'scene', the narrator's own understanding of her past is subject to repeated modification). Memory for Ernaux's narrator incorporates a performative element as present and past illuminate one another reciprocally. At the text's conclusion, the narrator provides a detailed account of the trip she made to Lourdes with her father, a trip which expands her horizons by taking her beyond the geographical parameters of Yvetot while rendering their limits glaringly obvious, in that the class hierarchy first encountered by the narrator at school is duplicated within the group her father and she are part of. The trip reifies the narrator's growing consciousness of class differences through her prolonged exposure to a middle-class girl of the same age. As in '*Je ne suis pas sortie de ma nuit*', it is a mirror which symbolises the gaze of the Other, reflecting the hierarchised norms of the social order: 'Je me suis vue dans la glace en face, pâle, l'air triste avec mes lunettes, silencieuse à côté de mon père, qui regardait dans le vague. Je voyais tout ce qui me séparait de cette fille mais je ne savais pas comment j'aurais pu faire pour lui ressembler' (LH, pp. 124–25). If *La Honte* highlights the fluid precariousness of the narrator's self-perception both during and after that summer of 1952 and the relativity of all subsequent attempts to transcribe it in writing, one constant uniting older and younger narrator – the one 'vérité' – as the title of the work suggests, is the overwhelming sense of shame which informs her existence after witnessing the 'scene', a shame fundamentally rooted in her awareness of social difference:

> Après chacune des images de cet été, ma tendance naturelle serait d'écrire 'alors j'ai découvert que' ou 'je me suis aperçue de' mais ces mots supposent une conscience claire des situations vécues. Il y a eu seulement la sensation de honte qui les a fixées hors de toute signification. Mais rien ne peut faire que je n'aie éprouvé cela, cette lourdeur, cette néantisation. Elle est la dernière vérité.
> C'est elle qui unit la fille de 52 à la femme en train d'écrire. (LH, pp. 125–26)

The metanarrative remarks on literary composition in *La Honte*, as elsewhere in Ernaux's corpus, express the narrator's desire to minimise the distortive effects the transcription of 'reality' in a literary medium entails, in this case through the eschewal of both clichéd literary language and a purely subjective interpretation of the events portrayed: '(Dire, "cet été-là" ou "l'été de mes douze ans" c'est rendre romanesque ce qui ne l'était pas plus que ne l'est pour moi l'actuel été

95, dont je n'imagine même pas qu'il pourra passer un jour dans la vision enchantée que suggère l'expression: "cet été-là".)' (LH, pp. 25–26). No longer willing to place her trust in the vagaries of memory (vagaries made clear in her initial recollection of the 'scene' – 'J'avais dû', 'sans doute' [LH, p. 13]), the narrator of *La Honte* chooses instead to capture her existence in 1952 through the evocation of specific items from her childhood environment. The objective ethnologist takes over the remembrancer more completely than in *La Place* and *Une femme*. The series of recollections and images which connote that universe in the earlier works are replaced by descriptive dissections of objects and, later, behaviour paradigms. This topography of class indices reinforces the work's objectivity by anchoring the narrator's account in externally verifiable items or codes of conduct which mould the behaviour and mores of a stratum of society. In this respect, the work goes beyond the consolidation not only of existent themes but also of narrative techniques in the corpus by signalling a development in Ernaux's writing practices, in that the objectivity which subtends the narrator's portrayal of the public domain in *Journal du dehors* and *La Vie extérieure* is successfully transferred to the private domain of *La Honte*. This historicising focus on individual objects serves to increase the objectivity of the narrator's account but also its fragmentation. In one of several references to Proust in Ernaux's writing, the narrator contrasts her reliance on transient and 'temporally-specific' objects to reflect different developmental stages of the self with the Proustian perception of the constancy of the self as reflected in nature:

> À moi – et peut-être à tous ceux de mon époque – dont les souvenirs sont attachés à un tube d'été, une ceinture en vogue, à des choses vouées à la disparition, la mémoire n'apporte aucune preuve de ma permanence ou de mon identité. Elle me fait sentir et me confirme ma fragmentation et mon historicité. (LH, p. 96)[15]

In *La Honte*, this enumerative approach may appear somewhat excessive, in that its greater objectivity engages the reader less fully than the more personalised portrayal of the parental microcosm in earlier works. While the narrator is conscious of the risk she has taken by beginning her work in such a dramatic fashion, and justifies her description of the classifying components of childhood as an attempt to contextualise the 'scene', the remainder of the text is inevitably anticlimactic. The portrayal of that universe may not only be familiar to the reader, but lacks the vividness which characterises its representation elsewhere. At times, the impression is of a grey universe analogous to the narrator's recollection of post-war Yvetot. In one such attempt to situate the 'scene' within a broader regional framework, the narrator looks up the newspaper *Paris-Normandie* for the year 1952. Given that she was 11 at the time of the newspaper's publication, it is hardly surprising that its content means little to her. However much the narrator seeks to make such tangential discussions relevant to the work, the very exercise of contextualisation is undermined by the all-encompassing nature of the 'scene' and its complete domination of her childhood landscape: 'aucun des milliards de faits qui s'étaient produits dans le monde ce dimanche-là ne pourrait être placé à côté de la scène sans me remplir de stupeur. Elle seule a été réelle' (LH, p. 36). The irrelevance of the main political or national events of 1952 to an understanding of the 'scene' and the narrator's inability to project herself into the mind of her younger self leave as her sole option a quasi-structuralist analysis of 'les lois et les rites, les croyances et les valeurs qui définissaient les milieux, l'école, la famille, la province' (LH, p. 37).

If *La Honte* returns to the childhood landscape which dominates the early trilogy, the work also incorporates metalinguistic features typical of Ernaux's writing from *La Place* onwards. Such features include the general role of metanarrative comments in illuminating the narrator's approach to writing, in particular, her desire to avoid fictionalisation in the drive to provide an objective account of her past – 'Être en somme ethnologue de moi-même' (LH, p. 38); and the italicisation of the oral working-class language of the narrator's domestic universe. Just as the narrator acknowledges the risk taken in the text's opening revelation, so too she recognises the superfluousness of certain metanarrative remarks: '(Sans doute n'est-il pas nécessaire de noter tout cela, mais je ne peux commencer à écrire réellement sans tâcher de voir clair dans les conditions de mon écriture)' (ibid.). The typographical gesture of enclosing such comments in brackets as if to make them less intrusive reinforces the reader's impression of their occasional redundancy in this work. In a further echo of earlier texts, the narrator of *La Honte* rejects the validity of a psychoanalytic or vaguely psychological interpretation of the 'scene', in that the abstract vocabulary prerequisite to such a reading would simplify and distort her sense of it. This resistance to the interpretative paradigms of the Other reflects the content of earlier metacommentaries, in which, implicitly or explicitly, the narrator posits a desired reading mode for the works in question. Mirroring the structure of previous texts, *La Honte* returns to the present at its conclusion, to the aims of writing the work and to the significance of the 'scene'. In keeping with the narrator's revised perception of literature post-*Passion simple*, her portrayal of the damaging effects of the internalisation of social inferiority is presented as an approximation – and attenuation – of her 'real-life' experience: 'Mais quelle honte pourrait m'apporter l'écriture d'un livre qui soit à la hauteur de ce que j'ai éprouvé dans ma douzième année' (LH, p. 132). In *L'Evénement*, the text with which this study concludes, this disparity in emotional intensity between 'reality' and its literary rendition is reduced, due in part to the recurrent parallels linking the act of abortion to the act of writing. Both *La Honte* and *L'Evénement* represent pivotal life events for the narrator, yet the unspoken, quasi-unspeakable nature of the 'scene' until its depiction in *La Honte* alienates the narrator from its eventual linguistic representation. The overwhelming sense of shame it elicits, and the narrator's perception of it as inherently linked to her family nucleus diminish any cathartic effect its public disclosure may entail. In *L'Evénement*, however, the abortion takes place when the narrator is a young adult and therefore more able to assume its traumatic ramifications; details of it have frequently been communicated to others, both privately and in the public forum of *Les Armoires vides* and *Passion simple*; and any secrecy surrounding the abortion stems above all from its previously illegal status rather than the narrator's sense of shame at having to procure one. The mature narrator continues to acknowledge the limitations inherent in any linguistic representation of 'reality', yet it is nonetheless the process of writing *L'Evénement* which sensitises her to the extensive repercussions of an event whose taboo status partially anaesthetised the emotional responses of her younger self.

L'EVENEMENT

The act of abortion may provide the catalyst for Denise Lesur's spiritual quest in Ernaux's first work, but the circumstances surrounding it and the experience of abortion itself are less important than the psychological journey they serve to galvanise. In *L'Evénement*, however, the narrator's abortion is not solely a narrative framing device but the subject proper of the work. As Chapter 1 argues, Denise's abortion in *Les Armoires vides* can be interpreted as heralding the demise of the narrator's younger working-class self and the birth of its bourgeois successor; it symbolises her severance from the working-class world of childhood and her definitive projection into middle-class adulthood in the form of attendance at university and participation in heterosexual relations. The abortion's dual life-denying/life-giving symbolism is expressed repeatedly in *L'Evénement*: 'Il me semble que cette femme [the backstreet abortionist] qui s'active entre mes jambes, qui introduit le spéculum, me fait naître. J'ai tué ma mère en moi à ce moment-là' (LE, p. 77).[16] Along with the foetus, the abortionist is shown to deliver the narrator into the world of adulthood.

The renaissance which the abortion represents for the narrator through its symbolic destruction of her childhood self is also reflected in her rejection of religion. When pregnant, the narrator briefly considers teaching at a private Catholic girls' school similar to the one in which she herself was educated. However, the taboo status of extra-marital sexual activity within the precepts of Catholicism and in the narrator's upbringing generally – and the particular vilification reserved for the unmarried mother – undoubtedly contribute to her decision to decline the post. As in '*Je ne suis pas sortie de ma nuit*', the oppressiveness of the narrator's religious education finds expression in the projected condemnatory gaze of the Other: 'je me suis vue dans la classe de seconde sous les regards des filles et j'ai eu envie de vomir' (LE, p. 20). If the narrator's prayers and repentance throughout her sexually aware adolescence can be read as a form of retrospective spiritual contraception in their endeavour to atone for, indeed, negate, sexual activity, their evident inefficiency in the shape of the narrator's pregnancy may further account for her rejection of religious succour after her abortion. The narrator prays not to suffer physically before her abortion, yet it is the Catholic Church's attempt to make her suffer psychologically afterwards which precipitates her decision to abandon religion: 'Je me sentais dans la lumière et pour lui [the priest] j'étais dans le crime. En sortant, j'ai su que le temps de la religion était fini pour moi' (LE, p. 108).[17] This rejection finds an allegorical echo in the figure of Sœur Sourire, a media singing star at the time of the narrator's abortion who later leaves the religious orders, replacing her conventionally religious conduct with a more sexually dissident lifestyle – the narrator's obligatory jettisoning of social norms in order to fulfil her personal wish to have an abortion is subsequently duplicated in this unknown woman's behaviour. Indeed, in a subversion of the religious teachings of childhood, the narrator perceives her abortion as 'une chose sacrée' (LE, p. 107), which brings about a form of absolution: 'Je me sentais sauvée' (ibid.).[18] After weeks of striving to overcome the numerous obstacles society throws in her path, the narrator perceives her abortion as a type of holy grail.

Like Denise, the narrator's perception of her pregnancy as inherently linked to her working-class origins endows it with a sense of inevitability, an inevitability highlighted in her interpretation of the environment as imbued with class-related indices: 'En regardant la silhouette frêle, en imperméable, du petit employé, ses humiliations, devant la désolation sans espoir du film, je savais que mes règles ne reviendraient pas' (LE, p. 18). The quasi-determinist significance of the material and human components which make up the narrators' environments throughout Ernaux's corpus reaches its logical conclusion in the narrator's belief that she too constitutes a sign of working-classness – her pregnancy is interpreted as the literal embodiment of her social origins, connoting the ultimate victory of the working-class physical over the bourgeois intellectual. The malediction of the *fille-mère* which so haunted her childhood has proved inescapable: 'Mais ni le bac ni la licence de lettres n'avaient réussi à détourner la fatalité de la transmission d'une pauvreté dont la fille enceinte était, au même titre que l'alcoolique, l'emblème' (LE, pp. 29–30). The narrator's sense of relief on learning that a professionally successful middle-class acquaintance has also undergone an illegal abortion testifies to the persistence of her association of unwanted pregnancy with working-class origins.

As in *La Honte*, the signifying function of the narrator's environment in *L'Evénement* invests her experience with a sense of permanence, of 'reality', which serves to counter 'l'immatérialité et [de] l'évanescence de ce qui traverse l'esprit' (LE, p. 68). The material consequence of her extra-literary 'reality' is repeatedly referred to: 'Seul le souvenir de sensations liées à des êtres et des choses hors de moi – la neige du Puy Jumel, les yeux exorbités de Jean T., la chanson de Sœur Sourire – m'apporte la preuve de la réalité. La seule vraie mémoire est matérielle' (ibid.). The reassuring role played by such concrete materiality for the narrator is mirrored in the backstreet abortionist's pragmatic approach to her 'profession', which focuses on the tangible physical repercussions of abortion, rather than its psychological effects, reinforcing parallels between the narrator's perception of the act of writing and that of abortion. As this study suggests, the influence accorded these classifying 'signes' and the environment generally in Ernaux's writing may explain her narrators' characteristically passive attitude to events. In *L'Evénement*, this attitude is exemplified in the narrator's search for a doctor capable of carrying out an abortion – 'Je ne me décidais pas à sonner. J'attendais un signe' (LE, p. 38) – or in her discovery that the address of the backstreet abortionist is not the nega-tive-sounding '"impasse Cardinet" (LE, p. 70) but the more optimisti-cally titled '"passage Cardinet", adding, 'c'était un signe qui me soulageait'.[19] While the material constituents of her previous universe – constituents which also include recorded examples of written and spoken language – are presented as the sole reliable source of recollec-tion for the mature narrator, so overpowering is her younger self's desire to abort that she exists in a quasi-dreamlike state, unable to register fully inter/national events occurring in the world around her:[20] 'Une semaine après, Kennedy a été assassiné à Dallas. Mais ce n'était déjà plus quelque chose qui pouvait m'intéresser' (LE, p. 23). Analo-gous to the all-encompassing nature of the narrator's personal experi-ence of the 'scene' in *La Honte*, the life event of abortion is shown to isolate her from more general political or social events.

The title of the work makes clear the significance of its content in the narrator's personal history, a significance further illustrated in the abortion's role as framing device in Ernaux's first book. The narrative of *Les Armoires vides* unfolds in the student bedroom described in *L'Evénement*: of all possible auto/biographical landscapes, Ernaux chooses that particular location and event with which to begin her writing trajectory. The abortion's importance for the narrator resides in its rep-resentative value, in that it incorporates not only class but gender con-notations, signalling both a break with her working-class origins and a reinforcement of her sexual identity in its testimony to her ability to conceive. Abortion may heighten the narrator's awareness of a primi-tive bond of femaleness uniting her with other women, yet, whatever its influential effect on the sexual identity of the women who experience it, abortion remains conspicuously absent from forms of ideological rep-resentation: 'Je ne crois pas qu'il existe un *Atelier de la faiseuse d'anges* dans aucun musée du monde' (LE, p. 82). Countering these representa-tive lacunae, the two epigraphs of *L'Evénement* articulate the narrator's belief in the symbiotic relationship between art and 'reality': however limited the political potential of a work of art and however 'unpalat-able' the subject it portrays, Ernaux's narrators desire that the detailed depiction of 'real-life' experiences have repercussions beyond the con-fines of the literary text. As the epigraph from Michel Leiris reads: 'Mon double vœu: que l'événement devienne écrit. Et que l'écrit soit événement.' The second quotation from Yûko Tsushima validates Ernaux's well-established aim to focus on the more disturbing, and consequently less represented, elements of human experience: 'Qui sait si la mémoire ne consiste pas à regarder les choses jusqu'au bout.' The literary text clearly facilitates the narrator's own assimilation of her experience, whether as producer or consumer of it:[21] her retrospective portrayal of the act of abortion in *L'Evénement* enables her to gauge the event's full significance in her maturation process, making it more 'real' for her. As this chapter suggests, the textual medium can be seen to replace the role of the confessional for Ernaux's adult narrators, allowing them to confront and assume past experiences and to reduce the judgemental role of the Other to a virtual presence.

Analogous to the text's personal function, *L'Evénement*'s projected public role can also be read as comprising religious overtones, overtones apparent in Ernaux's perception of writing as a form of mission and in earlier narrators' view of the portrayal of working-class experience as a moral obligation. While the metanarrative remarks which punctuate the text reveal the narrator's initial reticence in writing *L'Evénement*, they also articulate the sense of moral compulsion driving her depiction of abortion: 'Mais je me disais aussi que je pourrais mourir sans avoir rien fait de cet événement. S'il y avait une faute, c'était celle-là' (LE, p. 24).[22] The younger narrator's sole means of normalising her experience of abortion is to discuss it with another, to 'realise' her emotional and physical experience through its verbalisation. The literary text can be viewed as fulfilling a similar role for Ernaux generally in her endeavour to undermine the silence surrounding taboo subjects through a relentless exposure of them. This revelatory role further incorporates a classist impetus in the narrator's wish to shock her bourgeois interlocutor/reader by disclosing her impending 'crime'.[23] However, if the younger narrator's plight in *L'Evénement* renders her indifferent to the consequences of these verbal disclosures, the unknown repercussions of a literary description of the abortion proper engender fear in the mature narrator, and a desire to delay the act of writing. This desire is expressed in a characteristically 'Ernausian' analogy combining the sexual and the written, in which the narrator voices her concern that the textual inscription of the event may entail its anamnestic oblivion: 'Peur, peut-être, que l'écriture dissolve ces images, comme celles du désir sexuel qui s'effacent instantanément après l'orgasme' (LE, p. 69). This imbrication of sexual and literary expression for the narrator is further highlighted in her comparison of the initial secrecy and ultimate revelation of the act of writing to her abortion: 'Je n'aurai plus aucun pouvoir sur mon texte qui sera exposé comme mon corps l'a été à l'Hôtel-Dieu' (LE, p. 95).

The text opens with a climactic build-up of suspense as the narrator describes her arrival in a clinic (which the reader may erroneously presume is the one in which she is to have an abortion), foreshadowing the magnitude of the event shortly to be related. The reader, along with the various individuals who populate the clinic's waiting room, shares in the narrator's sense of anticipation, an anticipation fuelled by the discovery that she is in fact about to find out the result of an Aids test. The mounting narrative tension is only dispelled with the revelation that the test is negative. Echoing her younger self's reaction to abortion, the narrator employs religious vocabulary to illustrate her relief: 'j'étais sauvée encore' (LE, p. 15). The dramatic, cinematic quality of this initial scene is reinforced by the narrator's recollection of the sexual act which led to its occurrence in the first place – like the opening scene describing the pornographic film in *Passion simple*, the narrator's visual memory of it remains fuzzy. This recollective imprecision finds correspondence in the 'unrealness' which permeates her current experience, in that the mature narrator perceives the sexual act as somehow extrinsic to her everyday 'reality': as with her earlier response to news of her pregnancy, the narrator's discovery that her Aids test is negative is imbued with the surreal.[24] While this separation of the sexual from the everyday may have its origins in the oppressive censorship on sexual expression which characterised the young narrator's daily existence, the resultant denial of 'real-life' consequences to the sexual act may partly explain the narrator's need to abort and have an Aids test in the first place.[25]

The isolating limbo inhabited by the narrator prior to her abortion and the absence of any emotion other than fear may further contribute to the 'unrealness' of the event for her. She does little more than function in the weeks leading up to her abortion, suspended between past and future: her sole temporal measurement relates to the growth of the foetus inside her, as her term at university is spent trying to procure an illegal abortion, rather than pursuing her studies. Her inability to participate in the intellectual life of university is particularly distressing for the narrator in that she interprets it as her manual working-class origins regaining ground on her intellectual middle-class education: 'Elle [her inability to write her dissertation] était le signe indubitable de ma déchéance invisible' (LE, p. 46). The enforced surreptitiousness of the narrator's actions may also diminish her awareness of the consequentiality of what she is experiencing. That this obligatory dissimulation may result in the narrator's fictionalisation of her 'real-life' experience is reflected in the literary expressions which come to mind when the mature narrator recalls the period of her abortion. She retrospectively perceives herself in the role of novelistic heroine rather than 'real-life' individual, as conveyed in her references to 'la figure romanesque et sordide de la faiseuse d'anges' (LE, p. 61) and to her previous self as 'un personnage' (LE, p. 114).[26]

The contemporary experience of the Aids test corresponds to the role played by the abortion in *Les Armoires vides*, in that it acts as a catalyst for the subsequent narrative which describes that same abortion of January 1964. Like the allegorical function of the abortion itself, the love-making which leads to the Aids test is described as encompassing both vitality and mortality: 'L'enlacement et la gesticulation des corps nus me paraissaient une danse de mort' (LE, p. 14). This characterisation ratifies the Bataillean perception of heterosexual eroticism as a blurring of life and death through its exposure of the body, of the life force, to its potential violation by the Other. Equally, it echoes the narrator's recurrent blurring of pain and pleasure, of abortion and penetrative eroticism in *Les Armoires vides*. The dual symbolism of the abortion as incorporating elements of both life and death is further emphasised by the narrator's memory of the period during which it took place: 'j'ai vu une étendue éblouissante de soleil et de neige débouchant sur les ténèbres du mois de janvier' (LE, p. 67). In a similar vein, her description of 'passage Cardinet' can be seen as providing metaphorical representation of the narrator's sense of hope after the increasing emotional and physical isolation preceding her abortion, and, indeed, of the vaginal passage itself, 'de hauts murs se rapprochant, avec une déchirure au fond' (LE, p. 87). As epitomised in the Catholic Church's condemnation of abortion, it is only with the intervention of the outside world and its constraining morality that the narrator's more viscerally positive interpretation of abortion is compromised: 'D'expérience pure de la vie et de la mort, elle est devenue exposition et jugement' (LE, p. 93).[27] This compromised perception of abortion due to the intervening presence of the Other may partly account for the anxiety expressed by Ernaux's narrators prior to the release of the literary text into the public domain.

L'Evénement reveals a distinct feminist subtext in its portrayal of the narrator's network of female support during her abortion, a network which includes members of the medical profession – whose sensitivity contrasts dramatically with the attitude of their male colleagues; the – paradoxically – maternal backstreet abortionist to whom the narrator would have liked to dedicate *L'Evénement*; and the female friends, who unfailingly offer the narrator discrete practical and emotional aid, whatever their religious beliefs.[28] The narrator's indebtedness to these women is expressed in her desire to proclaim their identity publicly, a desire shared by her counterpart in *Passion simple* vis-à-vis her lover, but likewise rejected as an abuse of narratorial privilege. In contrast, her male friends receive news of her pregnancy with voyeuristic titillation, and show themselves unwilling to provide even moral support. Their supercilious 'superiority' is exemplified in the hypocrisy of a fellow student, Jean T., whose humanitarian espousal of revolutionary sentiments fails to translate into a modicum of 'real-life' philanthropy towards the narrator. Male members of the medical profession similarly demonstrate little or no understanding of the narrator's situation, and their different forms of verbal misogyny are remembered verbatim by the mature narrator. As Chapter 3 remarks, the emotive repercussions of certain terms cannot be eradicated for the narrator, eliciting the same emotional responses in her mature, as in her younger, self: 'D'entendre à nouveau chacune de ces phrases, indélébiles en moi, dont le sens devait être alors si intenable, ou à l'inverse si consolant, que les penser aujourd'hui me submerge de dégoût ou de douceur' (LE, p. 26).[29] While one doctor covertly overrides her wishes by prescribing her medicine which prevents miscarriages, another insists on being paid despite the fact that she is too ill to get out of bed.[30] Verbal misogyny can take the form of patriarchal pressure to keep the baby – '"les enfants de l'amour sont toujours les plus beaux"' (LE, p. 21) – or of mocking disdain in response to her questions: '"Je ne suis pas le plombier!"' (LE, p. 96). The attitude of the medical profession and male doctors in particular is also shown to be resolutely classist in *L'Evénement* – as elsewhere in the corpus – in that they view the narrator less harshly on learning that she is a (presumably middle-class) student.[31]

The absence of all regret or sentimentalisation surrounding the act of abortion can further be interpreted as reflecting a feminist ethos – indeed, the narrator perceives her abortion with a sense of pride once it is completed, in that she has survived a difficult event.[32] Returning to university after having aborted, the narrator has the impression of inhabiting an enlightened, dreamlike zone: the numbing loneliness she felt prior to abortion has been transformed into a more enriching sense of seclusion. The narrator's sanguine psychological state can be seen to originate both in the sheer relief at having finally procured an abortion and in the quintessentially 'Ernausian' validation of all experiential extremes: the narrator feels privileged to have undergone the relatively rare life event of abortion. The narrator recognises that her account may be considered 'de mauvais goût', yet presents her actual experience of abortion as justification for its literary inscription, further pointing to the centrality of 'reality' to Ernaux's conception of literature. Indeed, the sole guilt the narrator experiences vis-à-vis her abortion is that she has never written about it in detail before now. The narrator's dismissal of *bienséance* as a criterion for representation, while echoing the sentiments expressed in the work's epigraphs, has explicitly feminist origins: 'D'avoir vécu une chose, quelle qu'elle soit, donne le droit imprescriptible de l'écrire. Il n'y a pas de vérité inférieure. Et si je ne vais pas au bout de la relation de cette expérience, je contribue à obscurcir la réalité des femmes et je me range du côté de la domination masculine du monde' (LE, p. 53). Indeed, the narrator indirectly attributes the existence of her account to the success of feminism's campaign to legalise abortion. *L'Evénement* epitomises a fundamental tenet of the contemporary feminist movement – and of Ernaux's conception of the role of literature generally – in its foregrounding of the interrelation of the personal and political. While imbued with the personal symbolism of the narrator's entry into adulthood, the abortion has a wider symbolic value in that it crystallises the power relations between 'dominants' and 'dominés', between men and women, which Ernaux's corpus repeatedly denounces. *L'Evénement* makes clear that the legitimation and legalisation of abortion stem not from a humanitarian altruism which validates women's right to exercise choice, but are in response both to feminism's tenacious demands for women's reproductive rights and to the prevailing social climate: to have maintained the illegal status of abortion would have been to continue embracing a codified morality at odds with the existent economic and social conditions of women.

The abortion is presented not as an extraordinary, unique event, but as an 'épreuve ordinaire' (LE, p. 30) shared by thousands of women who have no choice but to entrust their physical well-being to a stranger. The narrator's sense of participating in an age-old female tradition strengthens her resolve to go through with her abortion. The abortion's symbolic role in incorporating common elements of women's existence mirrors the emphasis on the interchangeability of female experience articulated in '*Je ne suis pas sortie de ma nuit*': 'Elles forment en moi une chaîne invisible où se côtoient des artistes, des écrivaines, des héroïnes de roman et des femmes de mon enfance. J'ai l'impression que mon histoire est en elles' (LE, p. 40). The notion of a 'je transpersonnel' resurfaces throughout *L'Evénement*, as, once again, the representativeness of experience is endowed with greater significance than its idiosyncratic or subjective qualities, a representativeness substantiated by the work's focus on the material conditions of illegal abortion in 1964: 'Une foule ressuscite, dans laquelle je suis prise. C'est elle qui, plus que mes souvenirs personnels, me redonne mon être de vingt-trois ans' (LE, p. 50). Indeed, the narrator sees not only herself but also her abortionist, her abortionist's companion, and her university friend in others, extending her drive for representativeness to embrace an 'il/ elle transpersonnel(le)'.

The draconian measures adopted by the state in an endeavour to prevent, or at least to criminalise, abortion, are highlighted in the narrator's quotation from the 1948 edition of the *Nouveau Larousse Universel*, a technique also employed in earlier works when seeking to provide documentary evidence of ideological coercion. The narrator must remind herself that the time wasted looking for a backstreet abortionist – the abortionist is not even mentioned until over half-way through the work – as well as the medical profession's unwillingness to help her, and her subsequent reluctance to confide in others, stem principally from the illegal nature of her act; that the prohibitive constituents of her environment are in turn due to the illegality of abortion at the time. The ubiquitousness of the law and the fear its transgression provokes render it impregnable at even the most basic linguistic level, as exemplified in the narrator's exchanges with a doctor: 'Ni lui ni moi n'avions prononcé le mot avortement une seule fois. C'était une chose qui n'avait pas de place dans le langage' (LE, p. 54). Indeed, the retrospective narrator believes that the backstreet abortionist was also frightened of the consequences of her act.[33] This historicisation of abortion reflects the formative influence accorded to environment and social class throughout Ernaux's corpus. Her narrators repeatedly portray the expression of sexuality as an historically determined activity which differs depending on the individual's material conditions or social status. Yet, however much the narrator is at pains to historicise the issue of abortion and to comprehend the *huis clos* of the medical profession at the time, or even the presumption of male students that she will engage in sexual relations with them given that she is already pregnant, her constant desire to vomit throughout the text is not solely attributable to physiological nausea but is clearly sourced in the general intolerance and inhumanity of her environment. Whatever the narrator's attempts at contextualisation, that she is forced to try to abort using a knitting needle is condemnation enough of the anti-abortion regime in place at the time. It is in this portrayal of the class and gender hierarchies which impede an individual's access to knowledge and freedom of action as highlighted in the narrator's experience of abortion – the corpus's original point of departure – that *L'Evénement* exemplifies the 'circular continuity' characteristic of Ernaux's writing.

CONCLUSION

As the Introduction to this study suggested, the formative role played by both gender norms and, above all, class distinction in the socialisation process of Ernaux's narrators points to the relevance of Beauvoirian and Bourdieuian interpretative strategies when analysing her work. In Ernaux's writing, the social significance of cultural indicators – whether of 'femininity' or 'working-classness' – is dictated by existent cultural hierarchies: individuals *learn* how to valorise components of their social environment. It is this belief in the material and ideological influences of childhood – in the imbrication of external 'objective' social structures with internal 'subjective' thought structures – which accounts for the narrators' resolute deconstruction of them throughout Ernaux's corpus. Her narrators repeatedly expose the naturalised inferiority of the marginalised, and counter both the vilification of working-class experience – above all by the education system – and the interdiction on the expression of female sexuality through their representation in the quintessentially bourgeois medium of literature. The retrospective distance required to analyse the principal components of acculturation may be seen to provide an optimistic developmental paradigm in the narrators' positioning as subject of the writerly gaze. However, the cross-cultural locus inhabited by Ernaux's narrators produces a tension in her writing, in that, if the denial of inherent class or gender characteristics promotes an existential model of individual voluntarism – a *pour soi* – the quasi-determinist influence of environment both necessitates a constant return to the working-class childhood origins of the narrator and neutralises the potential power of the subject position. While, for both Beauvoir and Bourdieu, sexual and class differences stem from social context, they nonetheless demand the collusion of the dominated for their smooth perpetuation. The narrator may consciously decry the oppressive identity-forming structures of French society, yet her ultimate inability to perceive herself outwith culturally imposed hierarchies accounts for the circularity of both her narratives and her corpus: her self-definition as Other can be seen to result in a form of immanence, in a regressive developmental paradigm.

All of Ernaux's concentric narrative circles are firmly rooted in the pivotal period of childhood, and, whatever their brief divergences from that central point, her narrators unfailingly return to it. Ernaux's narrators seek to return to a period before the symbolic murder of the mother initiated their class migration to the bourgeoisie and consequent fragmentation of identity; they wish to relive the earlier contentment and sense of wholeness in the mother/daughter symbiosis. If works such as *La Place* and *Une femme* point to the redemptive potential of anamnesis, Ernaux's corpus also reveals its clear limitations in the narrators' continuing dependency on it. In Ernaux's writing, memory can only bring short instances of relief, necessitating an endless return to the past for 'memory fixes'. Her narrators may maintain that the death of their parents brings with it the assumption of adult consciousness and responsibility, yet Ernaux's texts bear witness to the lure that the world of childhood continues to exert upon them and to their recurrent desire to enclose themselves in the cocoon it represents. The narrators' recollection of the past is less to move beyond it than to reimmerse themselves in it, less to shake off its formative links than to strengthen them. The narrator's remark in *La Honte* apropos of the conditioning power Yvetot held over her as a young girl is equally applicable to her in adulthood: 'En 52, je ne peux pas me penser en dehors d'Y. [...] Il n'y a pas pour moi d'autre monde' (LH, p. 42). Like the outlying areas described in the town, the further the narrators depart from the childhood centre in the events of their life narrative, the less value they appear to accord these events. In Ernaux's writing, the fundamental interrelation of past and present in her narrators' sense of identity is epitomised in this repeated return to childhood origins.

Notes to Introduction
pp. 1–16

1 Interview with Smaïn Laacher, 'Annie Ernaux ou l'inaccessible quiétude', *Politix*, no. 14 (1991), pp. 73–78, p. 75.

2 Ernaux's humanist belief in the existence of an extralinguistic 'reality' produces an indifference to what she considers to be insular aesthetic debates: 'La solitude la plus grande vient peut-être de ce que la littérature – quand j'en entends discuter par les écrivains ou les critiques – n'est évaluée qu'en termes esthétiques purs. On débat de sujets comme: "Qu'est-ce que le roman?", "Y a-t-il encore de grands romanciers?", "Etes-vous postmoderne?", etc. Pour moi, l'esthétique n'est pas une fin, c'est un moyen pour mieux atteindre quelque chose, réalité, vérité, comme on voudra', 'Annie Ernaux ou l'inaccessible quiétude', *Politix*, no. 14, p. 78. In her article 'De corps à corps: réceptions croisées d'Annie Ernaux', Isabelle Charpentier argues that it is partly Ernaux's refusal to indulge in a more esoteric approach to literature which accounts for the criticism she has received from certain '*lectores*'. Her deceptively simple 'sociological' style and metanarrative comments diminish the professional usefulness and respect in which such *lectores* are held; *Politix*, no. 27 (1994), pp. 45–75, p. 75. In his article 'Pour une critique de la lecture', Pierre Bourdieu employs the term '*lectore*' to describe the literary commentator 'qui lit, commente, déchiffre un discours déjà produit, dont il tient son *auctoritas*', *La Lecture (II) – Approches*, Cahiers du séminaire de philosophie 2 (Strasbourg: Centre de documentation en histoire de la philosophie, 1984), p. 13.

3 For a detailed discussion of the reader response to Ernaux's writing, see the Charpentier article already mentioned and Lyn Thomas's *Annie Ernaux: An Introduction to the Writer and her Audience* (Oxford and New York: Berg, 1999).

4 However, as Chapter 3 argues, Ernaux's narrators may be seen to manifest an ambivalent attitude towards their literary heritage: while critical of its distorted representation of working-class experience, they repeatedly define themselves with reference to it.

5 Talk at Winchester College, 10 March 1988.

6 *Le Dictionnaire: Littérature française contemporaine*, ed. Jérôme Garcin (Paris: Editions François Bourin, 1989), pp. 179–83, p. 180.

7 Ernaux and her narrators employ both the terms 'ethnography' and 'ethnology' when foregrounding the representative significance of the works.

8 'Ecrire pour comprendre les choses', interview with Lucie Côté, *La Presse*, 26 March 1992. Ernaux may claim to view as largely irrelevant the precise category to which critics assign her work, yet, as Chapter 3 argues, her narrators are nonetheless at pains to impose their own definition on it. For further details on Ernaux's attitude to genre, see either the autobiographical entry in *Le Dictionnaire: Littérature française contemporaine* mentioned above, pp. 179–83 or Michèle Bacholle, 'An interview with Annie Ernaux: Ecrire le vécu', *Sites*, vol. 2, no. 1 (1998), pp. 141–51. Rita Felski perceives an indifference to aesthetic categories as intrinsic to the feminist confession:

'Aesthetic criteria are rejected as irrelevant; a conscious artistic structure is in fact suspect insofar as it implies distance and control rather than an unmediated baring of the soul', *Beyond Feminist Aesthetics: Feminist Literature and Social Change* (London: Hutchinson Radius, 1989), p. 97. Where Felski interprets the insignificance of aesthetic criteria or formal properties from a feminist optic, Pierre Bourdieu perceives such insignificance as characteristic of working-class taste in art: 'Tout se passe en effet comme si l'"esthétique populaire" [...] était fondée sur l'affirmation de la continuité de l'art et de la vie, qui implique la subordination de la forme à la fonction', *La Distinction: Critique sociale du jugement* (Paris: Editions de Minuit, 1979), p. V. Both perspectives are relevant to Ernaux's political aim of representing working-class women's experience.

  9   Mary G. Mason perceives the implication of the Other in female self-portraiture as linked to this lack of self-validation, just as women's peripheral social position typically requires mediation through the role of the Other: 'the self-discovery of female identity seems to acknowledge the real presence and recognition of another consciousness, and the disclosure of female self is linked to the identification of some "other"', 'The Other Voice: Autobiographies of Women Writers', in *Life/Lines, Theorizing Women's Autobiography*, ed. Bella Brodzki and Celeste Schenck, (Ithaca and London: Cornell University Press, 1988), pp. 19–44, p. 22.

  10   As Nellie Y. McKay remarks, auto/biographical writing may encompass a personal and political objective for women: 'Community identity permits the rejection of historically diminishing images of self imposed by the dominant culture; it allows marginalized individuals to embrace alternative selves constructed from positive (and more authentic) images of their own creation', 'Race, Gender, and Cultural Context in Zora Neale Hurston's *Dust Tracks on a Road*', *Life/Lines, Theorizing Women's Autobiography*, pp. 175–88, p. 175.

  11   In her essay 'Subject to Subject/Voice to Voice: Twentieth-Century Autobiographical Fiction by Women Writers', Janice Morgan relates this drive for representativeness to the psychoanalyst Nancy Chodorow's theory of gender development, which maintains that girls' ego boundaries are less rigid than boys': 'Rather than being unitary, monumental, and posited as either extraordinarily unique (à la Rousseau) or else thoroughly exemplary (à la Henry Adams), women's sense of self as portrayed in autobiographic texts has been much more locally-bound, tied to the exigencies of a particular place and time, tied especially to the key individuals who marked their development', *Gender and Genre in Literature: Redefining Autobiography in Twentieth-Century Women's Fiction*, ed. Janice Morgan and Colette T. Hall (New York and London: Garland Publishing, 1991), pp. 3–19, p. 8. For further discussion of the characteristics associated with women's autobiographical writing, see Liz Stanley's *The Auto/biographical I: The Theory and Practice of Feminist Auto/biography* (Manchester and New York: Manchester University Press, 1992), or Sidonie Smith's *A Poetics of Women's Autobiography: Marginality and the Fictions of Self-Representation* (Bloomington and Indianapolis: Indiana University Press, 1987).

  12   'Women's Autobiographical Selves: Theory and Practice', *The Private Self, Theory and Practice of Women's Autobiographical Writings* (London: Routledge, 1988), ed. Shari Benstock, pp. 34–62, p. 38.

  13   See 'Vers un Je transpersonnel', Autofictions et Cie, *Cahiers RITM*, no. 6 (1994) Université Paris X-Nanterre, pp. 218–21. Ernaux's theoretical conception of

the role of the first-person narrator has echoes of Cixous's definition of writerly 'bisexualité', which she views as a dynamic exchange, an ongoing 'cohabitation', in which both 'sexualities' coexist rather than dominate one another: 'Admettre qu'écrire c'est justement travailler (dans) l'entre, interroger le procès du même *et* de l'autre sans lequel rien ne vit, défaire le travail de la mort, c'est d'abord vouloir le deux, et les deux, l'ensemble de l'un et l'autre non pas figés dans des séquences de lutte et d'expulsion ou autre mise à mort, mais dynamisés à l'infini par un incessant échangement de l'un entre l'autre sujet différent', 'Le Rire de la Méduse', special issue of *L'Arc*, 'Simone de Beauvoir et la lutte des femmes', no. 61 (1975), pp. 39–54, p. 46.

14   Michèle Bacholle, 'An interview with Annie Ernaux: Ecrire le vécu', *Sites*, pp. 141–51, p. 145.

15   This aim for directness is also apparent in Ernaux's incorporation of metacommentaries; in her preference for the *passé composé* over the more literary *passé simple*; and in her general eschewal of conventional figures of speech such as metaphor or allegory, which she perceives as reinforcing cultural elitism and thereby exclusion. While the use of the *passé simple* is clearly incompatible with the interior monologues of the early trilogy, metaphors do exist in Ernaux's writing, particularly in her most linguistically colourful work, *Les Armoires vides*. Ernaux desires that the narrative form of her writing be accessible to the 'underclass' it represents: 'Mais je souhaite rester, d'une certaine façon, au-dessous de la littérature' (UF, p. 23).

16   While references to the same event in more than one text corroborate an auto/biographical reading of the works, they also serve to illustrate changes in narratorial perspective. One such event, mentioned by Claire-Lise Tondeur in *Annie Ernaux ou l'exil intérieur* (Amsterdam and Atlanta, GA: Rodopi, 1996), pp. 92–93, describes the narrator asleep on her mother's lap, and occurs in both *Ce qu'ils disent ou rien* and *La Femme gelée*. The first example reveals an angry young woman intent on vilifying her past: 'Penser que je l'ai adorée, une gosse qui était moi, quelle chose incompréhensible. Sa voix, les jours de gueuleton, je m'endormais contre sa poitrine, j'entendais les mots se former, ça grondait, comme si j'étais née de cette voix' (CDR, p. 129). The same event is given a quite different slant in *La Femme gelée*: 'Œdipe, je m'en tape. Je l'adorais aussi, elle. Elle, cette voix profonde que j'écoutais naître dans sa gorge, les soirs de fête, quand je m'endormais sur ses genoux' (LFG, p. 19). The latter representation exemplifies the narrator's more conciliatory attitude towards, as well as her 'bourgeoisisation' of, her mother. This change in perception reflects both the narrator's greater maturity and the influence exerted by her present social class when assessing the past, an influence apparent in the more 'classic' style of all subsequent works.

17   This focus on others and the absence of explicit nominal coincidence of narrator and author break with Philippe Lejeune's somewhat rigid autobiographical pact, which defines autobiography as a 'Récit rétrospectif en prose qu'une personne réelle fait de sa propre existence, lorsqu'elle met l'accent sur sa vie individuelle, en particulier sur l'histoire de sa personnalité', *Le Pacte autobiographique* (Paris: Editions du Seuil, 1996), p. 14.

18   In a review of *Une femme*, Maryse Rossi-Dutheil remarks: 'Ernaux use d'une phraséologie si dépouillée et si inexpressive qu'elle en devient symptomatique d'une sécheresse de cœur ou d'une impuissance à traduire ses sentiments', *L'Eveil Provence*, 2 April 1988, quoted in Marie-France Savéan, *La Place et Une femme d'Annie Ernaux*

(Paris: Gallimard, 1994), p. 193.

19   Ernaux, in common with Pierre Bourdieu, rejects the rationale behind Auguste Comte's description of a 'communisme linguistique', maintaining instead that it is relations of power which determine an individual's linguistic capital. See Bourdieu, *Ce que parler veut dire: L'Economie des échanges linguistiques* (Paris: Fayard, 1982), p. 24.

20   In her article 'Stylistic Aspects of Women's Writing: The Case of Annie Ernaux', Carol Sanders provides an additional gendered interpretation of Ernaux's disjointed syntax: 'the rejection of traditional syntax [is] seen as an attempt to resist the imposition of a male-defined rational ordering by those who equate logocentrism with phallocentrism', *French Cultural Studies*, no. 4 (1993), pp. 15–29, p. 17. Sanders is careful to distinguish between what she views as Ernaux's conformity to the general components of a 'feminine aesthetics' and the more deliberately experimental and radical *écriture féminine*. As Chapter 1 details, experimental aspects to Ernaux's writing do exist, as in Anne's deliberate abandonment of conventional gender usage in *Ce qu'ils disent ou rien*. (It is not merely Ernaux's use of syntax which may be viewed as illustrative of a 'feminine aesthetics', but equally her focus on the personal and everyday and her more general disjunctive or episodic narrative – particularly in works following *La Femme gelée* – which contrasts with the coherent, linear chronology associated with male autobiographical writing.)

21   For further discussion of this *mise en abîme*, see my article 'Recuperating Romance: Literary Paradigms in the Works of Annie Ernaux', *Forum for Modern Language Studies*, vol. 32, no. 3 (1996), pp. 240–50.

22   Given the conservative nature of the French literary establishment and canon, a conservatism acknowledged by both Ernaux and her narrators, it is tempting to speculate that her adoption of a more refined literary language in *La Place* in lieu of the slang vulgarities which pepper the early works may have contributed to her being awarded the *Prix Renaudot* for the work.

23   See the Bibliography for further details of all publications on Ernaux.

24   Recent publications on Beauvoir's *Le Deuxième Sexe* include *Simone de Beauvoir's* The Second Sex: *New Interdisciplinary Essays* (Manchester: Manchester University Press, 1998), ed. Ruth Evans, and *Simone de Beauvoir: A Critical Reader* (London and New York: Routledge, 1998), ed. Elizabeth Fallaize.

Notes to Chapter 1
pp. 17–47

1   Interview with Chantal Langeard, 'Annie Ernaux', *Vie ouvrière*, 8 October 1990, p. 45.

2   *Sexual/Textual Politics* (London: Methuen, 1985), pp. 86–87: 'As for the complex interactions of class and gender, they too have received little attention among Anglo-American feminist critics.' Moi's regret at this lack of critical attention may lie behind her interest in the sociologist Pierre Bourdieu, and the relevance of his work to feminist studies. See Moi's article 'Appropriating Bourdieu: Feminist Theory and Pierre Bourdieu's Sociology of Culture', *New Literary History*, no. 22 (1991), pp. 1017–49.

3   The topic of abortion and its legalisation was a particularly relevant one in France at the time of the text's publication. The abortion issue culminated in the appearance of a manifesto on 5 April 1971 in *Le Nouvel Observateur*, signed by 343 women claiming that they had had illegal abortions, and the ratification of the 'loi Veil' in 1974. In an interview with Mireille Dumas, 'Une femme dans l'engrenage', *Combat*, 13 March 1981, p. 14, Ernaux discusses the importance of this type of feminist action: 'Bien que je n'y milite plus, les mouvements féministes me semblent nécessaires. Ils font avancer les choses. J'ai moi-même participé au MLAC et me suis battue pour la reconnaissance de l'avortement. Mais il ne faut pas séparer l'évolution de la femme de l'évolution sociale et politique. Tout est lié.'

4   While the abortion has been interpreted as an allegorical cleansing of the narrator's links with the bourgeoisie, it is more convincingly read as a 'purification' of the narrator's 'emotional baggage' regarding her working-class background. Through-out the work, the narrator is far keener to sever ties with her working-class past, a past she associates with ignorance and oppression, than with her bourgeois present. Indeed, even at the work's conclusion, the narrator's questioning of the desirability of belonging to the bourgeoisie remains tentative. The narrator's defining characteristic is her resentful attitude towards her working-class origins; it is her repeated desire to understand, and thereby free herself from, the influence exerted by such origins which reinforces the parallels between the narrator's emotional and physical need to 'purge' herself of them. An intertextual reading of Ernaux's texts supports this interpretation of the abortion's symbolism in *Les Armoires vides*. In *La Honte*, the narrator locates the genesis of her sense of shame and consequent desire to escape her working-class origins in the moment in childhood when she witnessed her father attempting to mur-der her mother, and in *L'Evénement* the narrator remarks apropos of her abortion: 'J'ai tué ma mère en moi à ce moment-là' (LE, p. 77).

5   It is somewhat ironic, given the privileged status of Sundays in the young narrator's weekly routine and the concomitance of religion and sexuality for her – a concomitance explored later in this chapter – that the narrative is also related on a Sunday, as the narrator undergoes the 'purification' of abortion.

6   In her work *Annie Ernaux ou l'exil intérieur* (Amsterdam and Atlanta, GA: Rodopi, 1996), p. 24, Claire-Lise Tondeur attributes this latter remark to the clients in her father's café. While such clients may be portrayed as lecherous, their respect for

the narrator's parents would make such a remark highly improbable. Given the narrator's recurrent association of pain and pleasure, of abortion and sexual intercourse (see also LAV, p. 180), a more likely attribution would be to her boyfriend. This interpretation finds support in an imaginary remark addressed by the narrator to her boyfriend towards the text's conclusion, in which she employs an identical description of her genitalia, p. 172: 'Ta bouche méprisante, cornet pour les bonbons violacés.'

7   In *Le Deuxième Sexe II* (Paris: Gallimard, 1949; repr. 1976), p. 184, Beauvoir enumerates three recognised (and interrelated) forms of masochism, all of which, to varying degrees, are manifested by Ernaux's narrator: 'l'une [des formes] consiste dans la liaison de la douleur et de la volupté, une autre serait l'acceptation féminine de la dépendance érotique, la dernière reposerait sur un mécanisme d'autopunition. La femme serait masochiste parce qu'en elle plaisir et douleur seraient liés à travers défloration et accouchement, et parce qu'elle consentirait à son rôle passif.' As this chapter goes on to argue, however, the 'masochism' displayed by Denise in her relationships is unusually self-possessed.

8   The language employed by the narrator to describe her pleasure in eating – 'tentation', 'vagues douces', 'Je ne résistais pas' (LAV, p. 31) – is highly sensual, and the realisation of her eaterly desires produces a satisfaction with strong sexual overtones: 'la crème jaillie sur la langue' (LAV, p. 37). Food plays an important role throughout Ernaux's corpus – a role related to the working-class origins of her narrators – in that it connotes success and wealth, and acts as a focus for family reunions, as exemplified by the numerous 'repas de famille' described in her writing. Marie-France Savéan, in her study *La Place et Une femme d'Annie Ernaux* (Paris: Gallimard, 1994), p. 57, points to the continuing importance of food even as the narrator's parents approach death: her father has a stomach operation and suffers from serious digestive problems shortly before his death in *La Place*, while one of her mother's principal pleasures when she has Alzheimer's disease is eating cakes the narrator brings her. As Chapter 4 remarks, the narrators' own relationship to food has not been straightforward.

9   Beauvoir in *Le Deuxième Sexe II*, p. 331, comments on this absence: 'Il est peu de sujets sur lesquels la société bourgeoise déploie plus d'hypocrisie: l'avortement est un crime répugnant auquel il est indécent de faire allusion. Qu'un écrivain décrive les joies et les souffrances d'une accouchée, c'est parfait; qu'il parle d'une avortée, on l'accuse de se vautrer dans l'ordure et de décrire l'humanité sous un jour abject.' That the masculinist bias of the canonical texts on university syllabi contributes to this absence of representation of a specifically female experience is also acknowledged in *La Femme gelée*.

10   In *L'Evénement*, which provides a detailed account of the same abortion, the narrator makes a similar observation: 'J'espérais trouver des renseignements pratiques mais les articles ne parlaient que des suites de l'"avortement criminel", et celles-ci ne m'intéressaient pas' (LE, p. 37).

11   The role played by social conditioning throughout Ernaux's writing can be seen to reduce the potential for individual agency and, consequently, to discourage her narrators from assuming responsibility for their actions. As Chapter 5 argues with reference to *La Honte*, the narrator's religious education and the routine nature of her existence do little to instil a sense of empowerment in the individual.

12   These constraints are severe. Even more than *Les Armoires vides*, *La Honte* points to their all-consuming nature: 'Et je dois admettre ceci: rien ne pourra faire que,

jusqu'à l'adolescence, la croyance en Dieu n'ait été pour moi la seule normalité et la religion catholique la seule vérité' (LH, p. 80).

13   In *L'Invention du quotidien 2* (Paris: Gallimard, 1994), Pierre Mayol highlights the sexualised nature of these two domains: 'Le "café de quartier" […] peut être considéré, à certains égards, comme l'équivalent de la "maison des hommes" des sociétés traditionnelles. […] le café est une "chicane", un sas de rééquilibrage de l'atmosphère sociale, entre le monde du travail et la vie intime […]. A l'inverse, la boutique du commerçant joue le rôle d'une "maison des femmes" où ce qu'il est convenu d'appeler "le féminin" trouve le lieu de son exercise: échanges de paroles, de nouvelles familiales, menus propos sur la gastronomie, l'éducation des enfants, etc.' (p. 38).

14   The narrator partly attributes her growing preference for the educational over the domestic to maternal influence – once again ascribing responsibility to the Other – in that her mother prevents her from mixing with local working-class girls in order to maximise the benefits of the school environment. Interestingly, the incident which initiates this maternal interdiction and severance from early childhood centres on the narrator stealing roses – a further act of transgression involving the classic symbol of female sexuality – which prick her fingers and cause them to bleed, an incident immediately followed by her first sight of a penis. The symbolism of the rose is reinforced throughout the text by the narrator's association of the term 'fleur' with female sexual organs. See, for example, pp. 11, 30, 43, 65, and 181.

15   Ernaux's narrators frequently comment on, and resent, the omnipresence of customers during their upbringing. The narrator of *La Place* gives an indication of this lack of privacy: 'Au rez-de-chaussée, l'alimentation communiquait avec le café par une pièce minuscule où débouchait l'escalier pour les chambres et le grenier. Bien qu'elle soit devenue la cuisine, les clients ont toujours utilisé cette pièce comme passage entre l'épicerie et le café' (LP, pp. 51–52). In the domestic topography provided by *La Honte*, p. 50, we learn that there is not even a door separating the kitchen from the café.

16   The adolescent narrator's sense that her home is a transient location, that life proper will begin as soon as she leaves it, is shared by her counterpart in *Ce qu'ils disent ou rien*.

17   The narrator of *La Honte* perceives such shame as the driving force behind her entire corpus. As this quotation also intimates – and as the Introduction remarks – Ernaux's narrators repeatedly point to the innovative nature of their representation, whether it be the sexually explicit narrative of *Passion simple* which relates sexual pleasure from a female perspective, the unconventionality of the narrator's views on marriage and motherhood in *La Femme gelée*, or the accuracy of the portrayal of working-class experience in *La Place* and *Une femme*.

18   As Pierre Bourdieu observes apropos of a study of musical preferences: '*le goût "populaire"* représenté ici par le choix d'œuvres […] comme celles de Mariano, Guétary ou Petula Clark, trouve sa fréquence maximum dans les classes populaires et varie en raison inverse du capital scolaire', *La Distinction: Critique sociale du jugement* (Paris: Editions de Minuit, 1979), p. 16. In Ernaux's writing, working-class taste is characterised by a valorisation of modernity, and aesthetic appreciation is based on accessibility and price. In *La Place*, the narrator demonstrates her own middle-class certainty as to the constituents of taste, when, having described her father's modernisation of the café, she remarks that 'déjà les cafetiers qui avaient du flair revenaient au

colombage normand, aux fausses poutres et aux vieilles lampes' (LP, p. 84).

19   For Ernaux, as for Bourdieu, people learn how to 'appreciate' culture. As the narrator of *Journal du dehors* remarks on overhearing a conversation regarding an abstract painting, 'Impression qu'il me manque l'initiation à un savoir. Mais il ne s'agit pas de savoir puisque – en y réfléchissant – à la place "d'une telle sensualité", ils auraient bien pu dire "une telle fraîcheur!" ou "une telle violence!" sans que l'absence de rapport entre le tableau et l'appréciation soit modifiée: il ne s'agit que de l'acquisition d'un code' (JDD, p. 22). In *La Place*, the narrator observes that her working-class father never verbalises the emotions evoked by particular sights or sounds, and that her own articulation of aesthetic preferences signals her assimilation proper into the bourgeoisie.

20   As Bourdieu remarks: 'Quant aux classes populaires, elles n'ont sans doute pas d'autre fonction dans le système des prises de position esthétiques que celle de repoussoir, de point de référence négatif par rapport auquel se définissent, de négation en négation, toutes les esthétiques', *La Distinction*, pp. 61–62. Bourdieu also comments on the naturalisation of a culturally acquired aesthetics and on the negative social judgement which accompanies any indication of the learned properties of 'good taste' – properties which are, of course, most visible among members of the working class or petite bourgeoisie.

21   For this reason, the narrator of *La Place* – a work which aims to provide a representative account of working-class experience – seeks to avoid all use of irony when relating working-class characteristics, remarking apropos of her father's world, 'L'ironie, inconnue' (LP, p. 65). Her husband, however, is described as 'né dans une bourgeoisie à diplômes, constamment "ironique"' (LP, p. 96).

22   In this assessment of Denise, my emphasis differs slightly from that of Loraine Day, who in an article entitled 'Class, Sexuality and Subjectivity in Annie Ernaux's *Les Armoires vides*' remarks that 'it is tempting to speculate that once Denise allows her sexuality free rein, as she does only with Marc, an internalised model of female humiliation overcomes the assertive tendencies she has previously displayed', *Contemporary French Fiction by Women*, ed. Margaret Atack and Phil Powrie (Manchester: Manchester University Press, 1990), pp. 41–55, p. 52.

23   Shortly before losing her virginity, the narrator's perception of sexuality as a means of transcending her working-class origins is made clear when she compares penetration to a gesture made by her father, highlighting the 'cleansing' significance it has for her: 'Ça me fait un peu peur, ça saignera, un petit fût de sang, lie bleue, c'est mon père qui purge les barriques et en sort de grandes peaux molles au bout de l'immense rince-bouteilles chevelu' (LAV, p. 170). The removal of the 'grandes peaux molles' connotes the breaking of the hymen.

24   This description of the redemptive power of heterosexual activity is all the more striking, given that the narrator meets Guy on Sundays, instead of attending mass, despite having been taught that '"Quand on ne va pas à la messe pour partir en promenade, c'est péché mortel"' (LAV, p. 87). Her desire to be assimilated by the middle classes is far stronger than any fear of religious retribution.

25   *Ce que parler veut dire: L'Economie des échanges linguistiques* (Paris: Fayard, 1982), p. 64.

26   Throughout Ernaux's writing, linguistic adroitness is the ultimate aphrodisiac in that it indicates social superiority. In *Ce qu'ils disent ou rien*, any reservations

Anne may harbour vis-à-vis Mathieu are banished due to his language skills. He may present a patronising and distorted perception of the working class, yet Anne, despite belonging to the class described, does not contest his eloquent analysis of it. Analogous to the influence of literature on Denise's self-perception, Anne's identity is imposed upon her by an 'authoritative' representative of the patriarchal order. That the narrator's lover in *Passion simple* is not gifted linguistically provides further evidence that the relationship is a means of reliving her past, rather than escaping it, which is the function of heterosexual relationships in the early trilogy. See Chapter 2 for a more detailed discussion of the lover's role in *Passion simple*.

27   The narrator of *Les Armoires vides* refers to Balzac and Maupassant in what can be viewed as a further criticism of idealised representations of working-class experience: 'Ils [her parents' customers] nous montent dessus, ils nous envahissent, dix fois plus affreux que dans Balzac, pire que Maupassant' (LAV, p. 111). As both the Introduction and Chapter 3 suggest, Ernaux's narrators occupy an ambivalent position in relation to their literary predecessors and the French literary tradition generally, dismissing much of its patriarchal, classist content, yet simultaneously displaying an anxiety to be situated in relation to it.

28   In *La Place*, the narrator employs a similar image to describe the municipal library which is 'silencieux, plus encore qu'à l'église' (LP, p. 111). In *Les Armoires vides*, the narrator also refers to the library as 'le château de la belle au bois dormant' (LAV, p. 166), indicating her sense of entering a sacred realm, as well as her belief in university's ability to actualise her virtual selves instigated by reading and to provide them with an appropriate Prince Charming.

29   In her article 'Le Problème du langage chez Annie Ernaux', Christine Fau draws an analogy between the connotative power of the words Denise comes across in literature and those she overhears in conversations between her mother and her customers: both fuel the young narrator's imagination by portraying a world not yet accessible to her, *French Review*, vol. 68, no. 3 (February 1995), pp. 501–12. In *Le Deuxième Sexe II*, Simone de Beauvoir maintains that similar fantasies are the fruit of many young girls' imagination, not merely those from the working class: 'Souvent elles inventent des romans; elles supposent qu'elles sont une enfant adoptée, que leurs parents ne sont pas vraiment leurs parents' (p. 52).

30   Earlier in the work, the narrator comments on the freedom of expression which characterises her home life, and the fact that her 'natural' language contains 'du popu et du patois' (LAV, p. 66). As Chapter 3 discusses, Ernaux's narrators appear unwilling to acknowledge the possibility of working-class language infiltrating the domain of literature, unless it is spoken by others. Her narrators foreground the disparities between the spoken language of their parents and the written language of their bourgeois education, disparities which – as is the case in *Les Armoires vides* – appear overly pronounced, leading to the impression that the narrators are suffering from a form of willed linguistic amnesia. Ernaux has elsewhere remarked upon her own 'bilingualism': 'J'ai deux langues en fait, j'ai le langage oral qui était donc celui de la famille, des amis du quartier, et évidemment c'était un langage populaire et normand, avec des tournures en normand. [...] Par écrit, c'est un phénomène assez simple. Comme je lisais beaucoup, j'ai vite écrit très bien, j'avais un vocabulaire très étendu, j'avais les tournures grammaticales des livres', unpublished interview with Siobhán McIlvanney, 23 September 1993.

31   Eric Deschodt in 'Les Derniers Lauriers', *Spectacle du Monde*, no. 274 (1985), p. 70, interprets these features of Ernaux's writing as evidence of a distinct regional style: 'Il existe un style normand, viking plutôt: le style à la hache. Corneille, Flaubert, Maupassant, La Varende, Annie Ernaux, si différents que les siècles et leurs naissances les aient faits, utilisent tous, comme personne en dehors de leur province, la même brièveté meurtrière, le même sens de l'ellipse, la même économie décisive. La même conviction que les mots trompent toujours et qu'il faut se garder d'en trop employer.'

32   The different reading matter of family members illustrates this. If the detail that Anne is reading *L'Etranger* indicates her feelings of alienation in *Ce qu'ils disent ou rien*, the reading matter of her parents – *Paris-Normandie* and *France-Soir* – under-lines their interest in *faits divers*, and that of the narrator's grandmother – *Le Pèlerin* – her conservative Catholicism. These diverse literary tastes may be interpreted as reflecting Anne's increasing assimilation into the bourgeoisie in the form of gaining access to its culture: while she reads philosophical works in which the functioning of the social order is thrown into question, her family's limited education is manifested in their parochialism and concern with everyday 'banalities'. As in *Les Armoires vides*, reading is both a means of making the narrator's home life more tolerable and of alerting her to the power of language. However, following her unhappy sexual expe-riences, Anne feels betrayed by literature's representation of female sexuality and stops reading altogether. Just as her parents' language fails to construct a representation of her which coincides with her self-image, so literature offers no reflection of her expe-riences: '*Le Grand Meaulnes*, un type qui cherchait, mais ce sont toujours les garçons qui déambulent le nez au vent dans les livres, la grande meaulnesse, ça ne m'a pas fait rire' (CDR, p. 150).

33   It is interesting to speculate that the work's greater fictional content and more conventional narrative structure may have had some bearing on its reception, in that *Ce qu'ils disent ou rien* is probably the least successful of Ernaux's works; it can be viewed as sounding a rather false note in the search for 'authenticity' which charac-terises Ernaux's auto/biographical literary project.

34   In this deliberate sartorial provocation, the narrator resembles Marguerite Duras's heroine in *L'Amant*. Both narrators are the same age – 15½ – and both narra-tives relate the transition from childhood to adulthood through sexual awakening. Further parallels may be found in the maternal jealousy of the daughter's sexual pleas-ure, the articulation of the desire to write alongside that of sexual desire, and the theme of social deviance.

35   As Susan Koppelman Cornillon remarks in 'The Fiction of Fiction', *Images of Women in Fiction: Feminist Perspectives* (Bowling Green, OH: Bowling Green Uni-versity Popular Press, 1972), pp. 113–30, p. 127: 'Women in fiction only very rarely either deal with (i.e., touch, perform acts upon) their own bodies or experience their bodies directly, unless they are putting the finishing touches on a make-up job or suffering either labor pains or some non-genderally related agony. In fiction female bodies do not belong to females; they are male accessories, male possessions or reflec-tions. Perhaps one of the most significant bits of evidence we have of this state of affairs is the fact that women do not masturbate in fiction.' Beauvoir, too, comments on the taboos surrounding the sexually active, autonomous woman, whose conduct threatens to undermine the conventions (and inheritance laws) of patriarchal society, *Le Deuxième Sexe II*, p. 245.

36   This characterisation of her parents' speech as utterly lacking in interest points to a further possible interpretation of the work's title as conveyed in the expression 'Ce qu'ils disent ou rien, c'est la même chose.'

37   'Annie Ernaux, filial ambivalence and *Ce qu'ils disent ou rien*', *Romance Studies*, no. 24, (Fall 1994), pp. 71–84.

38   *The Reproduction of Mothering: Psychoanalysis and the Sociology of Gender* (Berkeley and Los Angeles: University of California Press, 1978), p. 135.

39   The narrator dismisses her mother's grieving as inauthentic, maintaining that, at the age of 48, she should have come to terms with the fact that the narrator's grandmother would soon die. Such a dismissal may be viewed ironically, in light of the profound and ineradicable repercussions the death of the mother has on the narrator in later works.

40   'On Female Identity and Writing by Women', *Writing and Sexual Difference*, ed. Elizabeth Abel (Brighton: Harvester, 1982), pp. 177–91, p. 186, note 18.

41   As Chapter 2 comments, the narrator's decision to espouse a heterosexual model of sexual relations in *La Femme gelée* is similarly anchored in a fear of social condemnation, rather than antipathy towards homosexuality.

42   Binary oppositions – as illustrated in the dichotomies masculine/feminine, culture/nature, rational/irrational, in which the 'opposition' is in fact an implicit hierarchy with the first component valorised over the second – have formed an important target for French feminist thought, which aims to uncover and deconstruct such hierarchies.

43   This lack of correspondence is given clear articulation in the opening remark of Irigaray's essay, 'Ce sexe qui n'en est pas un', in the collection of the same name (Paris: Editions de Minuit, 1977): 'La sexualité féminine a toujours été pensée à partir de paramètres masculins' (p. 23).

44   In certain respects, Anne's inability to relate to the public representation of her experience conforms to Edwin and Shirley Ardener's theory of muted and dominant linguistic groups, in which women fall into the first category and men, the second. According to this theory, the 'muted' group, while capable of formulating its own beliefs about the social reality it inhabits, is forced to adopt dominant modes of expression if it wishes to give them public articulation. See Shirley Ardener, ed., *Perceiving Women* (London: Dent, 1975) and *Defining Females* (London: John Wiley, 1978).

45   Monique Wittig, expressing a widely held feminist belief, comments on the detrimental effects of the generic masculine in language use, and considers the complete eradication of gender a prerequisite of sexual equality: 'Sex, under the name of gender, permeates the whole body of language and forces every locutor, if she belongs to the oppressed sex, to proclaim it in her speech, that is, to appear in language under her proper physical form and not under the abstract form, which every male locutor has the unquestioned right to use. The abstract form, the general, the universal, this is what the so-called masculine gender means, for the class of men have appropriated the universal for themselves,' 'The Mark of Gender', in *The Poetics of Gender*, ed. Nancy K. Miller (New York: Columbia University Press, 1986), pp. 63–73, pp. 65–66. The dismissal of the generic 'he' as an innocent grammatical construction has also been challenged by linguists such as Ann Bodine and Deborah Cameron. Simone de Beauvoir comments on the absurdity of generic conventions such as adjectival agreements, in

which the presence of one masculine noun – regardless of the number of feminine nouns present – requires a masculine adjective in French, introduction to 'Les Femmes s'entêtent' in *Les Temps modernes* (April–May 1974), pp. 1719–20.

Notes to Chapter 2

pp. 49–85

1   *The Mother/Daughter Plot: Narrative, Psychoanalysis, Feminism* (Bloomington and Indianapolis: Indiana University Press, 1989), p. 163.

2   In *La Femme gelée*, for example, the narrator condemns what she perceives as the romanticisation of self-sacrifice in a remark which could be seen to foreshadow the behaviour of her counterpart in *Passion simple*: 'Son exaltation du don total ne me bottait pas davantage, quand on aime un homme on accepte tout de lui, disait-elle, on mangerait sa merde. Plus tard j'en entendrai d'autres, plus évolué [sic], plus précieux, sur la passion, se perdre dans l'autre, mais pareil au fond' (LFG, p. 69).

3   In *Les Armoires vides*, the narrator twice mentions Simone de Beauvoir as one of the writers who most interested her when first introduced to 'serious' literature. She mentions her a third time when envisaging her future: 'Je serai agrégée de lettres, ça ressemblera presque à Simone de Beauvoir' (LAV, p. 175). In *La Place*, we learn that the narrator was reading *Les Mandarins* when her father died, and, in *Une femme*, emphasising the formative role both women played in her life, the narrator remarks apropos of her mother: 'Elle est morte huit jours avant Simone de Beauvoir' (UF, p. 105). Indeed, the work was commenced the day after Beauvoir's funeral and resembles Beauvoir's account of her own mother's death, *Une mort très douce*. Beauvoir is incorporated into the Parisian landscape in both *Journal du dehors,* which mentions the '*Beauvoir Hôtel*' (JDD, p. 37), and *La Vie extérieure*, which describes her gravestone and her ineradicable victory over the other women with whom Sartre was amorously involved in that she is buried with him (LVE, p. 104). Ernaux discusses Beauvoir's influence on her in her interview with Philippe Vilain, 'Entretien avec Annie Ernaux: Une "conscience malheureuse" de femme', *LittéRéalité*, vol. 9, no. 1 (1997), pp. 66–71.

4   Beauvoir's work aims to document 'le destin traditionnel de la femme' (LDS II, p. 9), a destiny which, as represented in *Le Deuxième Sexe*, is emphatically bourgeois. This normative thrust of Beauvoir's writing in which the middle-class model of womanhood denotes Womanhood *tout court*, while ironically duplicating the universalising tendency it denounces in relation to the sexes, perfectly illustrates the point made by Ernaux's narrator. That is, that the zenith of femininity is embodied by middle-class women, that it is they who represent the barometer against which all other women must be measured. Like Beauvoir, Ernaux's perception of femininity is unequivocally existential: 'J'en ai vraiment assez d'entendre parler de cette différence de nature qui entraîne une différence de rôle. Dans les milieux ruraux, la femme travaille depuis des siècles et porte la culotte … Tout le système pousse à la différenciation alors qu'au départ la féminité n'existe pas. Quant à la féminitude, c'est une notion bourgeoise', interview with Mireille Dumas, 'Une femme dans l'engrenage', *Combat*, 13 March 1981, p. 14.

5   Very few of the narrator's remarks regarding her working-class female relatives have a corresponding 'theoretical' remark in Beauvoir's work. Indeed, it is

189

somewhat ironic that, given her criticism of class bias in literature, Ernaux should admire Beauvoir's *Le Deuxième Sexe*, which only occasionally refers to working-class or rural women in its case studies and to the class-related differences governing their female condition. The predominantly negative portrayal of motherhood among the working-class women of the narrator's childhood in *La Femme gelée* illustrates Beauvoir's belief that a woman's class and financial resources play a key role in allowing her to assume motherhood freely or not. A further reference to class differences in *Le Deuxième Sexe II* occurs in Beauvoir's remark that the practice of urinating while standing – a practice both Ernaux and she perceive as more significant than penis envy in sexual differentiation between children (LDS II, p. 21; LFG, p. 43) – exists among peasant women. This observation finds validation in a comment about the narrator's grandmother in *La Femme gelée*: 'Il lui arrive de faire pipi debout, jambes écartées sous sa longue jupe noire, dans son bout de jardin quand elle se croit seule' (LFG, p. 12). Indeed, once she is married and confined within an oppressive domestic routine, the narrator's husband employs this sexual differentiation to justify his lack of participation in household chores, the essential vindicating the existential: '"Tu me fais chier, tu n'es pas un homme, non! Il y a une petite différence, quand tu pisseras debout dans le lavabo, on verra!"' (LFG, p. 133).

6   Throughout *La Femme gelée*, the narrator's use of terms such as 'modèle' (LFG, pp. 9, 33, 49, 131), or 'code' (LFG, pp. 68, 70, 72), when referring to the criteria which dictate a woman's adherence to one 'modèle' or another, foregrounds the learned aspect of feminine conventions, as does her recurrent use of verbs such as 'ignorer', 'ne pas savoir' and 'apprendre'.

7   As the Introduction remarks, Ernaux's more recent publication, *La Honte*, may attribute the onset of such 'corruption' to domestic rather than pedagogical circumstances, yet continues to locate it in her narrator's post-school existence. While the representation of her pre-school existence is extremely positive in *La Femme gelée*, there is also evidence of a less fortunate 'modèle' of working-class woman in the form of the narrator's Aunt Solange, whose miserable life at the hands of a violent husband leads her to regard suicide as the only option, and, to a lesser degree, her grandmother, who is forced to renounce all intellectual ambitions in order to support her family.

8   While the 'nous' in this quotation can be interpreted as referring specifically to mother and daughter, it equally has the effect of drawing in the female reader, reflecting a feminist desire for intimacy between narrator and reader. As the Introduction observes, this emphasis on relationality is perceived to run counter to the individualism common in male auto/biographical writings.

9   In *La Place*, the narrator acknowledges that she owes her existence to the death of her parents' first child, a daughter, who died aged seven from diphtheria. '*Je ne suis pas sortie de ma nuit*' comments on the emotional repercussions of this loss for the narrator's relationship with her mother.

10   This frustration with the passivity of dolls would appear to be a *topos* of much contemporary women's writing, as exemplified by the attitude of Sarraute's narrator in *Enfance*: 'Je n'ai jamais envie d'y jouer ... elle [the doll] est toute dure, trop lisse, elle fait toujours les mêmes mouvements' (Paris: Folio PLUS, 1995), p. 49.

11   Transcendence for Beauvoir represents an existentialist ideal, and is used to refer to an individual's potential for continual growth and redefinition, connoting a vertical movement upwards through the exercise of free choice, a projection of existence

into the future, while immanence can be understood as a more horizontal notion of repetition and non-progressive stagnation.

12   Michèle Le Doeuff, 'Simone de Beauvoir and Existentialism', *Feminist Studies*, no. 6 (1980), pp. 277–89, p. 286.

13   The normative influence of this pedagogical discourse is also apparent in less explicit references to it towards the work's conclusion. While motherhood is described as 'le plus beau métier du monde' (LFG, p. 55) when the narrator is at school, the older narrator repeats this description verbatim when she experiences motherhood for herself: 'A prendre ou à laisser le plus beau métier du monde, pas faire le détail' (LFG, p. 160). Whatever the narrator's responses to it, this discourse forms a point of reference to which she continually – if, at times, subconsciously – returns.

14   In *Maternal Thinking: Towards a Politics of Peace* (London: The Women's Press, 1990), Sara Ruddick comments on the ambivalent position the mother may occupy in the eyes of her children following such an awareness: 'The conjunction of maternal power and powerlessness is difficult for children to comprehend. They confront and rely on a powerful maternal presence whom they inevitably resent as well as love. This powerful presence becomes powerless in front of their father, a teacher, welfare worker, doctor, judge, landlord – the world' (p. 36). In *Les Armoires vides* and *Ce qu'ils disent ou rien*, that position is apparent in the narrator's criticism of her mother's obsequious behaviour towards those in authority.

15   Interestingly, Beauvoir's account of the mother's sometimes sadistic relationship with her daughter, stemming from her own frustrated ambitions, is occasionally reflected in the paternal attitude in Ernaux's writing, an attitude expressed in both *Les Armoires vides*, p. 181 – '"On aurait été davantage heureux si elle avait pas continué ses études!"' – and in *La Place*, when, with reference to the successful completion of her studies, her father is described as harbouring 'la peur OU PEUT-ÊTRE LE DÉSIR que [je] n'y arrive pas' (LP, p. 80; original capitals).

16   It is no coincidence that the narrator appears to make up for lost time in her candid representation of female sexual desire in *Passion simple*. In an interview with Claire-Lise Tondeur, Ernaux remarks: 'Ma mère, c'était la dernière censure. Une fois ma mère décédée, je voulais aller jusqu'au bout. Transgression et censure font partie de la mère. Ces femmes du quartier que j'évoque dans *Passion simple*, qui recevaient des hommes l'après-midi, il est évident que ma mère, elle, se joignait au chœur de celles qui condamnaient une telle conduite', 'Entretien avec Annie Ernaux', *French Review*, vol. 69, no. 1 (1995), pp. 37–43, p. 40.

17   Beauvoir comments: 'Le vocabulaire érotique des mâles s'inspire du vocabulaire militaire: l'amant a la fougue d'un soldat [...]; il parle d'attaque, d'assaut, de victoire' (LDS II, p. 151). In *Parole de femme* (Paris: Editions Grasset & Fasquelle, 1974), Annie Leclerc also draws attention to the use of military vocabulary to describe the sexual act: 'Don. Prise. Conquête. Abandon. Possession ... Où sommes-nous? Au marché? A la guerre? Tous les termes de l'amour sonnent le clairon de l'homme' (p. 63).

18   Chapter 1 mentions this dichotomy in relation to *Les Armoires vides* and *Ce qu'ils disent ou rien*. Vivien E. Nice in *Mothers & Daughters: The Distortion of a Relationship* (London: Macmillan, 1992), comments on the influence of the social perception of femininity on women's intellectual development: 'Psychological texts (e.g. Horner, 1972) have considered women's general lack of involvement in high

income positions as women's own fault related to their "fear of success". This "fear" is related to jeopardising one's "femininity", and certainly adolescent girls may devalue and deny their own academic abilities at a time when it is thought important to appear attractive to boys' (p. 43). In a similar vein, Susan Faludi's *Backlash: The Undeclared War Against Women* (London: Vintage, 1992), chapter 2, discusses the contemporary 'brain–womb' conflict in which higher education is blamed for producing an infertility epidemic.

19   Ernaux's narrator may closely mirror Beauvoir's adolescent girl in her increasing narcissism and sexual curiosity, yet differs in one key area of adolescence – her attitude towards menstruation. In *La Femme gelée*, the narrator views the onset of menstruation as 'un merveilleux événement' (LFG, p. 72), having imagined herself surrounded by a 'gloire rouge' (LFG, p. 46) with its advent. In *Le Deuxième Sexe II*, Beauvoir maintains that, for the adolescent girl, menstruation is always a traumatic event (LDS II, p. 68). These divergent accounts are due in part to generational differences between Beauvoir and Ernaux, to the fact that the taboo status of menstruation has been greatly reduced since 1949. Indeed, Beauvoir pre-empts Ernaux's more positive representation of menstruation in her belief that female physiological processes will be perceived as less constraining when women occupy a less socially subordinate position, which is undoubtedly the case for Ernaux's narrator. Beauvoir's more negative account of menstruation may also be attributed to her existentialist perspective, which cannot easily accommodate physiological manifestations over which the will holds no sway, a perspective also apparent in her description of pregnancy.

20   The disparity this sense of unreality produces finds illustration in much women's writing in the form of a 'divided' personality encompassing both an inner and outer self, a personality discussed in Chapter 1 with reference to *Les Armoires vides* and *Ce qu'ils disent ou rien*. As Rita Felski remarks in *Beyond Feminist Aesthetics: Feminist Literature and Social Change* (London: Hutchinson Radius, 1989), p. 130: 'This sense of remoteness from a preformed destiny which the protagonist feels helpless to alter is typically described as a splitting of inner and outer self, the heroine experiencing a powerful estrangement from the external appearance by which her social status as a woman in a patriarchal culture is largely determined.'

21   In *Le Deuxième Sexe II*, p. 266, we read: 'Il y a peu de tâches qui s'apparentent plus que celles de la ménagère au supplice de Sisyphe; jour après jour, il faut laver les plats, épousseter les meubles, repriser le linge qui seront à nouveau demain salis, poussiéreux, déchirés.'

22   Beauvoir makes the same point in *Le Deuxième Sexe I*, when she remarks that women feel solidarity above all with their husbands, rather than with other women: 'Bourgeoises elles sont solidaires des bourgeois et non des femmes prolétaires' (p. 19). Indeed, the content of *Le Deuxième Sexe* could be viewed as an endeavour to rectify this absence of solidarity in its aim to provide a representative portrayal of 'le destin traditionnel de la femme' from childhood to adulthood. While I have already highlighted the limits of such representativeness, by its very attempt to theorise and universalise the experience of individual women, the work validated that experience, and continues to do so. It provided a name for Betty Friedan's 'problem which has no name', giving women a lexicon with which to discuss and politicise their experience. Women suffering under the constraints of patriarchy learned that their feelings of frustration were shared by other women, an awareness which helped forge a sense of

unity and a communal apprehension of subjecthood not in evidence at the time of publication: 'Les femmes – sauf en certains congrès qui restent des manifestations abstraites – ne disent pas "nous"' (LDS I, p. 19).

23   The Capes stands for *Certificat d'aptitude au professorat de l'enseignement supérieur du second degré* and is a competitive teacher training examination which comprises both written and oral components.

24   See Sandra M. Gilbert and Susan Gubar, *The Madwoman in the Attic: The Woman Writer and the Nineteenth-Century Literary Imagination* (New Haven: Yale University Press, 1979). In her final chapter 'Vers la libération', Beauvoir also remarks that women writers have difficulty taking their work seriously: 'il est rare qu'elle envisage l'art comme un sérieux travail' (LDS II, p. 628). Ernaux acknowledges the integral role played by gender in the act of writing: 'Les plus forts coups contre ce désir [to write] me sont venus de ma condition de femme', unpublished interview with Siobhán McIlvanney, 23 September 1993.

25   In Ernaux's writing, the theme of abortion is most thoroughly treated in *Les Armoires vides* and in her recent work, *L'Evénement*. It is also mentioned in *Passion simple* and in *La Vie extérieure*, when the narrator's criticises what she perceives as the hypocrisy of Monica Lewinsky's anti-abortionist stance (LVE, pp. 105–06). Beauvoir's predominantly negative perception of motherhood stems from her view of woman as torn between her desire for a future of self-fulfilment, for transcendence, and her biological role which ties her to reproduction, to the future of the species and immanence, as well as from the conditions governing motherhood at the time of writing. Much debate has surrounded Beauvoir's remarks on women's biological functions, and critics such as Margaret Atack and Linda Zerilli have suggested that many of Beauvoir's more negative perceptions of female biology are actually ironic, and a rhetorical device to highlight misogynous representations of women's bodily experiences under patriarchy. In other words, woman's body is viewed more as 'situation' in a social and historical context than an ahistorical 'thing'. See Atack's 'Writing from the centre: ironies of otherness and marginality', *Simone de Beauvoir's* The Second Sex: New Interdisciplinary Essays, ed. Ruth Evans (Manchester: Manchester University Press, 1998), pp. 31–58, and Zerilli's 'A process without a subject: Simone de Beauvoir and Julia Kristeva on maternity', *Signs*, vol. 18, no. 1 (1992), pp. 111–35.

26   Beauvoir uses the same terminology in *Le Deuxième Sexe II*, p. 30: 'On la [the young girl] traite comme une poupée vivante.'

27   Throughout *La Femme gelée*, the narrator highlights the learned process of becoming a competent wife and mother – as with the terms 'modèle' and 'code', there are numerous references to 'apprentissage' and 'rôle' throughout the work. Indeed, the work's original title was *Les Années d'apprentissage*, highlighting both the 'unnaturalness' of marriage and motherhood for Ernaux's narrator, as well as the general perception of them as constituting a respectable career for women. The learned aspects of the narrator's role as wife and mother, and the 'doubling' of personality this results in, can also be interpreted from a specifically existentialist, as well as feminist, perspective. Margaret Atack, in her essay 'Writing from the centre: ironies of otherness and marginality', comments on the importance of role-playing in existentialism: 'It is no accident that, as has frequently been noted, metaphors of acting, putting on an act, play-acting, playing a role, dominate descriptions of the relations of self and other, and of bad faith in existentialist philosophy', *Simone de Beauvoir's* The Second Sex, p. 54.

28   Given the profound formative influence of the mother, her love of literature may also explain why the narrator aspires to become a writer. In *Une femme*, she remarks apropos of her mother: 'Les livres étaient les seuls objets qu'elle manipulait avec précaution. Elle se lavait les mains avant de les toucher' (UF, p. 57).

29   The narrator in *Passion simple* is similarly positive about the role of escapism generally in women's lives, when, in a footnote, she remarks, p. 26: 'Dans *Marie-Claire*, des jeunes, interviewés, condamnent sans appel les amours de leur mère séparée ou divorcée. Une fille, avec rancune: "Les amants de ma mère n'ont servi qu'à la faire rêver." Quel meilleur service?'

30   In an interview with Jacqueline Dana entitled 'Annie aime les romans à l'eau de rose', *L'Autre Journal*, no. 5 (1993), pp. 54–57, Ernaux expresses the belief that to condemn romantic literature as exercising a pernicious influence on its female readership is to underestimate the intelligence of that readership. This belief is one shared by Janice A. Radway in her analysis of romantic literature, *Reading the Romance: Women, Patriarchy, and Popular Literature* (London: Verso, 1987). For a more detailed discussion of the role of romantic literature and literature generally in Ernaux's writing, as well as of Radway's argument, see my article 'Recuperating Romance: Literary Paradigms in the Works of Annie Ernaux', *Forum for Modern Language Studies*, vol. 32, no. 3 (1996), pp. 240–50.

31   In *The Resisting Reader: A Feminist Approach to American Fiction* (Bloomington: Indiana University Press, 1978), p. xii, Judith Fetterley describes how 'the female reader is co-opted into participation in an experience from which she is explicitly excluded; she is asked to identify with a selfhood that defines itself in opposition to her; she is required to identify against herself.' In an interesting reversal of the tacit universalisation of the male narrator's experience, many male readers have told Ernaux that they identify with the female narrator of *Passion simple*. However, an explanation for that identification lies more in misogynistic tendencies than in the success of feminist reading strategies: 'Mais, vous savez, il y a une chose terrifiante, c'est qu'il y a des hommes qui m'ont dit "Mais on ne pensait pas qu'une femme puisse éprouver ces choses-là"', unpublished interview with Siobhán McIlvanney, 23 September 1993.

32   This quasi-dialogic exposition of the difficulties in achieving an 'authentic' representation of the past can be compared to Sarraute's masculine and feminine voices in *Enfance*, in that its corrective function aims to reduce the potential distortion in relating '"les beaux souvenirs d'enfance"' (p. 42), and, in the case of Ernaux's narrator, of early adulthood as well: 'Alors quoi, la perfection, elle est belle l'image d'avant, genre magazine pour femmes libérées, pubs dans le coup, les filles d'aujourd'hui ont horreur des entraves, elles vivent pleinement, avec coca-cola ou les tampons X. Pas juste. Faire la part de la faiblesse et de la peur' (LFG, p. 120).

33   The older narrator recognises, for example, that her conversations with her schoolfriend Brigitte, which formed the mainstay of her sex education, were significantly less radical than she believed at the time. These conversations may have centred on female sexuality, yet were based on the presumption that women should remain virgins until marriage and that their sexuality was of secondary importance to men's.

34   Beauvoir's authorial position in *Le Deuxième Sexe* has been viewed as similarly constraining. See, for example, Suzanne Lilar's *Le Malentendu du Deuxième Sexe* (Paris: Presses Universitaires de France, 1969), in which Beauvoir is accused of

browbeating the reader into intellectual submission through the sheer proliferation of examples she provides, rather than convincing them by the coherence of her arguments.

35   The importance of giving women the choice of motherhood for Beauvoir – 'Enfanter, c'est prendre un engagement' (LDS II, p. 386) – is signalled by the fact that she begins her chapter on 'La Mère' with a detailed discussion of contraception and abortion. Ernaux's narrator may make explicit mention of taking the contraceptive pill before becoming pregnant a second time in *La Femme gelée*, yet there is a sense in which anatomy is indeed destiny for her. In attributing some responsibility for her actions to the narrator of *La Femme gelée*, my analysis differs from that of Colette Hall, who, in her brief study of the work, 'De "La femme rompue" à *La Femme gelée*: *Le Deuxième Sexe* revu et corrigé' in *Thirty Voices in the Feminine*, ed. Michael Bishop (Amsterdam and Atlanta, GA: Rodopi, 1996), lays the blame for the narrator's 'frozen' condition squarely with the patriarchal socialisation process.

36   *Simone de Beauvoir: The Making of an Intellectual Woman* (Oxford and Cambridge, MA: Blackwell, 1994), p. 185.

37   'L'infortune d'être femme', *Le Monde*, 27 March 1981, p. 23.

38   Diana Holmes expresses the opinion of many feminist critics on Beauvoir when she writes: 'As in her representation of sexuality, underpinning Beauvoir's model of reality is a clear valorization of active progressive movement over passive stillness, or, for example, contemplative inactivity,' *French Women's Writing 1848–1994* (London: Athlone Press, 1996), p. 163.

39   As this chapter goes on to discuss, Alain Gérard's work, *Madame, c'est à vous que j'écris* (Paris: Albin Michel, 1995), published as a response to *Passion simple*'s gynocentric perspective, reveals the degree of unease this account generated among male readers. Gérard's work can be interpreted as an endeavour to undermine the female narrator's narrative dominance in *Passion simple* and to reassert phallocentric textual mastery. Philippe Vilain's *L'Etreinte* (Paris: Gallimard, 1997), can be read as constituting another response to *Passion simple* and also to 'Fragments autour de Philippe V.', *L'Infini*, no. 56 (Winter 1996), pp. 25–26, yet one based on a genuine relationship with the author, rather than motivated by a desire for retaliation (although it too can be viewed as indicative of male insecurity in that Vilain wishes to make public his brief 'mastery' of Ernaux herself). Nonetheless, Vilain's text pays homage to, rather than criticises, Ernaux's writing of *Passion simple* in its emulation of the work's literary style. Ernaux's later work, *La Honte*, is dedicated to Philippe V..

40   Monique Lang, 'L'amour Passion', *Marie-Claire*, May 1992, pp. 62–64, p. 64. In her article 'Erotica/pornorotica: *Passion simple* d'Annie Ernaux' in *Thirty Voices in the Feminine*, Claire-Lise Tondeur offers a nuanced reading of the work in which she also raises doubts about its feminist credentials.

41   'L'amour Passion', *Marie-Claire*, May 1992, p. 64. In an interview which appeared the day after Beauvoir's death in *Libération*, 15 April 1986, p. 5, Fouque expressed her hostility towards Beauvoir and her legacy, condemning what she viewed as Beauvoir's normalising, narrow-minded approach to combating women's oppression, the absence of which she finds so refreshing in Ernaux's work. Given Fouque's adherence to differentialist feminism, her praise of Ernaux's representation of passion is somewhat ironic, in that she adopts what may be viewed as Beauvoirean criteria of judgement: by emulating male conduct, Ernaux's narrator beats men at their own game.

42   This epigraph is taken from Barthes's dictionary of amorous states and associated terms, *Fragments d'un discours amoureux* (Paris: Editions du Seuil, 1977), many of which find ratification in the thoughts and conduct of the narrator in *Passion simple*. This particular remark comes under the entry 'L'obscène de l'amour', p. 211, in which Barthes remarks that it is sentimentality, rather than sexuality, which is nowadays considered obscene.

43   In her short text 'Fragments autour de Philippe V.', Ernaux's narrator employs the same analogy, remarking that the gesture of making sexual overtures to a man has the same impetus as beginning a written work – that of actively seeking to start something anew: 'Ecrire et faire l'amour. Je sens un lien essentiel entre les deux. Je ne peux l'expliquer, seulement retranscrire des moments où celui-ci m'apparaît comme une évidence', *L'Infini*, no. 56, p. 26. In this interpretation of the film, my emphasis differs from that of Lyn Thomas, who, in *Annie Ernaux: An Introduction to the Writer and her Audience* (Oxford and New York: Berg, 1999), p. 69, interprets the absence of a decoder as an allegory for the absence of a non-misogynous language to relate female sexual experience. It seems to me that the existence of *Passion simple*, with its description of female sexual relations from a female perspective, clearly refutes such an interpretation; whatever the reader may think of the narrator's conduct, the textual language describing the narrator's sexual relations is not misogynous. Moreover, the work makes clear that language is an inadequate tool with which to reflect 'reality' as a whole, not merely a specifically gynocentric aspect of it. This perception of language as generally inadequate finds further validation in *La Honte*, when the narrator employs an identical analogy to convey the inherent nebulousness of memory and its transcription in language. With reference to 'la scène' which forms the work's opening, she remarks: 'elle est grisée, incohérente et muette, comme un film sur une chaîne de télévision cryptée regardé sans décodeur' (LH, p. 30).

44   This lack of communication, which duplicates the parent/child model of earlier works, is given an imaginary bridge in *Madame, c'est à vous que j'écris*, in which the author projects himself into the persona of A. in order to provide his version of events. He rebukes the narrator of *Passion simple* for both her betrayal in publishing the work, and for misrepresenting 'his' character. Mirroring the form of *Passion simple*, with its introduction, account of the affair and postscript, Gérard's work, while making the occasionally astute observation about the content of Ernaux's work, is more the result of wounded male hubris than of a genuine interest in *Passion simple*.

45   As in the case of her parents in *La Place*, anonymity is supposedly safeguarded throughout the work by designating her lover with the letter 'A'. The effectiveness of this device is, however, somewhat dubious. We know that the narrator's lover is from the Eastern bloc, what type of cars he likes, his manner of dressing, that he is married, is aged 38, has green eyes and blond hair, is childless and looks like Alain Delon. Indeed, his name is one of the few things we do not learn. (In an interview, Ernaux revealed that her lover's first name began with the initial S, which may have subconsciously influenced her choice of adjective for the work's title, 'Entretien avec Annie Ernaux', Claire-Lise Tondeur, *French Review*, vol. 69, no. 1 [October 1995], pp. 37–43, p. 41.) Those in a position to know this man will recognise him from the portrait provided, and hence the narrator's wish to respect his private life is, at the very least, naïve. One possible interpretation of

Passion simple is that it functions as an open love letter to him. In the short text already referred to, 'Fragments autour de Philippe V.', the naming process is taken one step further.

46   The description of these various genres serves to illuminate the narrator's perception of her work: her reference to women's magazines highlights her drive for representativeness, for communication of a highly personal experience through a public medium, as well as her desire to deconstruct generic hierarchies; her defensiveness of her conduct and her awareness of the criticism it may elicit are demonstrated by her use of the terms 'manifeste' and 'procès-verbal'; and both the retrospective analysis and the somewhat unreal, at times clichéd, nature of her relationship are conveyed in the notion of 'commentaire de texte'. She subsequently makes reference to the 'text' of her life and to its written version: 'De ce texte vivant, celui-ci n'est que le résidu, la petite trace' (PS, p. 69).

47   Gérard provides a psychoanalytic angle on the text in *Madame, c'est à vous que j'écris*, p. 25: 'Peut-être n'ai-je été que la somme de vos refoulements. La voix d'un oncle, l'épaule d'un lointain cousin, la démarche d'un père ont peut-être davantage fait pour votre plaisir que nos réalités.' Beauvoir maintains that it is the more general framework of her childhood which a woman is seeking to rehabilitate through a lover, rather than attempting to recover her relationship with her father or other male representatives from childhood (LDS II, p. 550): 'la femme ne souhaite pas réincarner un individu en un autre, mais ressusciter une situation; celle qu'elle a connue petite fille, à l'abri des adultes; elle a été profondément intégrée au foyer familial, elle y a goûté la paix d'une quasi-passivité; l'amour lui rendra sa mère aussi bien que son père, il lui rendra son enfance.' This interpretation is borne out by the biographical events preceding the publication of *Passion simple*, namely the death of Ernaux's mother. If this death can be viewed as liberating the narrator from the sexual oppressiveness of her childhood, it may equally account for her need to anchor herself in that world once again, to have literature provide what reality no longer can. In *Fragments d'un discours amoureux*, Barthes draws analogies between the role of the lover and that of the mother, particularly in relation to the anguish and endless waiting characteristic of absence. It may be that the permanent absence of the author's mother has aggravated the sense of suffering and acute awareness of waiting experienced by the narrator in *Passion simple*. Chapter 3 comments on the mother/lover analogy in relation to *Une femme* and Chapter 4 discusses it more fully when analysing '*Je ne suis pas sortie de ma nuit*'.

48   For a more detailed discussion of Ernaux's views on psychoanalysis, see Michèle Bacholle, 'An interview with Annie Ernaux: Ecrire le vécu', *Sites*, vol. 2, no. 1 (1995), pp. 141–51, p. 147. She also rejects the relevance of psychoanalysis to her writing in an interview with Jean-Jacques Gibert, 'Le Silence ou la Trahison?', *Révolution*, 22 February 1985, pp. 52–53. Michael Sheringham, in his study *French Autobiography: Devices and Desires* (Oxford: Clarendon Press, 1993), pp. 27–30, remarks upon the viability of Peter Brooks's psychoanalytic transactional model of plot between analysand and analyst in defining autobiographical relations between narrator and reader. As Chapter 5 suggests, a transactional model appropriate to an understanding of Ernaux's writing may be that of the confessional exchange, in which the narrator seeks a form of absolution through the representation of past experiences.

49 *Journal du dehors* offers a nice analogy of the narrator's hesitation to 'go public' – as well as intimating the eroticism in the act of writing – in a description of the narrator awaiting a medical examination: 'La porte du box va s'ouvrir et je serai exposée en slip devant quatre ou cinq personnes. Mouvement d'arrêt avant d'oser sortir' (JDD, p. 38).

50 This desire to prolong a relationship through an aesthetic representation and permanent record of it is expressed in 'Fragments autour de Philippe V.'. In this case, the representation takes a more graphic form in the mélange of the narrator's menstrual blood with her lover's sperm, a form which may indicate the narrator's awareness of the proximity of the menopause. In *La Place* and *Une femme*, the act of writing can also be perceived as an act of both preservation and restitution of the lives of the narrator's parents. Like *Passion simple*, these texts begin with a description of the loss of a loved one, before re-presenting the narrator's past relationship with them.

51 Citing a case study from Pierre Janet's *Les Obsessions et la psychasthénie*, Beauvoir provides an apt description of the narrator's passion in the work, and one which incorporates its religious subtext: '"Combien j'envie l'amour idéal de Marie-Madeleine et de Jésus: être le disciple ardent d'un maître adoré et qui en vaut la peine; vivre et mourir pour son idole [...] tellement à lui que je n'existe plus"' (LDS II, p. 551).

52 Unpublished interview with Siobhán McIlvanney, 23 September 1993 a. Beauvoir's description of 'l'amoureuse' also incorporates this desire to experience extremes (LDS II, p. 556): 'Or l'amoureuse n'est pas seulement une narcissiste aliénée dans son moi: elle éprouve aussi un désir passionné de déborder ses propres limites et de devenir infinie, grâce au truchement d'un autre qui accède à l'infinie réalité.'

53 In her interview with me in September 1993, Ernaux commented on the vast number of letters she had received from readers endorsing the accuracy of her account. As mentioned in the Introduction, two useful sources for details on the reader response, both academic and lay, to *Passion simple*, are Lyn Thomas's *Annie Ernaux: An Introduction to the Writer and her Audience* and Isabelle Charpentier's 'De corps à corps: réceptions croisées d'Annie Ernaux', *Politix*, no. 27 (1994), pp. 45–75.

Notes to Chapter 3

pp. 87–115

1   As Ernaux remarked during a talk at Winchester College, 10 March 1988: 'A travers mon père, j'avais l'impression de parler pour d'autres gens aussi, [pour] tous ceux qui continuent de vivre au-dessous de la littérature et dont on parle très peu. Donc c'était une sorte de devoir, j'en ai jamais douté, pas plus que pour ma mère …'. In *La Place*, pp. 23–24, and *'Je ne suis pas sortie de ma nuit'*, p. 109, the narrator comments on her inability to provide fictional representation of the lives of her parents.

2   Loraine Day and Tony Jones, *Annie Ernaux: La Place, Une femme* (Glasgow: University of Glasgow French and German Publications, 1990), p. 1. Whatever the differences in genres separating the early trilogy from *La Place* and *Une femme*, the narrator can be viewed as resorting to a form of narrative ventriloquism in both types of writing, vindicating Mary G. Mason's observation that women writers tend to assume a variety of disguises when writing the autobiographical. If Ernaux's narrator employs a fictional façade to give voice to the autobiographical in the early trilogy, that façade is replaced by an emphasis on her parents and the parental heritage in the two texts under study. See 'The Other Voice: Autobiographies of Women Writers', *Life/Lines, Theorizing Women's Autobiography*, ed. Bella Brodzki and Celeste Schenck (Ithaca and London: Cornell University Press, 1988), pp. 19–44.

3   *Le Dictionnaire: Littérature française contemporaine*, ed. Jérôme Garcin (Paris: Editions François Bourin, 1989), pp. 179–83, p. 182.

4   'Annie Ernaux ou la femme blessée', interview with Josyane Savigneau, *Le Monde*, 3 February 1984, p. 15. A similar suspicion of categorisation, of the futile arbitrariness of naming, can be seen in *La Place*, when the narrator becomes impatient with the customers' desire to establish the precise nature of her father's illness: 'Pour nous, le nom n'avait plus d'importance' (LP, p. 108). This suspicion may be related to Ernaux's predominantly humanist perception of language – whatever her later qualifications of that perception – in which 'reality' always precedes its linguistic representation, and in which the overall effect produced by her writing is of greater significance than its generic breakdown.

5   As highlighted in the Introduction, in this desire to achieve a representative portrayal of her parents – which, ironically, the narrator endeavours to realise by foregrounding her writing's similarity to the traditionally male, 'objective' genres of history and sociology – Ernaux's narrator reflects what is considered to be a female emphasis on the importance of representativeness and relationality in women's auto/biographical writing – what Mary G. Mason refers to as the 'delineation of an identity by way of alterity', 'The Other Voice: Autobiographies of Women Writers', p. 41. Rather than focus on her parents' uniqueness, the narrator enumerates their points in common with others.

6   It is for the same reason that Ernaux's narrator is less concerned with the regional identity of her parents than with their class.

7   In his article, 'Invisible Presences: Fiction, Autobiography and Women's Lives – Virginia Woolf to Annie Ernaux', *Sites*, vol. 2, no. 1 (1998), pp. 5–24, p. 20, Michael

Sheringham interprets this emphasis on the role of the Other as foreshadowing narrative developments in *Journal du dehors*, in which the focus is on strangers the narrator encounters in her everyday life. The encounter between the narrator and an ex-pupil which concludes *La Place* can be viewed as having a similar function, particularly given the prominence accorded to *caissières* in *Journal du dehors*.

8   The intensity of that involvement is most clearly articulated in *'Je ne suis pas sortie de ma nuit'*, a work whose composition predates *Une femme*: 'Je me demande si je pourrais faire un livre sur elle comme *La place*. Il n'y avait pas de réelle distance entre nous. De l'identification' (JSN, pp. 35–36). In *La Honte*, the narrator returns to the use of initials when designating Yvetot.

9   The generic instability of these works is reflected in critical assessments of them. In Bernard Alliot's article in *Le Monde* of 13 November 1984, 'Renaudot: Annie Ernaux pour *La Place*', p. 48, he remarks that '*La Place* est aussi un roman de la déchirure sociale et un récit autobiographique.'

10   While we find a detailed dissection of the writing process in *La Place* and *Une femme*, the referential relationship between the 'real' and its literary transcription, between the world and the word, is presented as ultimately unproblematic: Ernaux's narrator may foreground the difficulties of that process, but does not question the possibility of attaining a truthful representation of her subject matter. As Chapters 2 and 4 demonstrate, that position is modified in later texts.

11   The narrator's repeated interventions in *La Place* in order to signal her detachment from her subject matter – whatever the effort required to achieve it – serve to emphasise her continuing involvement with it: 'Je rassemblerai les paroles, les gestes, les goûts de mon père, les faits marquants de sa vie, *tous les signes objectifs d'une existence que j'ai aussi partagée*' (LP, p. 24; emphasis added).

12   'Le Silence ou la Trahison?', *Révolution*, 22 February 1985, pp. 52–53, p. 52.

13   It is significant that the new information learnt about her mother relates to premarital sexual activity. Given the pivotal role played by the mother's sexual oppression and oppressiveness throughout Ernaux's corpus, the incorporation of this particular revelation would have profound repercussions for the narrator's self-perception and her perception of the mother.

14   This consciousness of the readerly Other which permeates Ernaux's writing has been viewed as particularly acute in female narrators, who, through the experience of objectification, are accustomed to projecting themselves into the imagined perception of others. In this respect, the example used by Michael Sheringham to illustrate the 'hidden presence' of the reader in *French Autobiography: Devices and Desires* (Oxford: Clarendon Press, 1993) is instructive. He draws an analogy between the Wim Wenders film *Paris Texas* and the narrator/reader relationship in autobiography. In the film, Nastassia Kinski, although only able to see her own reflection, is aware that she is being watched by Harry Dean Stanton and speaks into the darkness (p. 138). The self-conscious defensiveness of the narrator in *La Place* and *Une femme* is surely increased by her marginal position as a female narrator writing about the working class.

15   In this respect, Ernaux's narrator corresponds to Sidonie Smith's description of the 'diasporan subject' in *Subjectivity, Identity, and the Body: Women's Autobiographical Practices in the Twentieth Century* (Bloomington and Indianapolis: Indiana

University Press, 1993), pp. 123–24: 'The diasporan "I" lies simultaneously inside and outside identities, in a personal space of both appreciation and critique.'

16   For further discussion, see my article 'Annie Ernaux: Un écrivain dans la tradition du réalisme', *Revue d'histoire littéraire de la France*, no. 2 (March–April 1998), pp. 247–66.

17   Once again, the articulation of these objectives does not guarantee their realisation. Ernaux's narrator relates aspects of her father's existence which, by their rural unfamiliarity, cannot but poeticise it. The following quotation provides an example of such 'unwilled' poeticisation: 'Il reconnaissait les oiseaux à leur chant et regardait le ciel chaque soir pour savoir le temps qu'il ferait, froid et sec s'il était rouge, pluie et vent quand la lune était dans l'eau, c'est-à-dire immergée dans les nuages' (LP, p. 67).

18   As the Introduction and Chapter 1 observe, the association between middle-class male writers and the misrepresentation or absence of representation of working-class experience is a recurrent theme in Ernaux's works, as is her narrators' belief in the innovative nature of their own literary subject matter. See in particular Chapter 1, notes 9 and 17.

19   When quoting directly, the narrator also inserts her parents' speech in the narrative in inverted commas (pp. 36, 37, 86), without italicising it. Italics and inverted commas are equally used to indicate the mature narrator's retrospective distance from remarks made by her adolescent self, as in her condescending designation of her father as belonging to the category of '*gens simples*' (LP, p. 80). This distance is further exemplified in a comment relating her father's lack of discursive adeptness: 'Je croyais toujours avoir raison parce qu'il ne savait pas *discuter*' (LP, p. 82). The mature narrator's ironic detachment is again made clear in her use of inverted commas to relate her younger self's belief that only '"vraie"' literature (LP, p. 79) can provide expression of her deepest thoughts – her '"âme"' (ibid.). That the phrases she copies down from such literature are as trite as those found in her father's book, *Le tour de la France par deux enfants*, only more opaque, further corroborates the classist nature of 'good taste'.

20   A similar ambivalence exists with the use of inverted commas in *Une femme*, in that the reader is sometimes uncertain whether quoted speech is solely of maternal origin or whether the narrator shares its sentiments, an ambivalence fuelled by the greater intellectual and linguistic affinity between mother and daughter.

21   See, for example, the use of vulgar terms such as 'culot' (LP, p. 35), 'pissait' (LP, p. 27) or 'cuites' (LP, p. 67), as well as the transcription of oral French as in 'boire son petit verre' (LP, p. 25) or 'la solution la moins pire' (LP, p. 41).

22   In *La Place*, the narrator comments on the disparities between her parents' use of written and spoken language, disparities which highlight the importance of including oral aspects of their speech in any representative portrayal of them. With reference to her mother, the narrator remarks: 'Écrire comme elle parlait aurait été plus difficile encore, elle n'a jamais appris à le faire' (LP, p. 89). Throughout the narrator's childhood and adolescence, her father's sole written contribution was to sign letters written by her mother.

23   As Pierre Bourdieu remarks in *Ce que parler veut dire: L'Economie des échanges linguistiques* (Paris: Fayard, 1982), p. 85: 'L'hypercorrection s'inscrit [...] dans la logique de la prétention qui porte les petits-bourgeois à tenter de s'approprier

avant l'heure, au prix d'une tension constante, les propriétés des dominants.' He views women as particularly concerned with employing 'correct' language due to their inferior social status. This concern is apparent in the narrator's mother's attitude to language in *Une femme* – an attitude which may also stem from her professional requirements in dealing with the public – and in her readiness to be corrected by her daughter: 'Ma mère, elle, tâchait d'éviter les fautes de français, elle ne disait pas "mon mari", mais "mon époux"' (UF, p. 55).

24   The narrator's earlier disdain of her father's speech may also explain her endeavour to initiate a posthumous dialogue with him by incorporating some of his sayings in *La Place*. For example, the Cauchois expression '"elle pète par la sente"' (LP, p. 62) is one associated with her father and repeated in other texts (CDR, p. 73; LFG, p. 10). With reference to the first-person narrator of *La Place*, Ernaux has remarked: 'Le "je" qui s'y trouve encore dialogue déjà avec un "il" – la vie de mon père – et ce "je" ne sera, je le crois, plus jamais seul', interview with Jean-Jacques Gibert, 'Le Silence ou la Trahison?', p. 53.

25   The circular narrative structure of *La Place* is reinforced by the repetition of such remarks at the text's conclusion when the narrator is taking care of her dying father: '"Je peux faire cela" ou "Je suis donc bien grande que je fais cela"' (LP, p. 109). The narrator makes a similar comment in *'Je ne suis pas sortie de ma nuit'* in response to the increasing infantilism of her mother through Alzheimer's disease: 'Il est évident que c'est maintenant seulement que je suis adulte' (JSN, p. 70).

26   As Tony Jones points out in *Annie Ernaux: La Place, Une femme*, p. 34, note 4, the Capes is much more than a teaching qualification in that it guarantees the holder a lifetime post in the teaching profession, in other words, the permanent acquisition of a privileged social status. The narrator's success can be viewed as a symbolic approbation of her class, as well as of her pedagogical, credentials.

27   The differences between her past origins and her present social class are illustrated in the contents of her father's wallet after his death: a 'Photo typique des livres d'histoire pour "illustrer" une grève ou le Front populaire' (LP, p. 22) and a newspaper clipping announcing the narrator's success in the teaching examination.

28   Her husband's inability to empathise with the narrator's family and his obvious detachment from events may have further galvanised the narrator's desire to reconcile herself with her past, to valorise her working-class father over her middle-class husband. In her study, *La Place et Une femme d'Annie Ernaux* (Paris: Gallimard, 1994), Marie-France Savéan points out that, despite Ernaux having written many different versions of *La Place* from 1976 onwards, it is only after her separation from her husband that she devotes herself to completing the work: the 'removal' of the bourgeois replacement for her father as the principal male in her life allows her to return to her origins. See p. 176, and P. M. Wetherill's introduction, *La Place* (London: Methuen Educational, 1987), pp. 1–35, pp. 30–35, for further details on the different drafts.

29   This 1925 Russian film portrays a mutiny at sea, which stems from a sailors' revolt against the poor quality of their food. The narrator also mentions it in *L'Evénement* when describing a scene from the film which portrays food identical to that given to the farmworkers in *La Place*: 'Un énorme quartier de viande suspendu à un crochet, grouillant de vers, est apparu' (LE , pp. 89–90).

30   The echoes of Gervaise and Coupeau's situation in *L'Assommoir* are rein-

forced by the narrator's reference to her parents' café in Yvetot as an '"assommoir"' (LP, p. 54). Such literary resonances provide evidence that, whatever her opinion of their representation of working-class experience, male literary predecessors continue to exert an influence over her. Similarly, in *'Je ne suis pas sortie de ma nuit'*, p. 39, the narrator again mentions Proust's Françoise when she compares one of the women patients in the hospital to her.

31   In *Une femme* and *'Je ne suis pas sortie de ma nuit'*, p. 80, the narrator comments on the Norman usage of the term 'ambition', a usage which sheds light on her father's anxiety when forced to take part in events outside the familiar environment of the home: 'En normand, "ambition" signifie la douleur d'être séparé' (UF, p. 25).

32   Rivalry also governs interfamilial relations, in that relatives, having profited from the hospitality of the narrator's parents, accuse them of snobbery. It is apparent in the disdainful attitude of her father's sisters towards the narrator's mother. They consider women employed in factories to be unskilled in carrying out basic household tasks – which, ironically, is exactly the case of the narrator's mother. Her mother's lack of interest in housework – well-documented in *Les Armoires vides* and *La Femme gelée* – may be reflected in *La Place* in the choice of gravestone she makes for her husband: 'Sobre, et ne demande pas d'entretien' (LP, p. 111).

33   In *Une femme*, the narrator also provides an example of linguistic differences between mother and daughter, stemming from the daughter's gradual migration to the bourgeoisie and the petty adolescent rebellion this provokes: 'Pour ma mère, se révolter n'avait eu qu'une seule signification, refuser la pauvreté, et qu'une seule forme, travailler, gagner de l'argent et devenir aussi bien que les autres' (UF, p. 65).

34   While the dates provided at the end of the work indicate a composition period of seven months, as note 28 details, the writing process of the work comprised numerous drafts, the first of which was begun in 1976. It may be to these that the narrator is unconsciously referring.

35   According to Wetherill's introduction to *La Place*, p. 42, note 6, *L'Expérience des limites* was one of the original titles of the work, connoting the limitations of her father's social position.

36   In his article, 'Ecrire la différence sociale: registres de vie et registres de langue dans *La Place* d'Annie Ernaux', *French Forum*, vol. 19 (1994), pp. 195–214, Christian Garaud makes the point that, as a teacher, Ernaux's narrator is perpetuating the very system she holds responsible for so much social exclusion (p. 212).

37   In *Ce qu'ils disent ou rien*, pp. 32–33, the narrator makes a favourable comment about Camus's literary technique in *L'Etranger*, and, in many respects, *La Place* and *Une femme* emulate the work's sparse writing style and its directness – Ernaux also avoids employing the *passé simple*. However, it is perhaps Beauvoir's account of her mother's death in *Une mort très douce* which *Une femme* most resembles.

38   Indeed, there is some confusion over dates in the work, in that her mother dies on 7 April, the funeral is on 9 April and the work is begun on 20 April, yet, from remarks made in the early part of the book, the narrator can only bring herself to write that her mother is dead 22 days after her death (UF, p. 21). Prior to that, one can suppose that she must simply have made notes about the possible content of a book on her mother, an hypothesis which finds confirmation in *'Je ne suis pas sortie de ma nuit'*.

39   The epigraph is a quotation from Hegel and reads: 'C'est une erreur de prétendre que la contradiction est inconcevable, car c'est bien dans la douleur du vivant qu'elle a son existence réelle.' Guilt also surfaces in occasional instances of self-recrimination in the work: 'Plutôt que d'aller la voir, je préférais qu'elle vienne chez nous: il me semblait plus facile de l'insérer quinze jours dans notre vie que de partager trois heures de la sienne, où il ne se passait plus rien' (UF, p. 84).

40   That writing, by its continual restoration of the maternal, prohibits complete acceptance of the mother's death can be seen throughout Ernaux's corpus. The literary embalmment of the mother allows the narrator a form of perpetual access to her. As Chapter 2 remarks, a similar desire to prolong the relationship with her lover motivates the narrator's act of writing in *Passion simple*.

41   This mode of expression echoes Hélène Cixous's characterisation of writing in *Entre l'écriture* (Paris: Editions des femmes, 1986), p. 21: 'Ecrire? J'en mourais d'envie, d'amour, donner à l'écriture ce qu'elle m'avait donné, quelle ambition! Quel impossible bonheur. Nourrir ma propre mère. Lui donner à mon tour mon lait?' Indeed, the composition period of *Une femme* lasts 10 months, narrowly surpassing the gestation period of a healthy pregnancy.

42   That proximity is made clear when the narrator describes coming across her mother's sister drunk in the street: 'Je crois que je ne pourrai jamais écrire comme si je n'avais pas rencontré ma tante, ce jour-là' (UF, p. 35). The use of 'croire' again demonstrates the more tentative nature of her remarks apropos of the writing process in *Une femme*.

43   Ernaux considers the death of the mother as potentially more traumatic for a daughter than for a son, partly because of the physical similarities between them: 'Il ne reconnaît pas son propre corps dans le corps de sa mère, une fille reconnaît dans le corps de sa mère, dans son visage, même dans sa folie, quelque chose d'elle, c'est tout différent et c'est bien pire et jusqu'à dans ses rêves', 'Littérature pour tous', France Culture, 17 February 1990. From the voluptuous abundance of the mother figure during the narrator's early childhood to the frail, diminished woman she becomes, the changes in the revered maternal body are portrayed by the narrator of *Une femme*. This mother/daughter identification centring on the female body finds its most intense expression in *'Je ne suis pas sortie de ma nuit'*, which focuses exclusively on the final stage of her mother's life.

44   The narrator's self-representation as a medium through which working-class *histoire* can find expression echoes Balzac's analogy in his preface to *La Comédie humaine* in which he compares the role of the writer to that of a secretary chronicling 'reality': 'La Société française allait être l'historien, je ne devais être que le secrétaire', *La Comédie humaine* (Paris: Editions du Seuil, 1965), avant-propos, p. 52. In an interview with Roger Vrigny on France Culture, 21 June 1984, Ernaux characterised her role as writer in a similar manner: 'J'ai voulu travailler comme un ethnologue.' The narrator's reference to herself as a type of ethnologist of working-class experience is reiterated in different forms throughout Ernaux's writing, whether in the description of *Journal du dehors* as 'De l'ethnotexte' (JDD, p. 65), or in the expression of the narrator's aim in writing *La Honte* as 'Être en somme ethnologue de moi-même' (LH, p. 38).

45   While her mother is portrayed as occasionally over-indulging in alcohol, there is no sense in which this is viewed as problematic. *'Je ne suis pas sortie de ma*

nuit' reveals that alcoholism continues to affect members of the narrator's own generation in the form of her cousin, Claude (p. 52).

46   This description echoes Melanie Klein's belief in the child's inherently ambivalent attitude towards the mother who is perceived as 'good' (when satisfying needs) and 'bad' (when failing to do so). For a detailed discussion of Klein's relevance to *Une femme*, see Margaret-Anne Hutton's article, 'Challenging autobiography: lost object and aesthetic object in Ernaux's *Une femme*', *Journal of European Studies*, no. xxviii (1998), pp. 231–44.

47   Throughout Ernaux's writing, the narrator's parents are portrayed as neither verbally nor physically amorous to one another, but, instead, convey their feelings indirectly through sexual allusions or songs. This inability to discuss sexual or emotional matters openly also obstructs communication between parents and daughter. Indeed, as Claire-Lise Tondeur remarks, the mother/daughter model of communication in *Une femme*, by both its volume and lack of intimacy, can be viewed as duplicating the parental, *Annie Ernaux ou l'exil intérieur* (Amsterdam and Atlanta, GA: Rodopi, 1996), p. 104.

48   This quasi-divine characterisation of the protective mother figure, a characterisation reinforced by the narrators' frequent references to her all-seeingness in Ernaux's writing, finds confirmation in a remark made in the introductory section of *'Je ne suis pas sortie de ma nuit'*: 'Ce n'était plus la femme que j'avais toujours connue au-dessus de ma vie' (JSN, p. 13). In the same work, the whiteness in this image of her mother is related to her shopkeeper's white uniform, pointing to the dominant role played by the mother's job throughout the narrator's childhood, a role also signalled in *Une femme*: 'Elle était une mère commerçante, c'est-à-dire qu'elle appartenait d'abord aux clients qui nous "faisaient vivre"' (UF, p. 52).

49   Loraine Day observes that the mother's switch from dark to bright clothes following this move can be interpreted as indicating her joy at being reunited with her daughter, signifying the end of a mourning period of separation from her, *Annie Ernaux: La Place, Une femme*, pp. 55–56.

Notes to Chapter 4
pp. 117–51

1   See Michèle Bacholle, 'An interview with Annie Ernaux: Ecrire le vécu', *Sites*, vol. 2, no. 1 (1998), pp. 141–51, pp. 148–49. The narrator of *L'Evénement*, who bases the account of her abortion on diary entries, is 23 throughout the period in question and uses her diary as a form of confidant.

2   When recalling the past, Ernaux's narrator employs the verb '(re)voir' throughout the corpus, highlighting the importance of the gaze for her: 'Je raconte l'enfance, l'adolescence de ma mère, je la "vois" dans ma tête, la force, la beauté, la chaleur' (JSN, p. 94). In a metanarrative remark in *L'Evénement*, the narrator comments on the appropriateness of such visual imagery: 'Voir par l'imagination ou revoir par la mémoire est le lot de l'écriture' (LE, p. 58).

3   Virginia Woolf, 'A Sketch of the Past' (1941) , Sketch 90, in *Moments of Being*, ed. Jeanne Schulkind (London: Grafton Books, 1989). The usefulness of this term in discussing Ernaux's writing was first brought to my attention by Michael Sheringham in his article, 'Invisible Presences: Fiction, Autobiography and Women's Lives – Virginia Woolf to Annie Ernaux', *Sites*, vol. 2, no. 1 (1998), pp. 5–24. As Chapter 3 argues, the frequency with which Ernaux's narrators justify their adoption of a particular literary approach can be read as evidence of narratorial insecurity. This interpretation also accounts for the greater assertiveness of the metanarrative interventions in *La Place*, in that it is Ernaux's first work to abandon the security of the fictional framework.

4   Most of *'Je ne suis pas sortie de ma nuit'* was written before the narrator began to write *Une femme*, yet relates events which generally come after those portrayed in the earlier work, a large part of which is taken up with the mother's early life and marriage.

5   If *Une femme*, more than *La Place*, acknowledges the subjective component in the narrator's representation of a parent, the circumstances surrounding the production of *'Je ne suis pas sortie de ma nuit'* – the imminence of the mother's demise, the originally private genesis of the act of writing – result in an intensely subjective maternal portrait. The titles of the works reflect these differences in narrative approach: *Une femme* locates her mother in a generic sexual category, while the later work's transcription of a direct quotation from the narrator's mother intimates its greater subjectivity. The composition of *'Je ne suis pas sortie de ma nuit'* may not incorporate the self-conscious objectivity or detached writing style of *La Place* and *Une femme*, yet the narrator's characteristic writerly desire to exercise a degree of control over the finished product is present nonetheless: 'Eviter, en écrivant, de me laisser aller à l'émotion' (JSN, p. 38).

6   The narrator's focus on the corporeal could, however, also be read as reflecting the important dichotomisation of her childhood, in which her working-class origins were firmly associated with the physical and manual and her middle-class education with the intellectual.

7   The mother similarly projects herself into the persona of the daughter: 'Je remarque aussi qu'elle se prend souvent pour moi' (JSN, p. 42). While the narrator's awareness of the ageing process is understandably fleeting in the earlier works which centre on her early childhood and adolescence, it becomes more acute in *La Femme gelée*. In this work, the narrator repeatedly mentions her age when looking in the mirror, and projects her own physical and psychological degeneration on to the older women she sees in the hairdresser's at the work's conclusion. *Journal du dehors* also highlights both youthful indifference to, and mature concern with, the ageing process: 'Je commence à être à l'âge où l'on dit bonjour aux vieilles dames qu'on rencontre deux fois de suite, par prescience plus aiguë du temps où je serai l'une d'entre elles. À vingt ans je ne les voyais pas, elles seraient mortes avant que j'aie des rides' (JDD, p. 83).

8   In *The Reproduction of Mothering: Psychoanalysis and the Sociology of Gender* (Berkeley and Los Angeles: University of California Press, 1978), p. 169, Nancy Chodorow remarks: 'The basic feminine sense of self is connected to the world, the basic masculine sense of self is separate.' For Chodorow, girls, unlike boys, retain the primary attachment to the mother, and the mother/daughter relationship plays a pivotal role in female individuation and in the ongoing sense of relationality which underlies women's perception of, and relationships with, others.

9   It is only when the narrator puts her mother into care, where she is surrounded by the unfamiliar, that she recovers the ability to recognise her daughter. This form of address may also signify the mother's consciousness of the disparities in economic status between mother and daughter, disparities highlighted in *La Femme gelée* and *Une femme*: just as the adolescent narrator's assimilation of middle-class values distanced her from her working-class origins, so the narrator's mother felt alienated in the middle-class home of her daughter.

10   In *Ethique de la différence sexuelle* (Paris: Editions de Minuit, 1977), Luce Irigaray observes: 'Pour se faire désirer, aimer de l'homme, il faut évincer la mère, se substituer à elle, l'anéantir pour devenir même', p. 101. As Chapter 1 demonstrates, the constraining influence of the maternal on the young narrator's sexual relations is extensive.

11   As Chapter 1 remarks, food plays a key role in the narrator's early childhood and is endowed with a substitutive value, whether sexual or emotional, as in the following instance of 'comfort eating' which comes at the end of the narrator's relationship with Mathieu: 'j'ai commencé à manger vraiment beaucoup, de biscuits et du saucisson toute la journée' (CDR, p. 135).

12   This cyclical structure to her mother's existence can be viewed as 'feminine' in its eschewal of a linear, progressive model of development, and is particularly appropriate in a work so firmly grounded in the mother's body. As Annie Leclerc observes in *Parole de femme* (Paris: Editions Grasset & Fasquelle, 1974), p. 58: 'Mon corps revient à lui-même par un cycle de métamorphoses. Son appréhension du temps est circulaire.' Indeed, as this study remarks, Ernaux's corpus as a whole is characterised by circularity, in that its repetitions and recurrences defer a definitive dénouement.

13   The narrator's previous disregard of future developments is highlighted in a recollection evoking events portrayed in *Les Armoires vides* – a frequent point of reference in this work – a recollection which implicitly points to the superfluousness of fictionalisation, given the unpredictability of 'real life': 'Je songe à ma chambre de

la cité universitaire, il y a vingt ans. Maintenant, je suis ici, avec elle. On ne sait rien imaginer' (JSN, p. 47). The institutionalised isolation which characterises the narrator's experience of university in *Les Armoires vides* is duplicated in her mother's existence in *'Je ne suis pas sortie de ma nuit'*. The narrator's perception of her abortion as signalling the end of childhood, a perception articulated in both *Les Armoires vides* and *L'Evénement*, reinforces the narrator's association of the death of the mother with her own projection into adulthood in *'Je ne suis pas sortie de ma nuit'*.

14   In a similar vein, her sexual relationship with A. provokes the narrator's curiosity about her mother's sex life in *'Je ne suis pas sortie de ma nuit'*, as she draws parallels between her current corporeal experiences and those of her mother at the same age. As Philippe Vilain's *L'Etreinte* (Paris: Gallimard, 1997) reveals, the A. of *'Je ne suis pas sortie de ma nuit'* is not the A. of *Passion simple*.

15   Throughout Ernaux's writing, the female body acts as an important indicator of psychological health and well-being, as highlighted in the narrator's experiences of pregnancy and abortion, or in the cessation of menstruation at the end of *Ce qu'ils disent ou rien*. This portrayal of the body and bodily needs as playing an integral role in self-perception may also account for the extremely hostile reception accorded *Passion simple* among certain (predominantly male) French critics, whose adherence to 'enlightenment' values would privilege the intellectual and rational over the physical and 'irrational'.

16   This incident is mentioned in *Les Armoires vides*, p. 180, in *Ce qu'ils disent ou rien*, p. 152 and in *L'Evénement*, p. 89. Not only does *'Je ne suis pas sortie de ma nuit'* evoke events related elsewhere in Ernaux's corpus, but previous works such as *Les Armoires vides* and *La Place* are named. The narrator also refers to short stories she publishes in newspapers and journals, as well as to the fact that she is writing *Une femme* at the same time as keeping the diary entries which will form *'Je ne suis pas sortie de ma nuit'*.

17   It is interesting to note that, in both *Une femme* and *'Je ne suis pas sortie de ma nuit'*, the narrator suffers from stomach pains during the mother's deterioration and after her death.

18   It would appear that, in a manner similar to her relationship with the A. of *Passion simple*, the presumed working-class origins of A. in *'Je ne suis pas sortie de ma nuit'* testify to the narrator's desire to renew links with her working-class past, a desire substantiated by the heterosexual/familial parallels she draws. In her work, *L'Ecriture: lien de mère à fille chez Jeanne Hyvrard, Chantal Chawaf et Annie Ernaux* (Amsterdam and Atlanta, GA: Rodopi, 2000), Monique Saigal highlights similarities between the narrator's reaction to the departure of her lover in *Passion simple* and to her mother's death in *Une femme*, p. 158. Such similarities encompass the dominant role assumed by both the mother in childhood and the lover in *Passion simple*, and the narrator's association of them with active agency.

19   Throughout her corpus, Ernaux's narrators set store by the workings of 'fate' and 'destiny' in their belief that adherence to specific modes of conduct, frequently in the form of charitable deeds, will help bring about their desired future.

20   Continuity is also apparent in *La Vie extérieure*, which begins the year after *Journal du dehors*'s final entries.

21   See *L'Invention du quotidien* (Paris: Gallimard, 1994) a two-volume study in which Michel de Certeau, along with Luce Giard and Pierre Mayol, traces the

individual's interaction with the everyday. In its desire to represent an area neglected in traditional literature or sociology and its belief in the aesthetic value of the everyday; in its dismantling of the public/private dichotomy through the individual's gradual appropriation of the public domain by repeated insertion in it; and in its portrayal of public spaces as collective memory banks, de Certeau's work presents strong parallels to Ernaux's. Both *Journal du dehors* and *La Vie extérieure* represent a *mise en abîme* of consumerism, in which the narrator consumes the material and human components of her environment in the act of narration, as those portrayed consume the products of their commercial habitat. However, de Certeau's portrayal of the multifarious tactics of resistance adopted by the individual to refuse interpellation by the dominant social order offers a more positive reading of human behaviour paradigms than Ernaux's. *Journal du dehors*'s representation of snapshots of everyday life in suburban France has also led to comparisons being drawn between the work and Barthes's *Mythologies*. Such comparisons are of limited usefulness in that, while *Journal du dehors* does focus on manifestations of popular culture and their transformation into 'natural' indices, the narratorial desire for objectivity prohibits the descriptive detail and deconstructive relish found in Barthes's work.

22   De Certeau considers train travel particularly conducive to narrative creativity – a creativity reflected in the fundamental role played by storytelling in the everyday for Ernaux's narrators in *Journal du dehors* and *La Vie extérieure* – and to the deconstruction of the public/private divide. In an evocative passage, he remarks: 'La glace de verre et la ligne de fer répartissent d'un côté l'intériorité du voyageur, narrateur putatif, et de l'autre la force de l'être, constitué en objet sans discours, puissance d'un silence extérieur. Mais, paradoxe, c'est le silence de ces choses mises à distance, derrière le verre, qui, de loin, fait parler nos mémoires ou tire de l'ombre les rêves de nos secrets', *L'Invention du quotidien 1*, p. 167.

23   That criticism is again illustrated in her comment on Mitterrand's patronising elitism, an elitism foregrounded by her reference to him as 'Le président de la République' (JDD, p. 39), and which, given his socialist credentials, she may find all the more offensive. Analogous to other examples of mediatic representation in the work, Mitterrand's discourse perfectly illustrates the exclusion of the working class, in that, while appearing to express concern for their situation, his very language indicates that he does not even deem them worthy recipients of his speech.

24   In a similar vein, the most successful beggar portrayed in the work is one who colloborates in the public's willed misapprehension of the hardship he endures through his comic performance: 'C'est le clown, qui met une distance artistique entre la réalité sociale, misère, alcoolisme, à laquelle il renvoie par sa personne, et le public-voyageur' (JDD, pp. 78–79).

25   The narrator provides various examples of racism in French society in *Journal du dehors*, whether in the form of the poor housing given to immigrants, or in her descriptions of a Le Pen supporter or of a shopkeeper who treats an African customer as a potential shoplifter.

26   The reader is reminded of the narrator's stated intention in writing *Une femme*: 'je souhaite rester, d'une certaine façon, au-dessous de la littérature' (UF, p. 23). The narrator's desire to portray individual microcosms in an endeavour to reflect contemporary suburban society resembles the representation of her childhood universe in *La Honte*, in which each individual's *histoire* is shown to help define her

parents' milieu: 'Roman collectif, chacun apportant sa contribution, par un fragment de récit, un détail, au sens général' (LH, p. 62). This description also points to the role played by storytelling in daily life, a role highlighted in *Journal du dehors*.

27   Roland Barthes, *S/Z* (Paris: Editions du Seuil, 1970), p. 89. Ernaux's narrators may foreground the innovativeness of their subject matter relative to their literary predecessors and contemporaries, yet the corpus itself comprises numerous thematic repetitions and instances of intertextuality.

28   As this study remarks, the rectifying role played by Ernaux's writing is a recurrent, if implicit, theme of her corpus. Just as earlier narrators criticise existent literary representations of the working class for failing to reflect their childhood experiences, in *'Je ne suis pas sortie de ma nuit'* the narrator comments on the fact that pictorial representations of old age have little in common with her mother's experience of it: 'Vu *Les vieilles* de Goya. Mais ce n'est pas ma mère' (JSN, p. 56).

29   As the Introduction suggests, the narrator's attraction to those on the social periphery, those whose conduct is not subject to the usual norms, may have partly been fuelled by her experience of emotional and behavioural extremes in *Passion simple*.

30   The narrator can be seen to provide a Bourdieuian analysis of the sociology of cultural consumption in her condemnation of the more refined manifestations of social exclusion, a condemnation which is all the more ironic, in that she would also appear to enjoy the benefits of them: 'Aux Comptoirs de la Tour d'Argent, quai de la Tournelle, on n'entre pas librement, il faut sonner' (JDD, p. 67). Her disposable income is further illustrated by the fact that a number of vignettes are set in the hairdresser's, evoking the final scene of *La Femme gelée*, in which the narrator is loath to resemble the stereotypical middle-class women she sees there.

31   That desire for order is further exemplified in the general adherence to hierarchised social roles in *Journal du dehors* and *La Vie extérieure* – what Mayol terms the '"prêts-à-porter" sociaux', *L'Invention du quotidien 2*, p. 29. Even the subversive role adopted by certain beggars is in keeping with mainstream perceptions of the conduct of the marginalised.

32   The role played by narrative in everyday life endows verbal exchanges with a sense of theatricality, of dramatic performance – 'Théâtre spontané, avec unité de la forme et du fond' (JDD, pp. 59–60) – a theatricality also apparent in the discourse of the narrator's own mother, whose selling techniques are described as 'Du théâtre, du bagout' (LFG, p. 17).

33   As Chapter 2, note 43 remarks, the narrator also compares writing to eroticism in the short text 'Fragments autour de Philippe V.'.

34   This association is instilled in individuals from earliest childhood, as highlighted in the narrator's description of a young child she observes on a train: 'Le bonheur absolu d'arborer les premiers signes de "dame" et celui de posséder des choses désirées' (JDD, p. 64).

35   This analogy reveals the continuing influence of the narrator's childhood in the form of her traumatic experience of confession as portrayed in *Les Armoires vides*. In *Journal du dehors*, the narrator's sense of isolation and aberration following the machine's refusal to give out money is due to apparent material shortcomings rather than sexual ones. The narrator's feelings of guilt and inferiority have clearly not been eradicated, whatever her material security: 'À nouveau: "Votre carte est illisible."

Horreur du mot "illisible". C'est moi qui suis illisible, fautive' (JDD, p. 28). It is wholly appropriate that the judgemental gaze of the Other which figures so heavily in Ernaux's corpus take on an automated form in the anonymous, commercial environment portrayed in *Journal du dehors*.

36   Analogous to her desire to preserve the maternal in *'Je ne suis pas sortie de ma nuit'*, Ernaux's writing is further motivated by a desire to safeguard aspects of the constantly changing modern environment: 'Mon écriture cherche à fixer ce qui passe, à laisser une trace de soi mais aussi des autres, à lutter contre le caractère fugace de l'existence, la rapidité du changement dans la vie contemporaine', Claire-Lise Tondeur, 'Entretien avec Annie Ernaux', *French Review*, vol. 69, no. 1 (1995), pp. 37–44, p. 41. This desire is also intimated in a remark by Vincent Van Gogh quoted in *La Vie extérieure*: '"je cherche à exprimer le passage désespérément rapide des choses de la vie moderne"' (LVE, p. 81).

37   Ernaux has elsewhere underlined her perception of the narrating subject as temporarily inhabited by other subjects, as a type of medium through which others find articulation: 'Je suis un lieu de passage, un lieu de passage de l'amour, un lieu de passage de la mort d'une mère. Evidemment sur le moment toutes ces choses sont très fortes et très douloureuses ou, au contraire, exaltantes, mais, en même temps, c'est ce sentiment que c'est comme un fond commun qui passe à travers moi, et que je dois écrire là-dessus', unpublished interview with Siobhán McIlvanney, 23 September 1993. The narrator of *Les Armoires vides* expresses a similar belief: 'Pour moi, l'auteur n'existait pas, il ne faisait que transcrire la vie de personnages réels' (LAV, p. 80).

38   It also corresponds to the narrator's incomplete knowledge of the *Ville Nouvelle*'s geography, in that she is only familiar with particular areas of it and has no sense of its overall layout.

39   The narrator's positive perception of anonymity may account for her desire to live in a new town in the first place, given the constant invasion of privacy characteristic of her childhood. In *La Honte*, the mature narrator comments on the mental stasis which afflicts her as soon as she arrives in her home town of Yvetot, on her sense of engulfment by her surroundings (LH, pp. 43–44).

40   *La Honte* also highlights the importance of the gaze in validating the existence of the Other: 'On ne pouvait pardonner à ceux qui niaient l'existence des autres en ne *regardant personne*' (LH, p. 66). *La Vie extérieure* expresses this desire for integration through a form of visual appropriation more clearly: 'Aujourd'hui, pendant quelques minutes, j'ai essayé de *voir* tous les gens que je croisais, tous inconnus. Il me semblait que leur existence, par l'observation détaillée de leur personne, me devenait subitement très proche, comme si je les touchais' (LVE, p. 26). The narrator's desire to reduce the anonymity of her environment can be seen in her belief that the name of her hairdresser, 'Gérard Saint-Karl', refers to the owner of the shop – a bona fide, real-life human being – rather than designating a chain.

41   The narrator of *La Place* remarks: 'J'ai retrouvé dans des êtres anonymes rencontrés n'importe où, porteurs à leur insu des signes de force ou d'humiliation, la réalité oubliée de sa condition' (LP, pp. 100–01).

42   Autobiographical influences stemming from the narrator's religious education and Catholic upbringing are further apparent in her recurrent sense of shame – when buying condoms, she remarks: 'Répondre "deux préservatifs", c'est confesser dans une officine, devant tout le monde, qu'on va faire l'amour' (LVE, p. 37) – or in

Annie Ernaux: The Return to Origins

her desire for absolution when failing to acknowledge the social 'reality' of a beggar: 'Après je me dégoûte tant que, pour effacer la honte, je voudrais me rouler dans son manteau, embrasser ses mains, sentir son haleine' (LVE, p. 61). The narrator also describes cubicles in the social security office as 'le confessionnal des pauvres' (LVE, p. 98). The influence of the narrator's more recent past is illustrated when, as in *Journal du dehors*, members of the public remind her of her children.

43   See note 26. In *Journal du dehors*, the narrator employs a similar phrase – '"mettre au-dessus de soi"' (JDD, p. 36) – to refer to the intellectualisation of experience. This emphasis on the need for art to be an integral part of the everyday, rather than apart from it – and for the everyday to be an integral part of art – is echoed in de Certeau's focus on the 'sous-homme' and his/her *sous*-tactics of resistance, tactics which cannot be inserted into pre-established behaviour paradigms and therefore remain unrecognised by the dominant class. The marginalised subjects who figure in *Journal du dehors* and *La Vie extérieure* are likewise ignored by the dominant class and, consequently, by mediatic representation.

44   By her sheer longevity, Jeanne Calment – the oldest woman in the world, who forms the subject of two diary entries – is shown to blur the distinction between the two, constituting a living work of art.

45   While the work is infused with a sense of human powerlessness against the inexorable march of history, concrete political action in the form of demonstrations is presented as the most effective means of instigating social improvement. The narrator takes part in such demonstrations – whether protesting about the 'loi Debré' or appealing on behalf of a non-French immigrant for a visa extension – and this participation can be read as evidence of her democratic belief that political change begins at a grass-roots level. The narrator of *Journal du dehors* shares this pragmatic belief: 'La parole et la pensée n'ont pas la force du geste, de l'action sur un objet' (JDD, p. 77).

46   One diary entry describes a film about euthanasia which may be interpreted as combining both these emphases, in that it provides mediatic representation of what can be seen as a form of consumer choice.

47   The narrator's perception of the shopping centre as fulfilling the role played by the Church in the past further highlights its importance in instilling a – however tenuous – sense of community, even if principally through the purchase of consumer goods (LVE, p. 113). The significance of consumerism in influencing contemporary *moeurs* is reinforced by her description of Jean-Paul Gaultier as possessing 'le sourire de Dieu' (LVE, p. 124). If the commercial has usurped the role of the Church in modern life, the mediatic has taken over that of its moral guidance: 'La morale vient de la radio, par spots' (LVE, p. 37). In *L'Invention du quotidien 2*, Pierre Mayol also employs a religious analogy to describe the shopping centre, attributing the fragility of humanist values to the predominance of materialism: 'L'impression subjective d'être exposé au grand vent des objets, à leur amoncellement ordonné, dans ces cathédrales gigantesques que sont les halls des "grandes surfaces", fait peur car l'intimité, la confidence sont volatilisées au profit d'un système d'achat' (p. 150). In both *Journal du dehors* and *La Vie extérieure*, the narrator's association of the commercial with a sense of community may stem from the the fact that her parents' *café-épicerie* was a key meeting-place for the working-class people who populated her childhood.

48   The thematic emphases on the passing of time and the contiguity of past and present again find personification in the life of Jeanne Calment, whose existence acts

as a literal bridge between past and present.

49   The evocative power of songs in both *La Vie extérieure* and *Journal du dehors*, while presumably related to their prevalence in the narrator's working-class childhood – in early works, family get-togethers frequently turn into sing-songs – can be viewed as a form of aural equivalent to the Proustian perception of involuntary memory, permitting the narrator to re-experience aspects of her existence simply on hearing a particular song.

50   Past and present are again imbricated in her comparison of the current treatment of ethnic minorities with the Nazis' treatment of the Jews.

51   It is beggars who occasionally exemplify the 'sites of resistance' perceived by Michel de Certeau as characteristic of the individual's negotiations with the everyday. In *Journal du dehors* and *La Vie extérieure*, beggars participate in carnivalesque behaviour, both in their clown-like antics designed to attract the public's attention and in their constant insertion of discordant notes into a precarious social harmony.

52   It is not only beggars who are obliged to draw attention to their ostracisation by verbally confronting the dominant class of French society, but working-class individuals in *La Vie extérieure* manifest a similar need to have their existence acknowledged through their loud verbal performances in public, a need which contrasts with the confidently restrained conduct of the bourgeoisie in the work. These two different behaviour modes reflect the dichotomised characterisation of middle-class women as silent and working-class women as vociferous in *La Femme gelée*.

53   The term '"enfants des cités"' (LVE, p. 115) has similarly racist connotations for the narrator, while the acronym '"SDF"' dehumanises and desexes the homeless, turning them into an anomalous, undifferentiated mass (LVE, p. 110).

54   Such middle-class complacency is typified in Mazarine Pingeot's apparent presumption that, as the former president's daughter, she has the right to publish a book, whatever her literary talent (LVE, pp. 94–95). The self-regarding insularity of the writing profession is reflected in its title, *Premier roman*. The narrator of *Journal du dehors* is similarly critical of the social validation accorded to the literary persona: 'L'écriture ne suffit donc pas, il doit y avoir des signes extérieurs, des preuves matérielles, pour définir l'écrivain, le "vrai"' (JDD, p. 53).

55   The multifarious subjective interpretations of 'reality' and the consequent partiality of each individual's understanding of it, which form recurrent themes in the work, may further account for the absence of political solidarity it portrays.

56   During a radio interview, the director of an organisation which provides financial assistance to private businesses enounces her class status along with her detached syllables (LVE, p. 93), in a manner similar to the narrator's schoolteacher in *La Femme gelée* whose manner of speaking indicates her class as much as what she says: 'Tellement agaçante en plus la maîtresse à susurrer "votre mââman", chez moi et dans tout le quartier, on disait "moman". Grosse différence' (LFG, p. 60). As throughout Ernaux's corpus, the media in *La Vie extérieure* portray culturally acquired language skills as indicative of 'natural' class differences (LVE, p. 115).

57   Given the repeated emphasis on the imbrication of literature and 'reality' due to the public's constant exposure to a variety of mediatic representations, the narrator's argument that the public will seek a return to fiction when it has reached saturation point with 'real-life' programmes is somewhat contradictory, since, as she remarks, 'Le récit est un besoin d'exister' (LVE, p. 10).

58   The clichéd, predictable prejudices voiced in the documentary, as well as the dramatic/traumatic nature of its content, are highlighted in the predominance of theatrical terms in the narrator's description of it. That the narrator's memories of early childhood are in black and white, while recollections of the more recent past are in colour (LVE, p. 94), may further reflect the pervasiveness of mediatic influence.

59   The narrator's inclusion of *faits divers* in the work, which the earlier texts portray as one of the few examples of written representation of interest to working-class people, and, in particular, to her father, further validates working-class experience. By their representation of different aspects of the urban landscape, both *Journal du dehors* and *La Vie extérieure* make visible the '"villes invisibles"' – a term which echoes Woolf's 'invisible presences' – of the participants portrayed. As Pierre Mayol remarks in *L'Invention du quotidien 2*, p. 202: 'Dans les cafés, dans les bureaux, dans les immeubles, ils [les récits urbains] insinuent des espaces différents. Ils ajoutent à la ville visible les "villes invisibles" dont parlait Calvino.'

60   Parallels between the two diaries are reinforced by the narrator citing examples of grafitti and slogans which also appear in *Journal du dehors*.

Notes to Chapter 5
pp. 153–76

1 Interview with Jean-Jacques Gibert, 'Le Silence ou la Trahison?', *Révolution*, 22 February 1985, pp. 52–53, p. 53.

2 In her article, 'Le Problème du langage chez Annie Ernaux', Christine Fau perceives *Passion simple* as signalling a new beginning in Ernaux's writing, a beginning which the publication of *La Honte* reveals as illusive: 'Après cela, dans *Passion simple*, l'auteur peut se détourner de son enfance et explorer d'autres horizons', *French Review*, vol. 68, no. 3 (February 1995), pp. 501–12, p. 511. This readerly expectation is one shared by a number of critics, including Marie-France Savéan, who, in *La Place et Une femme d'Annie Ernaux*, remarks: 'Annie Ernaux, avec *La Place* et *Une femme*, semble avoir édifié le mausolée définitif consacré à ses parents, seul lieu où il lui soit désormais possible de visiter sa mémoire' (Paris: Gallimard, 1994), p. 143.

3 'Annie Ernaux ou l'écriture comme recherche' (reviews of *La Honte* and *'Je ne suis pas sortie de ma nuit'*), *LittéRéalité*, vol. 9, no. 1 (1997), pp. 111–13, p. 111. Such intertextuality can also be seen in *La Honte*'s dedication to Philippe V., the male protagonist of Ernaux's short text, 'Fragments autour de Philippe V.'.

4 There is some ambivalence as to the precise age of the narrator in *La Honte*: while references are made to her twelfth year, there are two remarks which indicate that she is only 11 when witnessing the scene (LH, pp. 16, 94). Annie Ernaux's own biography reveals her to have been 11 on the date of 15 June 1952, the day the 'scene' occurred.

5 The narrator's emphasis on the inevitable distortion in literature's translation of 'reality' should not be read as a rejection of all connection between the domains of art and 'real life'. Ernaux's narrators remain fundamentally humanist in their belief in the potentially beneficial reciprocity between these domains.

6 It is only in *'Je ne suis pas sortie de ma nuit'*, pp. 56–57, that the narrator conjectures as to the circumstances preceding the 'scene'.

7 The street is referred to as 'rue Clopart' in *Les Armoires vides*, which offers a less sophisticated analysis of the topography of habitat provided by *La Honte*, although one which reaches the same conclusion regarding the hierarchical structure – and structuring effect – of residential allocation, an effect which encompasses language, values and codes of conduct. If the narrator's *café-épicerie* denotes working-class proximity and lack of privacy, the opposite is true for the isolated, middle-class houses in 'rue de la République' (LAV, p. 38; LH, p. 46). In *La Honte*, this topographical approach is duplicated in the narrator's enumeration of particular objects in order to highlight their structuring significance in her environment and pivotal role in reflecting social position.

8 The formative role played by religion is foregrounded throughout Ernaux's corpus, whether in the narrator's quasi-mystical association of pain and pleasure in *Les Armoires vides*; in *Passion simple*'s association with the Passion in both the abjection of the narrator and her idolisation of A.; in her mother's religious beliefs described in *Une femme* and *'Je ne suis pas sortie de ma nuit'*; and in the narrator's comparison of

215

her own text to the text of Christ in *La Honte*, in which she explains the act of writing the 'scene' in the following rather opaque terms: 'Peut-être s'agit-il encore de cette chose folle et mortelle, insufflée par ces mots d'un missel qui m'est désormais illisible, d'un rituel que ma réflexion place à côté de n'importe quel cérémonial vaudou, *prenez et lisez car ceci est mon corps et mon sang qui sera versé pour vous*' (LH, pp. 38–39).

9   The important role played by the gaze in earlier works is also apparent in *La Honte*, and extends beyond the repercussions of the narrator's witnessing the 'scene'. Typically the object of the gaze within her domestic universe, the narrator finds a location in the family home which enables her to see others while remaining invisible to them. In a remark which unwittingly conveys her sense of claustrophobia, she states: 'De là, je vois tout à travers les barreaux, sans être vue' (LH, p. 51). At school, no gaze is allowed either to penetrate outside from within, or inside from without; it is a universe sealed off from the rest of the town, intensifying the atmosphere of religious and social superiority which permeates it.

10   The narrator partly attributes her mother's dominant role in the household to her religious convictions: 'Pour moi, en 52, ma mère *était* la religion' (LH, pp. 103–04). This quasi-divine characterisation of the mother echoes the references to her all-seeingness – and resultant omniscience – in earlier works.

11   The narrators of *Les Armoires vides*, p. 69, and *Ce qu'ils disent ou rien*, p. 37, indulge in similar games. These visual indicators of social status also play an important role in *Journal du dehors* and, less so, in *La Vie extérieure*, in which material possessions and physical appearance represent the principal criteria of social classification in the gaze of the Other. In *La Honte*, the narrator's post-'scene' belief in the material visibility of social class is confirmed when her schoolfriends and teacher see her mother in a dirty nightdress, an object indicative of her 'sullied' class status. Indeed, the narrator's overwhelming conviction of her class inferiority in *La Honte* leads her to reinterpret the 'scene' as consequential rather than causal in relation to that inferiority: like Denise in *Les Armoires vides*, she rereads the 'scene' as a sign of her family's 'vraie nature' (LH, p. 110), of their inherent working-class 'sinfulness'.

12   As Chapter 2 remarks, in a further parallel with *Passion simple*'s opening scene, the narrator describes her memory of the 'scene' once she has related it as resembling 'un film sur une chaîne de télévision cryptée regardé sans décodeur' (LH, p. 30). Language's fluidity in *La Honte*, coupled with the inevitable distortions of subjective memories and the impossibility of regressing, temporally and experientially, to one's previous self, result in an approximate self-representation: 'Mais la femme que je suis en 95 est incapable de se replacer dans la fille de 52 qui ne connaissait que sa petite ville, sa famille et son école privée, n'avait à sa disposition qu'un lexique réduit. Et devant elle, l'immensité du temps à vivre. Il n'y a pas de vraie mémoire de soi' (LH, p. 37). This avowal accounts for the work's topographical emphasis in the narrator's privileging of the 'stable' material components of her childhood universe.

13   In common with other photographs in Ernaux's writing, those described in *La Honte* reveal an acute self-consciousness on the part of their working-class subjects. An examination of the role of photographs throughout Ernaux's writing would prove illuminating.

14   See *Une femme*, p. 60, and *'Je ne suis pas sortie de ma nuit'*, pp. 56–57.

15   This quotation provides further evidence that, like her predecessors, Ernaux's narrator in *La Honte* repeatedly seeks confirmation, albeit indirectly, of the repre-

sentativeness of her feelings, including her sense of shame: 'Le pire dans la honte, c'est qu'on croit être seul à la ressentir' (LH, p. 109). One 'temporally-specific' object mentioned in the work is her mother's 'robe de crêpe bleue à fleurs rouges et jaunes' (LH, p. 95): 'Elle est partie et revenue habillée en deuil, enfilant seulement sur la plage sa robe bleue à fleurs rouges et jaunes, "pour éviter les commentaires des gens d'Y."' (LH, p. 113). In a characteristic intertextual manner, the same event – a trip to Étretat – is described in *Une femme* in similar terms: 'Elle grimpe sur la falaise à travers les herbes, dans sa robe de crêpe bleu [sic] à grandes fleurs, qu'elle a enfilée derrière les rochers à la place de son tailleur de deuil mis pour partir à cause des gens du quartier' (UF, pp. 59–60).

16   The concurrence of life and death throughout *L'Evénement* is further illustrated in the narrator's own urgent hospitalisation following her abortion and in accounts of other women who die as a result of theirs. If the act of abortion can be indicative of women's desire to keep alive a current self or to give birth to a new self, this desire entails occasionally mortal consequences. Similarly, the narrator's use of contraception – particularly in light of the Aids test with which the work opens – can be interpreted as signalling her wish both to prevent the creation of new life and to preserve her own: 'Ma vie se situe donc entre la méthode Ogino et le préservatif à un franc dans les distributeurs' (LE, pp. 15–16).

17   The Roman Catholic Church's strong opposition to abortion is well-documented, and partly finds expression through various so-called pro-life pressure groups and anti-abortion movements such as The Society for the Protection of Unborn Children.

18   As Chapter 1 remarks, the narrator describes the advent of her menarche and losing her virginity in similarly religious terms, pointing to the fundamental imbrication of religion and sexual activity in the narrator's psyche.

19   In *L'Evénement*, dreams are also interpreted as signs which justify or not the act of writing. Dreams constitute the most *vraisemblable* means of reliving the past for the narrator, offering an intense, if short-lived, duplication of past experience which writing can only approximate.

20   The mature narrator's verification of the accuracy of her account by checking diary entries for the period in question further foregrounds the importance of the 'real' as a foundation for Ernaux's literary project – hence the profusion of dates in the work.

21   The narrator is overcome by emotion when reading the rare literary accounts of abortion she comes across.

22   This point is expressed even more strongly at the work's conclusion: 'les choses me sont arrivées pour que j'en rende compte' (LE, p. 112).

23   A similar motivation – that of forcing him to confront an uncomfortable 'reality' – underlies the narrator's initial desire to continue her relationship with her middle-class boyfriend, who, given his key role in events, scarcely figures in the work. The class consciousness which permeates the narrator's sexual and textual discourses further manifests itself in the mature narrator's reluctance to analyse certain subjects in detail, a reluctance she attributes to a working-class suspiciousness of intellectualisation, to 'quelque chose de très ancien, lié au monde des travailleurs manuels dont je suis issue qui redoutait le "cassement de tête"' (LE, p. 46).

24   Further evidence of the narrator's sense of detachment from mainstream

existence during the period of her pregnancy and abortion can be found in her general intolerance of everyday conversations: as in *Passion simple*, she is astounded at the banality of much of their content, a banality which merely accentuates the 'abnormality' of her own situation.

25   It may also account for her earlier wish that all moral judgement be suspended when reading *Passion simple*, and for her sense of living her passion 'sur le mode romanesque' (PS, p. 30). That the abortion, like the sexual relationship portrayed in *Passion simple*, affects the narrator so profoundly points to the erroneousness of such a perception. If the narrator's separation of the sexual from the everyday may have contributed to her pregnancy, a further reason may lie in her feminist understanding of sexual relationships: in a manner analogous to the narrator's identification with male protagonists in literature in *La Femme gelée*, the young narrator in *L'Evénement* naively considers men and women as similar sexual entities until experience proves otherwise: 'Dans l'amour et la jouissance, je ne me sentais pas un corps intrinsèquement différent de celui des hommes' (LE, p. 21).

26   The 'unrealness' of her experience of abortion is again evoked in *Passion simple* when the narrator returns to 'passage Cardinet' where it took place: 'Je cherchais la différence entre cette réalité passée et une fiction, peut-être simplement ce sentiment d'incrédulité, que j'aie été là un jour, puisque je ne l'aurais pas éprouvé vis-à-vis d'un personnage de roman' (PS, p. 65).

27   The juxtaposition of life and death in the narrator's description of abortion is strikingly similar to the narrator's representation of diary writing in *'Je ne suis pas sortie de ma nuit'*, reinforcing the link between the death of the mother and the abortion/termination of childhood discussed in Chapter 4 and the perceived similarities between the act of abortion and the act of writing in *L'Evénement*: 'Je ne sais pas si c'est un travail de vie ou de mort que je suis en train de faire' (JSN, p. 94).

28   According to Rosalind Pollack Petchesky in *Abortion and Woman's Choice* (Verso: London, 1986; first published by Northeastern University Press, 1985), a female support network has historically been the fundamental condition of the availability of abortion: 'Where women are connected by strong ties of work and community, where they have access to non-domestic sources of support and livelihood, where mothering is not the only work culturally valued for them or their sense of their autonomy over "domesticity" is bolstered by feminist bonds, and where alternative systems of reproductive health care thrive because they are supported by vital women's communities – there, and mainly there, does a *culture* of fertility control, including abortion, develop' (p. 57).

29   The evocative power of language's ability to (mis)represent experience is further illustrated in the narrator's reference to her pregnancy as '"cette chose-là"' (LE, pp. 28, 36), as if to designate it correctly would render it ineradicable. On other occasions, words cannot do justice to the narrator's sense of the past – a form of visceral submersion in a visual image is all that can be achieved: 'Je suis parvenue à l'image de la chambre. Elle excède l'analyse. Je ne peux que m'immerger en elle' (LE, pp. 76–77). The secretive, 'unreal' nature of the abortion partly contributes to this linguistic shortfall.

30   Throughout the work, it is this flagrant insensitivity to the narrator's needs and removal of choice from her which are presented as criminal, not the abortion itself.

31   The attitude adopted by male members of the medical profession is quasi-Malthusian in its association of abortion or pregnancy with a working-class lack of morality, an association which, as this study has demonstrated, is shared by the narrator herself and originates in her grandmother and mother's anguish about extramarital pregnancy. Thus, the narrator initially seeks a doctor in a working-class area of Rouen and presumes that the backstreet abortionist is of working-class origin. For further details of the relevance of Malthus's ideology to working-class sexual relations and reproduction, see Petchesky's chapter on 'Fertility, Gender and Class', in *Abortion and Woman's Choice.*

32   Various medical studies on the after-effects of abortion demonstrate that, contrary to popular belief, particularly in the case of desired abortions this is not an uncommon reaction, and that notions of guilt or psychological damage are exaggerated. Rather, relief at avoiding an unwanted pregnancy and a sense of achievement at gaining control of reproductive rights are common reactions to abortion in these circumstances. As Sarah L. Minden and Malkah T. Notman remark in 'Psychotherapeutic Issues Related to Abortion', *Psychiatric Aspects of Abortion* (Washington and London: American Psychiatric Press Inc., 1991), ed. Nada L. Stotland, pp. 125–26: 'There is also evidence to suggest that like other major life events, pregnancy and abortion contain the potential for maturation and personal growth. The very process of making a difficult life decision like that about abortion can have positive effects on women's self-esteem and sense of autonomy.' In the preface to Lorette Thibout, *L'Avortement vingt ans après, Des femmes témoignent, des hommes aussi* (Paris: Albin Michel, 1995) p. vi, Benoîte Groult suggests that the sheer material difficulties confronting women seeking abortions before the ratification of the 'loi Veil' in 1974 in France may explain the frequent absence of psychological considerations. As many of the accounts in this work remark, the criminality of abortion is of less consequence when the act is financially necessary for women who cannot afford another child. Equally, the scientific notion of the foetus as constituting a life form is a relatively recent phenomenon, stemming from the same period. In *Abortion and Woman's Choice*, Petchesky cites *The Silent Scream* as a particularly graphic example of recent mediatic representation of this notion, in that it purports to present a 12-week-old foetus being aborted (p. x). This type of foetal imagery usurps the mother from the role of victim, as does the foetus's designation as an 'unborn child'.

33   Such fear is understandable, given that a backstreet abortionist was executed in France as recently as 1943.

Bibliography

Works by Annie Ernaux

Les Armoires vides (Paris: Gallimard, 1974).
Ce qu'ils disent ou rien (Paris: Gallimard, 1977).
La Femme gelée (Paris: Gallimard, 1981).
La Place (Paris: Gallimard, 1983).
La Place, introduction by P. M. Wetherill (London: Methuen Educational, 1987).
Une femme (Paris: Gallimard, 1988).
Passion simple (Paris: Gallimard, 1991).
Journal du dehors (Paris: Gallimard, 1993).
'Je ne suis pas sortie de ma nuit' (Paris: Gallimard, 1997).
La Honte (Paris: Gallimard, 1997).
La Vie extérieure, 1993–1999 (Paris: Gallimard, 2000).
L'Evénement (Paris: Gallimard, 2000).

Articles/Short Texts

'L'écrivain en terrain miné', *Le Monde*, 23 April 1985.
'Retours', *L'Autre Journal*, April 1985, pp. 70–71.
Entry in *Le Dictionnaire: Littérature française contemporaine*, ed. Jérôme Garcin, (Paris: Editions François Bourin, 1989), pp. 179–83.
'Lectures de *Passion simple*', *La Faute à Rousseau: Journal de l'Association pour l'Autobiographie et le Patrimoine Autobiographique*, no. 6 (June 1994), pp. 27–29.
'Vers un Je transpersonnel', Autofictions et Cie, *Cahiers RITM*, no. 6 (1994), Université Paris X-Nanterre, pp. 218–21.
'Fragments autour de Philippe V.', *L'Infini*, no. 56 (Winter 1996), pp. 25–26.

Academic Writing on Ernaux

Altounian, Janine, 'De l'Arménie perdue à la Normandie sans place', *Temps modernes* XLIII, nos 504–06 (juil.–sept. 1988), pp. 405–33.
Bacholle, Michèle, 'Annie Ernaux: Lieux communs et lieu(x) de vérité', *LittéRéalité*, vol. 7, nos 1–2 (1995), pp. 28–40.
—— '*Passion simple* d'Annie Ernaux: Vers une désacralisation de la société française?', *Dalhousie French Studies*, no. 36 (Fall 1996), pp. 123–34.
—— 'An interview with Annie Ernaux: Ecrire le vécu', *Sites*, vol. 2, no. 1 (1998), pp. 141–51.
Boehringer, Monkia, 'Ecrire le dedans et le dehors: dialogue transatlantique avec Annie Ernaux', *Dalhousie French Studies* no. 47 (1999), pp. 165–70.
Cairns, Lucille, 'Annie Ernaux, filial ambivalence and *Ce qu'ils disent ou rien*', *Romance*

221

Studies, no. 24 (Fall 1994), pp. 71–84.

Charpentier, Isabelle, 'De corps à corps: réceptions croisées d'Annie Ernaux', *Politix*, no. 27 (1994), pp. 45–75.

Day, Loraine, 'Class, Sexuality and Subjectivity in *Les Armoires vides*', in Margaret Atack and Phil Powrie, eds, *Contemporary French Fiction by Women* (Manchester: Manchester University Press, 1990), pp. 41–55.

——and Tony Jones, *Annie Ernaux: La Place, Une femme* (Glasgow: University of Glasgow French and German Publications, 1990).

Fallaize, Elizabeth, *French Women's Writing: Recent Fiction* (Basingstoke and London: Macmillan, 1993), pp. 67–87.

Fau, Christine, 'Le Problème du langage chez Annie Ernaux', *French Review*, vol. 68, no. 3 (February 1995), pp. 501–12.

Fernandez-Récatala, Denis, *Annie Ernaux* (Monaco: Editions du Rocher, 1994).

Garaud, Christian, 'Ecrire la différence sociale: registres de vie et registres de langue dans *La Place* d'Annie Ernaux', *French Forum*, vol. 19 (1994), pp. 195–214.

——'*Il n'est héritier qui ne veut*: Danièle Sallenave, Annie Ernaux et la littérature', in Michael Bishop, ed., *Thirty Voices in the Feminine* (Amsterdam and Atlanta, GA: Rodopi, 1996).

Golopentia, Sanda, 'Annie Ernaux ou le don reversé', in J. Brami, M. Mage and P. Verdaguer, eds, *Regards sur la France des années 80*, Stanford Italian and French Studies (ANMA Libri, 1994), pp. 84–97.

Hall, Colette, 'De "La femme rompue" à *La Femme gelée*: *Le Deuxième Sexe* revu et corrigé', in Michael Bishop, ed., *Thirty Voices in the Feminine* (Amsterdam and Atlanta, GA: Rodopi, 1996).

Holmes, Diana, 'Feminism and Realism: Christiane Rochefort and Annie Ernaux', *French Women's Writing, 1848–1994* (London: Athlone Press, 1996), pp. 246–65.

Hutton, Margaret-Anne, 'Challenging autobiography: lost object and aesthetic object in Ernaux's *Une femme*', *Journal of European Studies*, no. xxviii (1998), pp. 231–44.

Kimminich, Eva, 'Macht und Magie der Worte: zur Funktion des Schreibens im Werk Annie Ernaux', in *In* S1660, pp. 149–59.

Laacher, Smaïn, 'Annie Ernaux ou l'inaccessible quiétude', *Politix*, no. 14 (1991), pp. 73–78.

Laubier, Claire, ed., *The Condition of Women in France, 1945 to the Present: A Documentary Anthology* (London and New York: Routledge, 1990), chapter 9.

Lebrun, Jean-Claude and Claude Prévost, *Nouveaux territoires romanesques* (Paris: Messidor, Editions Sociales, 1990), pp. 51–66.

McIlvanney, Siobhán, 'Ernaux and Realism: Redressing the Balance', in Maggie Allison, ed., *Women's Space and Identity*, Women Teaching French Papers 2 (Bradford: Department of Modern Languages, University of Bradford, 1992), pp. 49–63.

——'Recuperating Romance: Literary Paradigms in the Works of Annie Ernaux', *Forum for Modern Language Studies*, vol. 32, no. 3 (1996), pp. 240–50.

——'Ernaux, Annie: *La Honte* and *'Je ne suis pas sortie de ma nuit'* (reviews), *Dalhousie French Studies*, no. 42 (1998), pp. 200–02.

——'Annie Ernaux: Un écrivain dans la tradition du réalisme', *Revue d'histoire littéraire de la France*, no. 2 (March–April 1998), pp. 247–66.

——'Writing Relations: The Auto/biographical Subject in Annie Ernaux's *La Place* and *Une femme*', *Journal of the Institute of Romance Studies*, vol. 7 (1999), pp. 205–15.

Mall, Laurence, '"Moins seule et factice": la part autobiographique dans *Une femme* d'Annie Ernaux', *French Review*, vol. 69, no. 1 (1995), pp. 45–54.

Marrone, Claire, 'Past, Present and Passion Tense in Annie Ernaux's *Passion simple*', *Women in French Studies*, no. 2 (1994), pp. 78–87.

Meizoz, Jérôme, 'Annie Ernaux, une politique de la forme', *Versants: Revue Suisse des Littératures Romanes*, no. 30 (1996), pp. 45–61.

Miller, Nancy K., 'Autobiographical Others: Annie Ernaux's *Journal du dehors*', *Sites* (Spring 1998), pp. 127–39.

Montfort, Catherine R. '"La Vieille Née": Simone de Beauvoir, *Une mort très douce*, and Annie Ernaux, *Une femme*', *French Forum*, vol. 21, no. 3 (1996), pp. 349–64.

Morello, Nathalie, 'Faire pour la mère ce qu'elle [n']avait [pas] faire pour le père: étude comparative du projet autobiographique dans *La Place* et *Une femme* d'Annie Ernaux', *Nottingham French Studies*, vol. 38, no.1 (spring 1999), pp. 80–92.

Motte, Warren, 'Annie Ernaux's Understatement', *French Review*, vol. 69, no. 1 (1995), pp. 55–67.

——'Annie Ernaux's Understatement', in *Small Worlds* (Lincoln, NE: University of Nebraska Press, 1999), pp. 54–69.

Naudin, Marie, '*Passion simple* Annie Ernaux' (review), *French Review*, vol. 67, no. 2 (1993), pp. 386–87.

Orel, Orietta, '*Journal du dehors* di Annie Ernaux. La letteratura come etnotesto', *Cristallo: Rassegna di Varia Umanità*, year 38, no. 2 (August 1996), pp. 89–98.

Saigal, Monique, *L'Ecriture: lien de mère à fille chez Jeanne Hyvrard, Chantal Chawaf et Annie Ernaux* (Amsterdam and Atlanta, GA: Rodopi, 2000).

Sanders, Carol, 'Stylistic Aspects of Women's Writing: The Case of Annie Ernaux', *French Cultural Studies*, no. 4 (1993), pp. 15–29.

Savéan, Marie-France, *La Place et Une femme d'Annie Ernaux* (Paris: Gallimard, 1994).

——'Dossier: *La Place*' (Paris: Gallimard, 1997).

Sheringham, Michael, 'Invisible Presences: Fiction, Autobiography and Women's Lives – Virginia Woolf to Annie Ernaux', *Sites*, vol. 2, no. 1 (1998), pp. 5–24.

Thomas, Lyn, 'Women, Education and Class: Narratives of Loss in the Fiction of Annie Ernaux', in M. Hoar, M. Lea, M. Stuart, V. Swash, A. Thomson and L. West, eds, *Life Histories and Learning: Language, the Self and Education: Papers from an Interdisciplinary Conference* (Brighton: University of Sussex, 1994), pp. 161–66.

——*Annie Ernaux: An Introduction to the Writer and her Audience* (Oxford and New York: Berg, 1999).

——and Emma Webb, 'Writing from Experience: The Place of the Personal in French Feminist Writing', *Feminist Review*, no. 61 (Spring 1999), pp. 27–48.

Tondeur, Claire-Lise, 'Entretien avec Annie Ernaux', *French Review*, vol. 69, no. 1 (1995), pp. 37–44.

——'Le passé: point focal du présent dans l'oeuvre d'Annie Ernaux', *Women in French*

Studies, no. 3 (Fall 1995), pp. 123–37.

——'Relation mère/fille chez Annie Ernaux', *Romance Languages Annual*, no. 7 (1995), pp. 173–79.

——*Annie Ernaux ou l'exil intérieur* (Amsterdam and Atlanta, GA: Rodopi, 1996).

——'Erotica/pornorotica: *Passion simple* d'Annie Ernaux', in Michael Bishop, ed., *Thirty Voices in the Feminine* (Amsterdam and Atlanta, GA: Rodopi, 1996).

Vilain, Philippe, 'Entretien avec Annie Ernaux: Une "conscience malheureuse" de femme', *LittéRéalité*, vol. 9, no. 1 (1997), pp. 66–71.

——'Annie Ernaux ou l'écriture comme recherche' (reviews of *La Honte* and *'Je ne suis pas sortie de ma nuit'*), *LittéRéalité*, vol. 9, no. 1 (1997), pp. 111–13.

Wetherill, P. M., Introduction to *La Place* (London: Methuen Educational, 1987), pp. 1–35.

Journalistic Articles on Annie Ernaux

Alliot, Bernard, 'Renaudot: Annie Ernaux pour *La Place*', *Le Monde*, 13 November 1984, p. 48.

Alphant, Marianne, *'Une femme apparaît'*, *Libération*, 21 January 1988, p. 36.

Amette, J.-P.,'Enfance et adolescence', *Le Point*, no. 1269, 11 January 1997.

Cicco, Anne and Bruno Peuchamiel, 'La littérature doit attaquer', *L'Humanité*, 22 April 1993.

Clavel, André, 'Annie Ernaux, une romancière dans le RER', *L'Evénement du jeudi*, 29 April 1993.

——'L'enfance à nu d'Annie', *L'Express*, 30 January 1997.

Côté, Lucie, 'Ecrire pour comprendre les choses', *La Presse*, 26 March 1992.

Courchay, Claude, 'L'infortune d'être femme', *Le Monde*, 27 March 1981, p. 23.

Dana, Jacqueline, 'Annie aime les romans à l'eau de rose', *L'Autre Journal*, no. 5 (1993), pp. 54–57.

Delbourg, P., 'Annie Ernaux: le bovarysme est un humanisme', *L'Evénement du jeudi*, 23–29 January 1997.

Deschodt, Eric, 'Les Derniers Lauriers', *Spectacle du Monde*, no. 274 (1985), p. 70.

Dumas, Mireille, 'Une femme dans l'engrenage', *Combat*, 13 March 1981, p. 14.

Gibert, Jean-Jacques, 'Le Silence ou la Trahison?', *Révolution*, 22 February 1985, pp. 52–53.

Langeard, Chantal, 'Annie Ernaux', *Vie ouvrière*, 8 October 1990, pp. 45–47.

Manceaux, Michèle, 'L'amour Passion', *Marie-Claire*, May 1992, pp. 62–64.

Matignon, Renaud, 'Annie Ernaux: Les Banlieues du romanesque', *Le Figaro littéraire*, 23 April 1993, p. 1.

Mazingarbe, D., 'Récits: *La Honte*, *"Je ne suis pas sortie de ma nuit"*, d'Annie Ernaux', *Madame Figaro*, 25 January 1997.

Pélegrin, Dominique Louise, 'La Vérité, simplement', *Télérama*, 5 February 1992, pp. 34–35.

Poncet, Mireille, 'Une année en livres-service: Interview d'Annie Ernaux', *Phosphore*, 92 (1988), pp. 52–54.

Royer, Jean, 'Pour que s'abolisse la barrière entre la littérature et la vie, *Le Devoir*, 26 March 1988.

Savigneau, Josyane, 'Annie Ernaux ou la femme blessée', *Le Monde*, 3 February 1984,

p. 15.

——'Annie Ernaux, dans les marges', *Le Monde*, 23 April 1993, p. 25.

——'Ethnologue de soi', *Le Monde des livres*, 24 January 1997.

General Works

Abel, Elizabeth, ed., *Writing and Sexual Difference* (Brighton: Harvester, 1982).

——Marianne Hirsch and Elizabeth Langland, eds, *The Voyage In: Fictions of Female Development* (Hanover and London: University Press of New England, 1983).

Aebischer, Verena, *Les Femmes et le langage: Représentations sociales d'une différence* (Paris: Presses Universitaires de France, 1985).

Amossy, Ruth, *Les Idées reçues: Sémiologie du stéréotype* (Paris: Editions Nathan, 1991).

Ardener, Shirley, ed., *Perceiving Women* (London: Dent, 1975).

——*Defining Females* (London: John Wiley, 1978).

Ascher, Carol, *Simone de Beauvoir: A Life of Freedom* (Brighton: Harvester, 1981).

Assiter, Alison, *Althusser and Feminism* (London: Pluto Press, 1990).

Atack, Margaret and Phil Powrie, eds, *Contemporary French Fiction by Women: Feminist Perspectives* (Manchester: Manchester University Press, 1990).

Badinter, Elisabeth, *L'Amour en plus: Histoire de l'amour maternel* (Paris: Flammarion, 1983).

Bakhtin. M. M., *The Dialogic Imagination, Four Essays by M. M. Bakhtin*, ed. Michael Holquist, trans. Caryl Emerson and Michael Holquist (Austin: University of Texas Press, 1981).

——*Speech Genres & Other Late Essays*, trans. Vern W. McGee (Austin: University of Texas Press, 1986).

Balzac, Honoré de, *La Comédie humaine* (Paris: Editions du Seuil, 1965).

Barthes, Roland, *S/Z* (Paris: Editions du Seuil, 1970).

——*Mythologies* (Paris: Editions du Seuil, 1970).

——*Le Plaisir du texte* (Paris: Editions du Seuil, 1973).

——*Fragments d'un discours amoureux* (Paris: Editions du Seuil, 1977).

——Leo Bersani, Philippe Hamon, Michel Riffaterre and Ian Watt, *Littérature et Réalité* (Paris: Editions du Seuil, 1982).

Beauvoir, Simone de, *Le Deuxième Sexe*, 2 vols (Paris: Gallimard, 1949; repr. 1976).

——*La Femme Rompue* (Paris: Gallimard, 1968).

Belsey, Catherine, and Jane Moore, eds, *The Feminist Reader: Essays in Gender and the Politics of Literary Criticism* (London: Macmillan, 1989).

Benjamin, Jessica, *The Bonds of Love, Psychoanalysis, Feminism and the Problem of Domination* (London: Virago, 1990; first published by Pantheon Books, New York, 1988).

Benstock, Shari, ed., *The Private Self, Theory and Practice of Women's Autobiographical Writings* (London: Routledge, 1988).

Berger, John, *Ways of Seeing* (London and New York: Penguin, 1973).

Bodine, Ann, 'Androcentrism in prescriptive grammar', in Deborah Cameron, ed., *The Feminist Critique of Language: a Reader* (London: Routledge, 1990).

Bonvoisin, Samra-Martine and Michèle Maignien, *La Presse féminine* (Paris: Presses Universitaires de France, 1986).

Boose, Lynda E. and Betty Flowers, eds, *Daughters and Fathers* (Baltimore, MD and London: Johns Hopkins University Press, 1989).

Bourdieu, Pierre, *La Distinction: Critique sociale du jugement* (Paris: Editions de Minuit, 1979).

——*Ce que parler veut dire: L'Economie des échanges linguistiques* (Paris: Fayard, 1982).

Brodzki, Bella and Celeste Schenck, eds, *Life/Lines, Theorizing Women's Autobiography* (Ithaca, NY and London: Cornell University Press, 1988).

Brooks, Peter, *Reading for the Plot: Design and Intention in Narrative* (Oxford: Clarendon Press, 1984).

Buck, Claire, ed., *Bloomsbury Guide to Women's Literature* (London: Quality Paperbacks Direct, 1992).

Cameron, Deborah, ed., *The Feminist Critique of Language: A Reader* (London: Routledge, 1990).

——*Feminism & Linguistic Theory*, 2nd edn (London: Macmillan, 1992).

Camus, Albert, *L'Etranger* (Paris: Gallimard, 1974; 1942).

Cardinal, Marie, *Les Mots pour le dire* (Paris: Editions Grasset & Fasquelle, 1975).

——*Autrement Dit* (Paris: Editions Grasset & Fasquelle, 1977).

Certeau, Michel de, *L'Invention du quotidien 1. arts de faire* (Paris: Gallimard, 1990).

——Luce Giard and Pierre Mayol, *L'Invention du quotidien 2. habiter, cuisiner* (Paris: Gallimard, 1994).

Chodorow, Nancy, *The Reproduction of Mothering: Psychoanalysis and the Sociology of Gender* (Berkeley and Los Angeles: University of California Press, 1978).

——*Feminism and Psychoanalytic Theory* (New Haven, CT and London: Yale University Press, 1989).

Cixous, Hélène, 'Le Rire de la Méduse', special issue of *L'Arc*, 'Simone de Beauvoir et la lutte des femmes', no. 61 (1975), pp. 39–54.

——*Entre l'écriture* (Paris: Editions des femmes, 1986).

——and Catherine Clément, *La Jeune Née* (Paris: Union Générale d'Editions, 1975).

Conley, Verena A., *Hélène Cixous: 'Writing the Feminine'* (Lincoln, NE: University of Nebraska Press, 1984).

Cornillon, Susan Koppelman, *Images of Women in Fiction: Feminist Perspectives* (Bowling Green, OH: Bowling Green University Popular Press, 1972).

Culler, Jonathan, *On Deconstruction, Theory and Criticism after Structuralism* (London: Routledge & Kegan Paul, 1983).

Dardigna, Anne Marie, *Les Châteaux d'Eros ou les infortunes du sexe des femmes* (Paris: F. Maspéro, 1981).

DeJean, Joan and Nancy K. Miller, eds, *Displacements: Women, Tradition, Literatures in French* (Baltimore, MD: Johns Hopkins University Press, 1991).

Didier, Béatrice, *L'Ecriture-femme* (Paris: Presses Universitaires de France, 1981).

Dinnerstein, Dorothy, *The Rocking of the Cradle and the Ruling of the World* (London: The Women's Press, 1987).

Duchen, Claire, *Feminism in France: From May '68 to Mitterrand* (London: Routledge & Kegan Paul, 1986).

Dudovitz, Resa L., *The Myth of Superwoman: Women's Bestsellers in France and in the United States* (London: Routledge, 1990).

DuPlessis, Rachel Blau, *Writing beyond the Ending* (Bloomington and Indianapolis:

Indiana University Press, 1985).

Duras, Marguerite, *L'Amant* (Paris: Editions de Minuit, 1984).

Ellmann, Mary, *Thinking about Women* (London: Virago Press, 1979).

Eluard, Paul, *La Rose publique* (Paris: Gallimard, 1934).

Evans, Martha Noel, *Masks of Tradition* (Ithaca, NY: Cornell University Press, 1987).

Evans, Ruth, ed., *Simone de Beauvoir's* The Second Sex: *New Interdisciplinary Essays* (Manchester: Manchester University Press, 1998).

Fallaize, Elizabeth, *French Women's Writing: Recent Fiction* (Basingstoke and London: Macmillan, 1993).

——'Reception Problems for Women Writers: The Case of Simone de Beauvoir', in Diana Knight and Judith Still, eds, *Women and Representation* (Nottingham: WIF Publications, 1995), pp. 43–56.

——ed., *Simone de Beauvoir: A Critical Reader* (London and New York: Routledge, 1998).

Faludi, Susan, *Backlash: The Undeclared War Against Women* (London: Vintage, 1992).

Felski, Rita, *Beyond Feminist Aesthetics: Feminist Literature and Social Change* (London: Hutchinson Radius, 1989).

Fetterley, Judith, *The Resisting Reader: A Feminist Approach to American Fiction* (Bloomington: Indiana University Press, 1978).

Foucault, Michel, *Les Mots et les Choses* (Paris: Gallimard, 1966).

——*Power/Knowledge: Selected Interviews and Other Writings, 1972–1977*, ed. Colin Gordon, trans. Colin Gordon and others (Brighton: Harvester, 1980).

Francis, Claude, and Fernande Gontier, *Les Ecrits de Simone de Beauvoir* (Paris: Gallimard, 1979).

Freud, Sigmund, 'Family Romances', in A. Richards, ed., *On Sexuality: Three Essays on Sexuality and Other Works* (London: Penguin, 1977; 1909), pp. 217–25.

——'Female Sexuality', in A. Richards, ed., *On Sexuality: Three Essays on Sexuality and Other Works* (London: Penguin, 1977; 1931), pp. 367–92.

Freund, Elizabeth, *The Return of the Reader: Reader-Response Criticism* (London and New York: Methuen, 1987).

Friedan, Betty, *The Feminine Mystique* (London: Victor Gollancz, 1963).

Fullbrook, Edward and Kate, *Simone de Beauvoir, A Critical Introduction* (Cambridge: Polity Press, 1998).

Genette, Gérard, *Figures II: Essais* (Paris, Editions du Seuil, 1969).

Gérard, Alain, *Madame, c'est à vous que j'écris* (Paris: Albin Michel, 1995).

Gilbert, Sandra M. and Susan Gubar, *The Madwoman in the Attic: The Woman Writer and the Nineteenth-Century Literary Imagination* (New Haven, CT: Yale University Press, 1979).

Gilmore, Leigh, *Autobiographics: A Feminist Theory of Women's Self-Representation* (Ithaca, NY and London: Cornell University Press, 1994).

Greene, Gayle and Coppélia Kahn, *Making a Difference: Feminist Literary Criticism* (London and New York: Methuen, 1985).

Gusdorf, Georges, 'Conditions et limites de l'autobiographie', in *Formen der Selbstarstellung* (Berlin: Duncker & Humbolt, 1956).

Herrmann, Claudine, *Les Voleuses de langue* (Paris: Editions des femmes, 1976).

Hirsch, Marianne, *The Mother/Daughter Plot: Narrative, Psychoanalysis, Feminism* (Bloomington and Indianapolis: Indiana University Press, 1989).

Holmes, Diana, *French Women's Writing, 1848–1994* (London: Athlone Press, 1996).
Hughes, Alex and Kate Ince, eds, *French Erotic Fiction, Women's Desiring Writing, 1880–1990* (Oxford and New York: Berg, 1996).
Hutcheon, Linda, *Narcissistic Narrative: The Metafictional Paradox* (Waterloo, ONT: Wilfred Laurier University Press, 1980).
Irigaray, Luce, *Ce sexe qui n'en est pas un* (Paris: Editions de Minuit, 1977).
——*Ethique de la différence sexuelle* (Paris: Editions de Minuit, 1984).
Jacobus, Mary, *Women Writing and Writing Women* (London: Croom Helm, 1979).
Jardine, Alice A., *Gynesis: Configurations of Women and Modernity* (Ithaca, NY: Cornell University Press, 1985).
Jelinek, Estelle C., *The Tradition of Women's Autobiography: From Antiquity to the Present* (Boston: Twayne Publishers, 1986).
Jenkins, Richard, *Pierre Bourdieu* (London and New York: Routledge, 1992).
Jouve, Nicole Ward, *White Woman Speaks with Forked Tongue: Criticism as Autobiography* (London and New York: Routledge, 1991).
Kenyon, Edwin, *The Dilemma of Abortion* (London: Faber & Faber, 1986).
Képès, Suzanne and Michèle Thiriet, *Femmes à 50 ans* (Paris: Editions du Seuil, 1981).
King, Adèle, *French Women Novelists: Defining a Female Style* (London: Macmillan, 1989).
King, Josephine and Mary Stott, eds, *Is This Your Life? Images of Women in the Media* (London: Virago, 1977).
Knight, Diana and Judith Still, eds, *Women and Representation* (Nottingham: WIF Publications, 1995).
Laubier, Claire, ed., *The Condition of Women in France: 1945 to the Present, A Documentary Anthology* (London and New York: Routledge, 1990).
Leclerc, Annie, *Parole de femme* (Paris: Editions Grasset & Fasquelle, 1974).
Lejeune, Philippe, *Je est un autre: L'Autobiographie de la littérature aux médias* (Paris: Editions du Seuil, 1980).
——*Moi aussi* (Paris: Editions du Seuil, 1986).
——*Le Pacte autobiographique* (Paris: Editions du Seuil, 1975; 2nd edn, 1996).
Lemoine-Luccioni, Eugénie, *Partage des femmes* (Paris: Editions du Seuil, 1976).
Lilar, Suzanne, *Le Malentendu du Deuxième Sexe* (Paris: Presses Universitaires de France, 1969).
Lionnet, Françoise, *Autobiographical Voices: Race, Gender, Self-Portraiture* (Ithaca, NY and London: Cornell University Press, 1989).
Lyotard, Jean-François, *La Condition postmoderne: Rapport sur le savoir* (Paris: Editions de Minuit, 1979).
Mackinnon, Catharine A., *Feminism Unmodified, Discourses on Life and Law* (Cambridge M.A. and London: Harvard University Press, 1987).
McConnell-Ginet, Sally, Ruth Borker and Nelly Furman, eds, *Women and Language in Literature and Society* (New York and London: Praeger, 1980).
Mahon, Joseph, *Existentialism, Feminism and Simone de Beauvoir* (Basingstoke: Macmillan, 1997).
Marcus, L., *Auto/biographical Discourses: Theory, Criticism, Practice* (Manchester and New York: Manchester University Press, 1994)
Marks, Elaine, and Isabelle de Courtivron, eds, *New French Feminisms: An Anthology* (London: Harvester, 1981).

Mercier, Michel, *Le Roman féminin* (Paris: Presses Universitaires de France, 1976).

Miller, Jane, *Women Writing about Men* (London: Virago, 1986).

Miller, Jean Baker, *Toward a New Psychology of Women*, 2nd edn, (London: Penguin, 1978).

Miller, Nancy, K., ed., *The Poetics of Gender* (New York: Columbia University Press, 1986).

——*Subject to Change: Reading Feminist Writing* (New York: Columbia University Press, 1988).

——'Personal/autobiographical criticism', in E. Wright, ed., *Feminism and Psychoanalysis: A Critical Dictionary* (Oxford and Cambridge, MA: Blackwell, 1992), pp. 306–11.

——*Bequest and Betrayal: Memoirs of a Parent's Death* (New York and Oxford: Oxford University Press, 1996).

Mills, Sara, Lynne Pearce, Sue Spaull and Elaine Millard, *Feminist Readings/Feminists Reading* (Hemel Hempstead: Harvester Wheatsheaf, 1989).

Moi, Toril, *Sexual/Textual Politics* (London: Methuen, 1985).

——ed., *French Feminist Thought* (Oxford: Blackwell, 1987).

——*Feminist Theory and Simone de Beauvoir* (Oxford: Blackwell, 1990).

——*Simone de Beauvoir: The Making of an Intellectual Woman* (Oxford and Cambridge, MA: Blackwell, 1994).

Montefiori, Jan, *Feminism and Poetry: Language, Experience, Identity in Women's Writing* (London: Pandora, 1987).

Morgan, Janice and Colette T. Hall, eds, *Gender and Genre in Literature: Redefining Autobiography in Twentieth-Century Women's Fiction* (New York and London: Garland Publishing, 1991).

Newton, Judith L. and Deborah Silverton, eds, *Feminist Criticism and Social Change: Sex, Class, and Race in Literature and Culture* (New York: Methuen, 1985).

Nice, Vivien E., *Mothers & Daughters: The Distortion of a Relationship* (London: Macmillan, 1992).

Pearce, Lynn, *Feminism and the Politics of Reading* (London, New York, Sydney and Auckland: Arnold, 1997).

Petchesky, Rosalind Pollack, *Abortion and Woman's Choice* (Verso: London, 1986; first published by Northeastern University Press, 1985).

Phillips, John, *Forbidden Fictions, Pornography and Censorship in Twentieth-Century French Literature* (London and Sterling, VA: Pluto Press, 1999).

Picq, Françoise, *Libération des femmes: Les Années-mouvements* (Paris: Editions du Seuil, 1993).

Planté, Christine, *La Petite Sœur de Balzac: Essai sur la femme auteur* (Paris: Editions du Seuil, 1989).

Pratt, Annis, *Archetypal Patterns in Women's Fiction* (Bloomington: Indiana University Press, 1981).

Prince, Gerald, *Narratology, The Form and Functioning of Narrative* (Berlin: Walter de Gruyter, 1982)

Radway, Janice A., *Reading the Romance: Women, Patriarchy and Popular Literature* (London: Verso, 1987, first published by the University of North Carolina Press, Chapel Hill, NC,1984).

Rich, Adrienne, *Of Woman Born: Motherhood as Experience and Institution* (London: Virago, 1977).

Robinson, Lilian, *Sex, Class and Culture* (Bloomington: Indiana University Press, 1978).

Ruddick, Sara, *Maternal Thinking: Towards a Politics of Peace* (London: The Women's Press, 1990).

Sarraute, Nathalie, *Enfance* (Paris: Folio PLUS, 1995).

Schor, Naomi, *Breaking the Chain: Women, Theory, and French Realist Fiction* (New York: Columbia University Press, 1985).

Sellers, Susan, *Language and Sexual Difference: Feminist Writing in France* (London: Macmillan, 1991).

——ed., *Feminist Criticism: Theory and Practice* (Hemel Hempstead: Harvester Wheatsheaf, 1991).

Sheridan, Susan, ed., *Grafts: Feminist Cultural Criticism* (New York: Verso, 1988).

Sheringham, Michael, *French Autobiography: Devices and Desires* (Oxford: Clarendon Press, 1993).

Sherzer, Dina, *Representation in Contemporary French Fiction* (Lincoln, NE: University of Nebraska Press, 1986).

Showalter, Elaine, ed., *The New Feminist Criticism* (London: Virago, 1986).

Simons, Margaret A., ed., *Feminist Interpretations of Simone de Beauvoir* (Philadelphia: Pennsylvania State University Press, 1995).

Smith, Sidonie, *A Poetics of Women's Autobiography: Marginality and the Fictions of Self-Representation* (Bloomington and Indianapolis: Indiana University Press, 1987).

——*Subjectivity, Identity, and the Body, Women's Autobiographical Practices in the Twentieth Century* (Bloomington and Indianapolis: Indiana University Press, 1993).

Smith, S. and J. Watson, eds, *Women, Autobiography, Theory: A Reader* (Madison: University of Wisconsin Press, 1998).

Stanley, Liz, *The Auto/biographical I: The Theory and Practice of Feminist Auto/biography* (Manchester and New York: Manchester University Press, 1992).

Stotland, Nada L., ed., *Psychiatric Aspects of Abortion* (Washington and London: American Psychiatric Press, 1991).

Suleiman, S. R. and I. Crosman, eds, *The Reader in the Text: Essays on Audience and Interpretation* (Princeton, NJ: Princeton University Press, 1980).

Sullerot, Evelyne, *La Presse féminine* (Paris: Armand Colin, 1963).

Thibout, Lorette, *L'Avortement vingt ans après, Des femmes témoignent, des hommes aussi* (Paris: Albin Michel, 1995).

Todd, Janet, *Feminist Literary History: A Defence* (Cambridge: Polity Press, 1988).

Tompkins, J. P., ed., *Reader Response Criticism: From Formalism to Post-Structuralism* (Baltimore, MD and London: Johns Hopkins University Press, 1980).

Vilain, Philippe, *L'Etreinte* (Paris: Gallimard, 1997).

Wandor, Michelene, ed., *On Gender and Writing* (London, Boston, Melbourne and Henley: Pandora Press, 1983).

Waugh, Patricia, *Metafiction: The Theory and Practice of Self-conscious Fiction* (London: Methuen, 1984).

Woolf, Virginia, 'A Sketch of the Past' (1941), Sketch 90, Jeanne Schulkind, ed., *Moments of Being* (London: Grafton Books, 1989).

Yaguello, Marina, *Les Mots et les femmes* (Paris: Editions Payot, 1978).

Additional Articles

Althusser, Louis, 'Idéologie et Appareils idéologiques d'état, (Notes pour une recherche)', *La Pensée*, 151 (1970), pp. 3–38.

Beauvoir, Simone de, 'Les Femmes s'entêtent', *Les Temps modernes*, April–May 1974, pp. 1719–20.

Bourdieu, Pierre, *La Lecture (II) – Approches*, Cahiers du séminaire de philosophie 2 (Strasbourg: Centre de documentation en histoire de la philosophie, 1984), p. 13.

Günther, Renate, 'Fifty years on: the impact of Simone de Beauvoir's *Le Deuxième Sexe* on contemporary French feminist theory', *Modern & Contemporary France*, vol. 6, no. 2 (1998), pp. 177–88.

Le Doeuff, Michèle, 'Simone de Beauvoir and Existentialism', *Feminist Studies*, no. 6 (1980), pp. 277–89.

Mauger, G. 'Les autobiographies littéraires: objets et outils de recherche sur les milieux populaires', *Politix*, no. 27 (1994), pp. 32–44.

Moi, Toril, 'Appropriating Bourdieu: Feminist Theory and Pierre Bourdieu's Sociology of Culture', *New Literary History*, no. 22 (1991), pp. 1017–49.

Wenzel, Hélène, ed., *Simone de Beauvoir: Witness to a Century*. Special issue of *Yale French Studies*, no. 72 (1986).

Signs, vol. 18, no.1 (1992), including Zerilli, Linda, 'A process without a subject: Simone de Beauvoir and Julia Kristeva on maternity', pp. 111–35.

Radio Interviews

With Roger Vrigny, France Culture, 21 June 1984.

'Littérature pour tous', with R. Favier, France Culture, 17 February 1990.

'Des livres et nous', with O. Barrot and V. Sommer, France Inter, 25 April 1993.

Other interviews

Unpublished interview with Siobhán McIlvanney, 23 September 1993.

Index

233

Printed and bound by CPI Group (UK) Ltd, Croydon, CR0 4YY

09/06/2025

14685803-0003